PIMLICO

778

GROWING UP IN A WAR

GROWING UP IN A WAR

BRYAN MAGEE

PIMLICO

Published by Pimlico 2007

4 6 8 10 9 7 5 3

First published in Great Britain by
Pimlico in 2007

Pimlico
Random House, 20 Vauxhall Bridge Road,
London SW1V 2SA

www.randomhouse.co.uk

Addresses for companies within The Random House Group Limited
can be found at: www.randomhouse.co.uk

The Random House Group Limited Reg. No. 954009

A CIP catalogue record for this book
is available from the British Library

ISBN 9781845950873

The Random House Group Limited
makes every effort to ensure that the papers used in its books
are made from trees that have been legally sourced
from well-managed and credibly certified forests.
Our paper procurement policy can be found at:
www.randomhouse.co.uk/paper.htm

Printed and bound in Great Britain by
Mackays of Chatham plc, Chatham, Kent

to
Richard Cavendish

CONTENTS

CHAPTER ONE

I was sitting in a tree with Teddy Green, talking about what I was about to discover were the facts of life. At the top of it was an intertwining of branches that formed a wide-bottomed, broad-backed place to sit, like a throne; and whenever this was our tree for climbing, whichever one of us got there first took possession of the throne, while the other one sat astride a branch. It was a favourite place of ours. We would talk there for hours.

Today I was in the throne. One of us had just told a dirty joke, and I was reflecting aloud that these sorts of jokes were funny all right, but it was such a pity we had to base them on a silly pretence about some ridiculous thing that grown-ups were supposed to do.

Teddy gave me a look. He was a village boy, and was used to animals. The conversation went something like this.

'It's not silly. It's true.'

'Garn.'

'Yes it is.'

'Can't be.'

'They really do.'

'Gercha.'

'Really.'

'Corse they don't.'

'They do.'

'Get away.'

'I promise you.'

And so on, for a long time. Why I ever did start believing him I don't know. Perhaps it had something to do with his manner and expression (he did, after all, know) and something to do with our ages (I was nine, he ten) and the fact that I had for so long been familiar with the ideas, and the meanings of all those naughty words (since I was about five), although it had never occurred to me to take them seriously. When, after many refusals, I accepted the truth of what he was saying, there was still a sense in which I could not believe it. How could grown-ups, of all people, do such a thing? Children, perhaps, yes, but grown-ups . . . How could they do it for laughing, quite apart from anything else? Did they titter and giggle all the time they were doing it? *Why* did they do it, if they wished they didn't have children? Come to think of it, it was a dirty thing to do, as well, joining up the things they pissed with. How could they *want* to do that? I was mystified. Enthroned at the top of the tree I gazed out over a wide, sunlit green field, awestricken by these revelations, struggling to take them in.

No doubt Teddy and I went on chattering, but I have no memory of what we said. I remember only my thoughts, though I expect I was putting them into words. If this really was how babies were born then it must be how I was born. And that . . . no . . . yes . . . they couldn't . . . they must . . . it meant my parents had done it!! The realisation was a thunderbolt. Never in my life had I been so gobsmacked. I tried to picture my mum and dad at it, and found this impossible. Yet I wouldn't be here if they hadn't, so I was a sort of living proof that they had. They must've.

In spite of my inability to conceive it, I arrived at the conclusion that my parents must have done it not once but twice – once for my sister and once for me. Of course, this was a very long time ago, and they had been different people then. Even so, it remained baffling beyond anything I had ever tried to get my mind round. And of course, there was the fact that they disliked one another, so that may have helped and made it easier for them.

But I kept coming back to the question of *why* they did it. My mother had never wanted children, and she certainly wished she'd never had us. Perhaps it had been my father who wanted us. He loved us, that was for sure; but what a thing to have to do to get us!

I felt like a traveller on foot who finds a range of mountains springing up around him. Problems heaved up on every side, whichever way I looked. *Everybody* had been born the same way. So my parents had. And this meant that my grandparents had done it . . . And Norman Tillson's parents . . . And all the boys' parents at school . . . And everyone's parents in the village . . . And everybody's in Hoxton . . . Everybody's . . . All the people that had ever existed since the beginning of the world. Obviously everybody who had ever had children had done it. And then, when the children grew up, most of them did it too; and then *they* had children themselves, and that's how the world carried on – in fact it's what the world *was*. Without it there wouldn't be a world, or at least there wouldn't be any people. It was a flabbergasting picture. The entire human world suddenly seemed phantasmagoric to me, grotesque.

I wandered around lost in these thoughts for days. As incredulity faded, it gave way to curiosity. I was sharing a bedroom with a girl called Gwen, a cousin of the Pammie Ainsworth who had wheeled me about in a pushchair when I was two. Gwen, who was eleven, slept on a divan in the diagonally opposite corner of my bedroom. I realised now that my grandmother was keeping us as far apart as she could. These were the earliest weeks of the Second World War, and we were having to go to bed by torchlight because of the blackout. Gwen and I would always natter together in the darkness before falling asleep, and sometimes, after my grandmother had gone to bed, we would get up again and play by the light of our torches, which we thought were fun in themselves.

Gwen was a whole year older than Teddy, so one night I asked her if she knew about this incredible thing grown-ups were supposed to do. She said she did. But did she realise, I persisted, that they actually did it? Yes, she said, she did know that. I found this disconcerting and encouraging at the same time. Why should you have to be grown up to do it, I wondered aloud – I mean, what would there be to stop the two of us doing it, right now? She said she couldn't think of anything that was stopping us. Well shall we have a go at it, I suggested, and see what it's like? She was game, in a way that gave me the impression that she had wondered about it already.

The first thing we needed to do was get our pyjama trousers off. Then we used our torches to examine the situation. I found she had something I had never seen before, pubic hair, and this held me up a bit. I was familiar with pubic hair as an idea, because it came into the jokes, but it had never occurred to me that people actually had it. I had frequently seen girls of my own age showing off what was under their knickers, and none of them had it. I moved the torch in to a close-up, and examined the hair in detail, fingering it with fascination. It made such an impression that it is the only part of Gwen I now remember – I have only the vaguest recollection of her face. When I questioned her about the hair she told me that all girls got it at about her age – and then, she supposed, they must have it for the rest of their lives. This was another revelation – my grandmother . . . my mother . . . my sister . . . they must all have this hair. In some huge, secret way everything was turning out to be different from what I thought – and altogether more gamy.

Eventually we moved on to the main agenda – or rather we tried to. My attempts to insert my penis into Gwen's vagina were completely unsuccessful. We tried and tried, but it was impossible to get it in. She did everything she could to help, holding herself open with the fingers of one hand while trying to stuff me in with the other, but it was hopeless. My penis was a tiny little squashy thing that just flattened itself against her, while her vagina was dry and tight-lipped. It was as if we were trying to force a blancmange through a blocked keyhole. After trying and retrying, and re-retrying, we were flummoxed. How did people do it? Assuming they did, which we accepted, there must be some trick to it that we were missing. We were unable to think what it could be. It was all so hopeless that we never tried again. But the mystery went on puzzling me for quite some time. It was more than another year before someone (a seventeen-year-old girl) explained to me that erections made the difference. I had had erections, naturally, ever since I could remember, but only occasionally, and they had seemed to happen out of the blue, unconnected with anything else, like having a pain that then went away. It had never occurred to me to think of them in such a connection as this. In any case, they happened so seldom that I did not see how someone could expect to be having one just at the moment he needed it. Nor did I see, still, how he would be able to get it in to that tightly closed lock, even if he had one.

♥

CHAPTER TWO

Towards the end of the 1930s it was obvious to most people in Britain that war was going to break out soon, and the only question was when. It was expected that Hitler would launch immediate air attacks against Britain's cities. (The air attacks came, but not immediately.) So the peacetime government began making plans for the defence of the civilian population, organising air-raid shelters and gas masks, and preparing the evacuation of children from those cities most likely to be targeted. To anyone with low expectations of bureaucracy, the high quality of the planning was disconcerting. Within three days of the outbreak of war something like one and a half million children had been removed by train in good order from the most vulnerable cities, and were billeted with families in safe areas. The organisation of the evacuation was based on schools, not on individual children or residential areas: whole schools, together with their teachers, moved to small non-industrial towns, or to cities beyond the range of bombing, and carried on their activities in makeshift surroundings such as church halls and assembly rooms, or disused large buildings of other kinds.

It was only because the civilian population had been put into a high state of preparedness beforehand that all this worked. There had been, inevitably, people who said that a Tory government was manipulating the population to prepare for a war it was planning; but this was the usual nonsense from what had become the usual quarters: few governments in history have tried harder to buy off aggression by appeasement than that pre-war Conservative government. The critics of what were in fact highly civilised and sensible precautions were only too often apologists for Stalin's Russia, which at that juncture entered into an alliance with Nazi Germany, and was even then preparing a secret agreement with Hitler to divide up Poland and the Baltic states.

That is how it came about that in the summer of 1939 ordinary British families were discussing over their breakfast tables what action they were going to take when war broke out. Our family shop – which my grandfather owned, and worked in with my father – sold men's and boys' clothes. Since people were obviously going to go on needing clothes, it was assumed that the shop would continue trading. At the age of thirty-seven my father was unlikely to be called up early, and that was a blessing, because my grandfather would not have been able to run the shop by himself. If Dad were to volunteer, it was not likely that Grandad would be allowed to hire another able-bodied man to replace him. So the decision was reached that Dad would continue working in the shop until ordered by officialdom to do something else, at which point the family would reassess the situation in the light of whatever turned out to be the prevailing circumstances. But meanwhile, what about the children, my sister and me? The shop, which was where we lived, was in Hoxton, in the very heart of inner-city London, which everyone expected to be the most heavily bombed area. All the local schools were now forming plans to evacuate themselves on the outbreak of war, to as yet unknown destinations. Joan and I were automatically invited to go with ours. But there was nothing compulsory about all this. So should we go? If not, and our schools went, what would we do instead?

These questions were gone over repeatedly. My parents decided quickly enough to send us away from London for our own safety, but they were uncertain on what basis to do that. In the end,

differing decisions were made for the two of us. Joan, just now
becoming a teenager, was at a good grammar school in Highbury,
and it was decided that she should stay with it, because of the
unlikelihood of finding a better school. At her age she would be
able to manage if sent beyond the reach of visits by parents. But
I was still only nine, and at a bog-standard elementary school
round the corner from the shop, a school to which there was no
reason for me to remain attached; so it was decided that there
was no need for me to stay with my school. Perhaps it is worth
remarking that these considerations, although they turned out to
be less pressing than was thought, were by no means superfluous
or unrealistic. Although the bombing did not begin until a year
after the outbreak of war, when it came it demolished a third of
Hoxton, which was one of the most heavily bombed areas in the
country. The rooms in which we lived above our shop had their
roof torn off by the blast from a direct hit on my school, which
was totally demolished.

My grandparents were now in their sixties, and had been planning to retire quite soon in any case to a cottage in the country.
At least, my grandmother regarded herself as having made this
decision: with this in mind she had rented one of three newly built
bungalows in a tiny village called Worth, in West Sussex. She got it
on the cheap because a speculative builder had been left with it
on his hands. It was a mile or so outside Three Bridges, and two
or three miles from Crawley. The way you got there was by taking
a train to Three Bridges from Victoria. In those days Three Bridges
was little more than a railway junction, Crawley was a small and
charming country town, and Worth a single street. Various members
of the family, including me, had already been there for weekends.
I have memories of a longer stay over the Easter of 1939, when I
recall my delight at the colourfulness of the birds, and my pride
and surprise at being able to identify many of them from a set of
pictures I had collected from my parents' cigarette packets.

The family decision was that, when war began, I and my grandmother should go down to Worth and live together there. It would be an already familiar home for me, within easy reach of London, in a place that my parents knew how to visit – whereas my school could well go to somewhere inaccessible. Worth had its village school, in which, we were told, all the children over eleven were taught in one room; but there was no junior school, so my father arranged that, like other Worth children of my age, I should go to school in Three Bridges.

Actually, I and my grandmother travelled down to Worth the day before war broke out. My father's sister Peggy had a friend, a secretary in Whitehall, who telephoned her to tell her that Germany was about to invade Poland; that Britain would immediately issue an ultimatum to Hitler to withdraw; that Hitler was expected to ignore the ultimatum; and that we would then declare war on Germany; and that all this was going to happen within the next few days. It did, but none of it was explained to me in advance, and I complained clamorously about being sent away from home when there was not even a war. My father, whom I trusted in everything, assured me that I could rely on war breaking out in a few days, and that it would be a good idea to go before the rush. So, at the age of nine, I left what had been my world until then, never to live in it again.

Since birth my home had been my birthplace, 276 Hoxton Street. This street was both the main and the market street of a whole distinctive area called Hoxton, one of London's Domesday Book villages that for centuries had nestled just outside the northern gates of the City. With the expansion of London after the Industrial Revolution it became the westernmost part of the East End; and by the time I came on the scene it was notorious throughout the country for its combination of poverty and crime. A report published when my grandparents were young adults had famously declared: 'Hoxton is the leading criminal quarter of

9

London, and indeed of all England.' But for me it had up to now been where I felt I belonged. I was at home in it, it was the only place I knew really well, and I loved it. It was to be largely wiped off the face of the earth in the few years after I left: what was not destroyed by German bombing was swept away in the post-war slum-clearance programmes; so today almost nothing of the Hoxton I grew up in remains. What goes under that name now is a quite different place even physically, with mostly different buildings and even different streets, in which much of the population is black; and what were warehouses when I was there have been turned into lofts and artists' studios.

The first whisper of a realisation that everything had changed for me for ever did not sound until after Jimmy Ainsworth, who kept the pub nearest our shop, came down to Worth to bring his niece, Gwen, to stay with us. He told us confidently that the war would be over by Christmas, so the first time I saw my father after that I asked him if this was true, and he said no, the war would last for several years. *Years*, I thought. *Years!* How could a war last for years? Surely you had a jolly good fight, which settled everything, and then it was over. *What* could possibly go on for years? Still, if my father said so, it must be true. But I could form no understanding of it. And somehow the first beginnings of a realisation crept into my head that in these circumstances I could not form any expectations about going home again – in fact, I could not form any expectations about the future at all, neither the future in general nor my own in particular.

On the morning after my grandmother and I arrived in Worth, soon after eleven o'clock, an air-raid siren sounded. I knew what this meant, because we had had air-raid drill at school in London, and I assumed that the village was having a drill. But my grandmother went into a panic such as I had never seen her in before. 'Shut the windows! Shut the windows!' she screamed, rushing to the nearest window and slamming it. For a moment I goggled at her uncomprehendingly; but she went on shouting at me while running from window to window (I had never seen her run before): 'Don't just stand there! Shut the windows in the bedrooms or we'll be having poison gas in here!' I opened my mouth to protest, but she yelled at me hysterically, and I did as I was told.

When every window had been tightly closed, checked and double-checked, I rejoined her in the living room, nonplussed that she should be reacting in such a way to a drill that she and I, there being no one else with us, had no need to take part in at all. What was the point, I wanted to know, of getting worked up like that about poison gas until there was a war on and there could actually *be* some poison gas?

'There'll be some gas all right,' she said, still terrified. 'Where's your gas mask?'

'But there isn't a war yet.'

'Yes there is.'

'No there isn't. It's only a drill.'

'It's not a drill. It's real.'

'It can't be real. The war hasn't started yet.'

'Yes it has.'

'Eh?'

'It started this morning.'

'This *morning*?'

'Yes.'

'When?'

'Eleven o'clock.'

'Why didn't you tell me?'

'I didn't want to upset you. Run and get your gas mask.'

Even as a nine-year-old I was engulfed by a sense of the inanity of it. How could she have imagined she could keep secret from me the fact that there was a war on? And if I was going to find out anyway, why not straight away?

At last, after what seemed an eternity of sitting in our living room, gas masks at the ready, waiting for the terrifying noise of aeroplanes, we heard the siren sound the all-clear. That unnecessary alert on the outbreak of war took place all over the country, and became a notorious event, because a population that was expecting instant air attack thought, *By Jesus, here it is!* and panic was widespread. Apparently some senior bureaucrat thought it would be a good idea, now that war had begun, to make sure that all the air-raid sirens were in good working order.

For the whole of the time I was with her, my grandmother tried to shield me from the war. Either she did not take a newspaper or, if she did, it was kept from me. When I was around she never listened to a radio news bulletin. When we went to the cinema in Crawley she timed our arrival so that we missed the newsreel; and if it came round as soon as the main film was finished she chivvied me out of my seat in an agitated manner: 'Quick! Quick! We must go. We must leave.' Since the newsreel always started with exciting action shots – bombs falling, guns firing, tanks charging – I always wanted to stay and see it, so I objected, and tried to dig in, but she would bundle me out physically. 'Come on! Don't hang about! We'll miss the bus. We've got to go.' It was against nature that I should be made actually to leave a cinema in the middle of a battle scene – and it could even be, in those earliest weeks of the war, a scene with horses, which was better still.

I was also at an age when I was beginning to follow intelligently some of the feature films I was seeing, instead of just absorbing them like blotting paper. The fact that I was for the first time seeing grown-up films without my parents made a difference. I became very aware of the music on the soundtrack, perhaps because I was getting so much less music than I had been used to at home. The string tremolando that usually accompanied suspense fascinated me, and I assumed that there must be one instrument that made that sound. I asked people, 'What is the instrument that goes *diddle-iddle-iddle-iddle-iddle?*' but they could never answer the question to my satisfaction. To those who suggested it might be violins I said: 'No, it doesn't sound like a violin at all.'

CHAPTER THREE

Immediately outside the back door of our cottage was a low hedge, then an open field. This was used by the children of the village as their playground. There would usually be separate groups of them, all ages and both sexes, doing different things. Even if something got under way that took up most of the space, like a football game, other children would go on playing round the edges of it, and get shouted at when they got in the way.

My grandmother kept a permanent eye on all this through the kitchen window. A couple of days after our arrival she led me out into the field through a gap in the hedge and shouted to the nearest children who looked as if they were roughly my age: 'Here's somebody for you to play with.'

They stopped what they were doing to gawp at me. They had seen me before, but only for a day here and a day there, with long absences in between, to forget.

'His name's Bryan,' she said as she turned and went back into the house, leaving me standing there. Once she was out of the way they loosened up. 'We're playing so-and-so,' said one of the boys, who remembered me. Two girls started talking at once to explain what they were doing. And before I knew where I was, I was in the game. It had been much the same on earlier visits. When my grandmother yelled to me from the kitchen door to come in and eat, I did not want to go.

'Coming tomorrow?' asked one of the boys as I walked away.

''Spec' so.'

And so I was recruited, in what seemed an entirely natural way, into the gang of village children. We played together more or less every day after school, most often in the field, though frequently some of us would get up to some mischief elsewhere. My special friend became Teddy Green, who lived in one of the railway cottages at the far end of the field, fronting the main road. All the wage-earners there worked at the railway station in Three Bridges. Teddy said that when he grew up he was going to work for the railway in Three Bridges, just like his dad, and he did.

The hero among the children was a boy who played with them only occasionally, and I heard him talked about before I saw him. I took them to be calling him King Constable, and asked if that was really his name, and they said yes, it was. What a splendid name, I thought, for the chap who is obviously the chap of chaps. Actually they were saying Ken Constable, but I found this out only when he came to play with us and I heard them address him as Ken. He was a good-looking, strongly built fourteen-year-old who had left school that summer. This meant he was looked on by the rest of us as more or less grown-up. He had known the other children all their lives, but because they were younger he played with them only when he could find no one better to hang around with. Then he dominated them. He did everything better than they did, and they idolised him for it, and tried to emulate him. I, like the rest, imitated the way he played football. I had never played with such a big boy before – no such persons had ever deigned to take notice of me. I was overawed by him. Four years later he was drafted into the navy and killed. A plaque in the village church commemorates him.

The church played an essential part in our lives as the chief source of pocket money. I was told that if I joined the choir and attended regularly I would be given half a crown for the period up to Christmas. The children in the choir got half a crown for each of the three terms in the year. I could scarcely believe it. I had never possessed anything like such a sum of money at once: I was used to getting money in ha'pennies and pennies, plus fourpence on Saturdays. Teddy told me he went to the vicarage every Saturday morning and cleaned all the boots and shoes, including those of the servants, and for this he was paid the unbelievable sum of sixpence. On top of that he got money from his parents. The village children were wallowing in money, it seemed to me, and the biggest sums of all came from the church. This was a revelation. I joined the choir immediately. Thus choir practices and church services became part of my life.

It was the first time I had been to grown-up services – I had been to weddings and Sunday school, but no one in my family went to ordinary church, so it was new to me. It surprised me that grown-ups were expected to kneel, though I noted that the hassocks provided for them to do it on were so high that they didn't have to do a really proper kneel. As a choirboy I was provided with a scarlet cassock and white surplice, an outfit I thought snazzy, especially the cassock. We processed a lot, walking behind a man carrying a cross, out of the main door, round the outside of the church, then back in again, singing as we went. No matter where we started, we always ended up in the same place as we began. I had no idea why we did this, nor indeed what any of it was about, but I was never bored, because there was always so much going on. There were the people in the church, for a start – although never full it was usually well attended. And there seemed to be some sort of indoor autumnal mist, so that the lights shining through it on to our red cassocks made everything look shimmery in a cheerful, Christmassy way. It was the first time I ever noticed chandeliers. And of course there was the music. But I discovered that my voice was awkwardly positioned between treble and alto: if I sang with the trebles I could not get the high notes, and if I sang with the altos I could not get the low ones.

What I did was sing treble and stop whenever it got too high. This meant I missed out on the best bits, the climaxes. On the other hand, if I got carried away, and strained to stay with the others to get up there, I made a croak that brought grimaces and shushing from the choirmaster. I half expected to be dropped from the choir for not fitting into it properly, but I never was. I went on having the same trouble with singing until my voice broke – whereupon I became too low for the tenor part and too high for the bass.

My grandmother came once to see me in my cassock and surplice, and told my father I looked angelic. Next time he visited us from London he came to church to see for himself. I could not take my eyes off him. His presence seemed to fill the church. He was, and always had been, the lodestar of my life, and I must have been missing him more than I consciously realised. Actually, I think he visited us on most Sundays, often with my grandfather, occasionally with my mother; but I was used to living with him and seeing him every day, and all I knew was that he was not there most of the time. But anyway, here he was now, and in a church of all places, something I knew he would not have done if it had not been for me. I noticed that he did not kneel. Afterwards he said how awful those hassocks were – people should either kneel or not kneel, not fudge it. From him I learnt that the church was unusually old – Saxon, he said – and famous with people who knew about churches. It was surprisingly big, apparently, for something as old as it was, and this showed that, although it was now in the middle of nowhere, the area round Worth must have been important at one time. It so happens that the church is considered by many the most beautiful cruciform Saxon church in England; but there would have been no way in which that could have been made to mean anything to me. I just liked it, that was all. And it remains to this day the only church I have ever attended voluntarily and regularly.

The vicar was an irascible, dislikeable man. In the village it was said that more people would have gone to church had it not been for him. Teddy heard new gossip about him every Saturday morning from the servants in the vicarage: they said he had fits of uncontrollable temper in which he sometimes threw his dinner at his wife. When Teddy told my grandmother this it impressed her so much that she made occasional references to it in conversation with me for the rest of her life.

Teddy was my chief source of information about most things. It was he who introduced me to the crimes (literally) of scrumping and smoking. There was a few yards of the village street that constituted a bridge over one of the railway lines into Three Bridges, and Teddy and I liked to clamber down at that point and play along the line. Beside the railway, not far off, was an orchard and, this being autumn, apples were ripening. We raided that orchard several times, climbing over the wire fence with special joy because its purpose was to keep us out. It was the first time I felt my heart in my mouth. Climbing back again with armfuls of apples was much trickier, and we always managed to drop most of them. Even those we clung on to were a problem, because we could not eat them all, yet neither of us dared to take them home. We ended up stuffing ourselves with as many as we could – enough to make us ill, sometimes – and throwing the rest away. I found scrumping by far the most thrilling of all the things there were for us to do, and I wanted to do it more and more. A couple of times we were spotted by the man who owned the orchard, and he screamed at us through the trees, rushing towards us waving his arms. When this happened we panicked and hurtled like rabbits over the fence. Once I was not quick enough, and he grabbed me by the collar and gave me a clip round the ear while yelling abuse into it. I was surprised to be let free – I expected something terrible and final to happen; to be arrested, handed over to the police. He must have complained to my grandmother, though, because she said something about it a day or two later. After that the scrumping expeditions became more exciting, because more forbidden and dangerous.

Smoking presented us with the same basic problem as scrumping. Cigarettes were sold only by the packet, and not even between us could we get through a whole packet at once, yet neither of us dared to take cigarettes home. So the question was, what to do with those we had not smoked? We felt the dilemma more keenly with cigarettes because they were so dear that it hurt us to throw them away. In the end, most often, we did – though only after having puffed our way frantically through enough to make us ill. We naturally discovered that the more fiercely we sucked a cigarette the quicker it burnt. And we lit one from another. They made us far sicker than the apples. There was a Saturday morning when we got through most of a packet of Craven A like this, and when I got home I was monumentally sick. My head in that lavatory bowl is almost as present to me now as it was then. I heaved my heart out, my grandmother standing over me, and me realising that I stank of cigarettes. The nausea felt terminal, like seasickness. The experience must have been something of a trauma for me, because never again, not even in my thirties when I was an addicted smoker, was I ever able to bring myself to touch a Craven A cigarette.

The shop where we bought our cigarettes was just outside the village. The man there explained to us that because the law forbade him to sell them to us he could let us have only the largest and most expensive packets, those of twenty, since to sell us fives or tens was not worth the risk to him. He could not even let us have the cheaper packets of twenty – the smaller, more elegant cigarettes 'for ladies': it would have to be the bigger, full-priced ones. In Hoxton no sales would have been possible on that basis, but he made quite a lot of money out of the children of Worth.

Although as the offspring of two heavy smokers I had been preprogrammed, in the womb, for addiction, I had never smoked until now. At home there had been cigarettes lying about all over the place, and I had constantly been sent out to buy them, but my parents would have punished me so harshly if I had smoked that I never did. In fact I do not remember any children of my age in Hoxton smoking. It was probably a matter of money more than anything. It was an everyday thing to see grown-ups scavenging for cigarette ends in the gutter, in the same way as there were always children who would pick up apple cores. Nearly all grown-ups smoked, but it was a luxury for them, most of all for those who bought cigarettes in ones and twos. When I started smoking, at Worth, I could not understand why anyone did it. Cigarettes tasted disgusting, and caused my head to swim, and made me feel sick almost from the first puff. They also gave me a headache, and a burning throat, and made me cough. So why did people smoke if they were allowed to? How could anyone like it? I was aware that the only reason I smoked was that I was forbidden to, and thought that as soon as I was allowed to smoke I would stop.

Smoking was so much a part of everyday life in those days that it was a matter for remark if someone did not smoke. Like drinking, smoking was thought to oil the wheels of ordinary life. When people were offered cigarettes they said things like: 'All right, I'll have one just to be sociable.' I knew only one or two grown-ups who did not smoke; but my grandmother was one of them, so any telltale signs of smoking in her bungalow would have been noticed. In any case, she did know I smoked – she asked me, and I denied it, but I could see from her eyes that she knew I was lying.

The only other adult I knew who did not smoke was Miss Rutland, our neighbour in the bungalow next door. She was a thin little woman with a face like parchment, and seemed to me unimaginably old, at least ninety. In fact she must have been about sixty. She dressed always in black from head to foot, in clothes appropriate at the time of Queen Victoria's death, in mourning for her fiancé, who had been killed in the Boer War – which of course had taken place less than forty years earlier. However, although she looked ancient and funereal, she was on easy, friendly terms with the village children, and particularly with me, simply because I lived next door. She bought sweets and chocolate from a yellow van that used to come round – to give to 'the bairns', as she called us in her Scottish accent – and this may have had something to do with the fact that I would sometimes wander into her home. The two of us played games of our, or rather her, invention. She introduced me to one in which each in turn had to guess a tune from its rhythm. We sat beside a chest of drawers that had metal rings on its handles, and with one of these we tapped out the rhythm of a tune in staccato clicks. I started with the popular songs of the day, but she did not know them, she knew only hymn tunes, so I changed over to those. I was surprised at how often – sometimes almost immediately – I was able to identify one, out of the hundreds of tunes I knew, from just these tuneless taps; the words would come leaping into my head during the first line. I was receiving the lesson, without realising it, that there was a great deal more to even the simplest of tunes than its melodic line.

On my first visit to Miss Rutland, she showed me round her house, which included many photographs and other mementos of her fiancé. The man in the photographs was young enough to be her son or grandson now, and his funny old-fashioned army uniform located him in the world of silent film comedy. One of her mementos was a paperknife he had given her, the handle of which was a military cartridge in its case. I was chilled by the sight of it: even to me as a nine-year-old it looked a horribly evil thing, obviously intended to kill someone like the young man himself. When I commented on it to my grandmother, she said that this was typical of the way people had thought during the Boer War, and even during the First World War, but no one would think like that nowadays.

My grandmother seemed not to know many people in the village, apart from Miss Rutland, but she was perfectly happy about that. Grandma was a tough old party, hard in character, and tightly closed up. Traumatic poverty in childhood had turned self-reliance and self-sufficiency into absolutes: you must never, never depend on others, never *need* others, because if you did you were done for. She had not much imagination, and no sense of humour; but very surprisingly, to me at least, she was aware of this: she was the only person I have ever known who said unaffectedly and truthfully that she had no sense of humour. When she said it, her voice had a note of wistfulness, almost of yearning: others were laughing, sparkle-eyed, and she would have loved to join in, but she remained outside it, not understanding. Her basic form of self-protection was to keep herself beyond reproach: always tell the truth, always keep your word, always be on time, always be meticulously honest about money, always obey the rules – not out of concern for others, but to keep yourself invulnerable. If you did these things no one would be able to get at you – or, if they did, you would be in the right, not they. To preserve this position she avoided anything that might bring pressure on her to compromise – discussion, explanation, consultation – and just got on with doing what she thought right, and presented everyone with fait accomplis. This was the thing I found hardest about living with her: I was never allowed to make a choice or express a preference. Everything was presented to me as a settled decision, and all I could do was come to terms with it. Inevitably it made me feel excluded, alienated. But from her point of view, everything was being done in my best interests, as she thought it should be.

Throughout the time we were together at Worth, she seemed to me to be living in her own little air bubble. Most Sundays her son, my father, would come tootling down from London in his second-hand Austin 10, occasionally bringing her husband, my grandfather, with him, and thankfully seldom her daughter-in-law, my mother. And that made her content. On one such Sunday my grandfather was sitting in a deckchair in the garden reading a newspaper, my parents were in the house with my grandmother, and the car was parked outside the front gate. Teddy Green and I were playing in the street; and I, trusting that the garden hedge would prevent my grandfather from seeing us, started to show the car off to Teddy in whispers. 'And this,' I said, 'is the handbrake,' operating it to show how it worked – at which, in slow motion, the car rolled into the ditch under the hedge. My grandfather stirred. Teddy and I scuttled off into the brushwood opposite the house and hid behind trees, waiting in fear to observe the consequences of our actions (my action). Grandad emerged from the front gate and looked at the car, his jaw in his hand. Then he went into the house. Then everyone came out. My father was exasperated. 'How could that have happened? Did you see anybody?'

'No,' said my grandfather.

'Or hear anything?'

'No.'

It took all four of them a lot of heaving, and a lot of time, to get the car back on to the road, all talking at once while they were doing it, speculating on how this could have happened. At last, when it was done and the handbraking double-checked, they went back into the house. When I rejoined them later I looked, or hoped I looked, the picture of innocence, and had to be told what had happened in my absence. When the time came for our visitors to leave, my grandfather said his goodbyes to me out of earshot of the others, and his last words to me were: 'I saw you. But don't worry. I won't give you away.'

CHAPTER FOUR

Worth was just a single stringy, straggly street off a not-very-main road. It was a cul-de-sac, so no one passed through it: the street just ended with the church, and then there were miles of unusually thick woodland (in which I and my friends spent a lot of time). I have since found that there are people who live not all that far away yet are unaware of the village's existence. To them the name Worth is associated with a Roman Catholic abbey and boarding school, round which they assume any village of the same name is bound to be clustered; but in fact the abbey and school are some miles from the village, on the other side of the woodland; and during the time I lived in Worth I never even heard of them.

Another thing that added to the isolation of Worth was that it did not contain a single shop or pub. This was because the woman who owned the village would not allow them. She wished to keep it, she said, unspoiled. She lived somewhere called Wentworth Park, on the other side of the main road. I have no memory of seeing a house there, but in any case I did not envisage her as living in a house but living in a park, as it might have been a London park. She was pointed out to me one day driving past in her car, and looked a nice woman. She was rarely mentioned, though; she was too remote. This has since suggested to me that people who own villages probably figure less in the minds of the villagers than they imagine. I am quite sure that scarcely anyone in Hoxton would have known who owned the land there. It would not have entered most of their heads to wonder – though critics of slum landlordism might expect effigies of the landlords to be burnt every Bonfire Night in the slum streets.

The nearest shop, the little corner store that sold cigarettes, was a short way up the main road, at the crossroads from which Pound Hill ran down into Three Bridges. Although the shop was oddly isolated, it prospered. My grandmother went there for every thing she needed at short notice, and bought the rest of her provisions from the yellow van that came to the village every day – a general store on wheels that stopped at each house. For big items she would walk to Crawley and bus back, as we did when the two of us went to the pictures there. (Of the films we saw, the one I always remember is *Stagecoach*.) Only one or two people in Worth had cars. Several had bicycles, but these were not of much use across fields, so most of the time people walked. This, of course, must have been so since the beginning of time, and no doubt it never entered people's heads to question it, but it did mean that their horizons were narrow by the standards of the post-war world. During the three and a half months I spent in Worth, the only other places I went to were Three Bridges and Crawley. Other nearby towns I heard mentioned were Horsham and Horley – I used to mix the two up – and East Grinstead; but I never went to any of them; and there were quite a few grown-ups in the village who never went to any of them either. Some had never been to London.

Although Worth was a backwater, it was less rustic and remote than the village in Dorset where I had been for a couple of holidays when I was younger. That had been an exotic world of buzzing heaviness and flies, of farmyards and outdoor privies, with the reek of dung everywhere, and few roads, whereas this was comparatively well tailored. Even so, my experience in Dorset was of great help to me in Worth. It had made me used to being in the country, and hearing country accents all round me, and playing with village children, mostly in fields, or clambering in trees; and it had taught me such basic skills as how to make a bow and arrow. Having enjoyed it before helped me to feel at home in Worth – more at home, I suspect, than my grandmother, who probably had less experience of being outside London, except at some of the cockney seaside resorts. Even so, I went on thinking of London as real life, the real world, from which I was now separated because of the war. But I did not feel homesick, perhaps because I was relieved to be away from my mother.

Homesickness was something I never experienced as a child, despite the fact that after the age of nine my base was always away from my family. I was pleased to see them during school holidays, but never longed for them when I was not with them. One thing I do remember, though, that may be connected with living away from home for the first time, is that at Worth I took a new kind of interest in reading. I had always gobbled up comics greedily, unable to put one aside until I had read every word of it, and secretly spending forbidden sums of money on them. But in the area round Worth the shops did not sell the comics I was addicted to – the *Wizard*, above all, and also the *Hotspur* – and I regarded the others as inferior, so I was forced now to move on to something halfway between comics and books. They were novelettes, actually, though no one used that word. They looked like very thin paperbacks, were aimed at grown-ups, cost tuppence, and were probably the crudest as well as the cheapest adult fiction outside magazines. The leading genres were romantic, adventure, detective and cowboy, and I opted for detective, these being mostly Sexton Blake stories. But I was prepared to try anything, except romantic. I became as addicted to novelettes as I had been to comics – in fact I thought they were better, because they were longer and more grown-up. I remember one about the Ku Klux Klan (the first time I heard of it) in which its members were the goodies as against the dirty niggers who were the baddies. This makes me wonder now about the provenance of some of them. There was one about airmen in the First World War in which, as in my comics, pilots were represented brandishing pistols and shooting at one another from their cockpits – wonderfully exciting. This, I thought, was what I wanted to do when I grew up. Once in the bungalow, when my grandmother thought I was out, I heard her in the next room praising me to a visitor and wondering aloud what I was going to be in life, and I bawled out to them: 'An airman!'

For my grandmother I felt no positive affection, unlike the way I did for my grandfather and Aunt Peggy. Although I accepted the other aspects of my life in Worth, I was not happy about living with Grandma. It gave me problems which I did not know how to cope with. At home in London my mother's indifference to me had always had the back-handed advantage of leaving me to grow up in freedom. She cared little what I did, and never wondered where I was, provided I came home for meals. On days when there was no school she would shoo me out on to the pavement of Hoxton Street after our midday dinner and say: 'I don't want to see you again till it gets dark.' And from that moment I was at liberty to do whatever I liked, go wherever I liked – anywhere, that is, except home. If I got into trouble it would not matter provided my parents never heard about it, so for me the important thing was not keeping out of trouble but keeping the trouble from my parents. This was how I had become used to living; so when I found myself in Worth I went on behaving like that. However, my grandmother was not like my mother. She felt responsible for my welfare, and wanted to know where I was going, and what I would be doing when I got there; and she became angry if I did not tell her. Furthermore, because the village was a village, the scrapes I got into reached her ears. She genuinely tried to do what was best for me, but without asking me what I thought or wanted. Her decisions boxed me in at every turn, and it became intolerable. She was, it seemed to me, behaving as if I were a well-treated prisoner.

A day came when I exploded. Shouting through floods of tears, I denounced her for 'the way you treat me'. She was dumb-founded, and in righteous outrage said things like: 'But every-thing that happens here is done for your benefit. I do everything I can think of for you.' I knew this to be true – in fact I under-stood the situation clearly – but at that age I was incapable of putting such thoughts into words. The frustration this induced was itself intolerable – I knew exactly what was wrong but did not know how to say it. So I carried on accusing her of treating me badly when I knew that this was not what it was, and not what I really meant.

I think this scene may have played a decisive role in bringing my period at Worth to an end. When Christmas showed its funnel over the horizon, my father said that, since the anticipated bombing of London was not taking place, it would be all right for me to come home at least for Christmas. After that, I would not return to Worth but would rejoin my old Hoxton school, which had been evacuated to Market Harborough in Leicestershire. Then, he said, I would once more be with my old mates and my old teachers. The reason he gave for this change was that the school in Three Bridges had turned out not to be good enough. It was not educating me properly, he said. I imag-ined this must be true if he said it, but was puzzled how he could know, since he was not living with us and had never been to the school. It seemed to me I was learning more there than I had at my school in Hoxton. Certainly I was finding it more interesting. But I supposed what he said must be true in some grown-up sense beyond my comprehension. Only now, as I write this chapter, over sixty-five years later, do I find myself reflecting that the real truth was probably otherwise.

What I think now, when I look back, is that my grandmother felt herself inadequate to the task of controlling me. There were my scrumping and smoking, both of which were crimes and could have led to trouble with the police, perhaps even (in her mind) to my being sent to a borstal. There were probably whispered, giggling sounds in the night telling of who-knows-what going on between me and Gwen. I was roaming all over the countryside getting up to mischief, and then lying about it when I got home. I was misbehaving about the house – on one occasion I tore up all her rose bushes. And finally there was my explosion of direct rebellion, and my denunciation of her. I suspect she told my father that she simply did not know what to do with me. And he would have decided the rest.

The first thing to happen was that Gwen was taken away from us and returned to her family in London. When she was no longer there I started waking up in the night crying, but I had no idea what I was crying about. I had only the vaguest of recollections of what might have been bad dreams, and was not sure I had been dreaming at all. During the day I was a happy enough child, but in my sleep I would be overwhelmed by the same feelings of grief and loss as had afflicted me when I slept alone in London. One night I woke myself with the noise I was making, howling and sobbing at the top of my voice. When I was fully awake I sat up in bed and stopped crying. Immediately my grandmother's voice came to me in the blackness, calling from her bedroom: 'What's the matter, Bryan? Are you all right? You've just woken me up.' I shouted back: 'It's all right, Grandma. Don't worry. I'm all right now. Go back to sleep.' And she did. So did I. What strikes me now is that incidents like this must have made her think I was desperately unhappy in Worth, when actually I was not.

CHAPTER FIVE

School in Three Bridges was more fun than I had known school to be before. But, as usual, the really enjoyable thing was getting there. Half a dozen or more of us in Worth went to the junior school in Three Bridges every day, and we walked there and back together. This may have originated as a protective measure, for none of us was older than eleven, and we had no adult supervision. The one who lived nearest the church started out alone, and picked up the rest as he walked through the village, so by the time the group reached the main road it was complete. We would make the long walk down Pound Hill into Three Bridges, chattering and playing as we went. For reasons I cannot quite explain, I have always associated those daily walks with feelings of happiness – perhaps it was a sense of freedom at being out of the house and with other children. I remember the scenes as autumnal – golden leaves underfoot, which there never were in Hoxton, and appealing mist in place of fog, turning all the colours to pastel shades – with all of us larking about together the whole way down, girls as well as boys. Each morning I would look eagerly out of my window for the group to approach along the village street, impatient to be going out and joining them.

One morning I was late, and missed them. Out of the house I pelted, in a hurry to catch them up. So heedlessly did I scuttle across the main road – looking the wrong way, because I was looking for my friends – that I ran almost under the wheels of a car. There was a screaming of brakes as the car knocked me to the ground. Because I had my back to it I was thrown forward on my knees. I picked myself up, thinking I was unhurt, and assured the driver I was okay. But then, as he drove away, I began to shake uncontrollably. So I turned and headed back home. As I was approaching my front gate I felt a stinging in my knees. This caused me to look down for the first time, and I saw blood pouring down the front of both legs. At this I broke into howls and sobs, not having been in the least disposed to cry up to that point. Even at the time I knew that it was seeing my legs streaming with blood that was making me yell, not the pain. My injuries were superficial – I had simply scraped a lot of the skin off my knees – but I carry the scar tissue to this day.

On our daily walks down Pound Hill each of us carried a gas mask at the hip, its stiff cardboard box in a bag slung from the shoulder. The whole population of England was carrying these things now. No one ever needed to use them for a gas attack because there never were any gas attacks, but we children often had a gas-mask drill at school, and that came to be what I thought of gas masks as being for. Their boxes had a practical use, too, which was to carry our sandwiches. There were no such things as school dinners, only school milk, so we took sandwiches to school. My grandmother, who remains to this day the worst cook I have ever known, was also the worst sandwich-maker. She cut the bread thick, to keep me well nourished, and had no understanding that for sandwiches to be appetising they need to be moist.

The school was in a street behind the main road. It was the first time since infant school that I had been in a class with girls, and I regarded this as an improvement. It made the atmosphere more interesting, without preventing the boys from having their usual fun among themselves. There was one girl of about the same age as me who aroused in me feelings that were new and strange. Whenever I looked at her I felt a rosy glow all over, with an odd sort of pleasure that made not only my skin go warm but my insides as well. I enjoyed this feeling so much that I tried to get it with other girls – I looked at each one in the class in turn, hoping to find it, but that was no good. It happened only with this one. Her name was Morag Macdonald. She was pretty, quiet, perhaps a little on the plump side but not too much so; her skin was unusually white, her eyes and hair dark. I spent hours looking at her secretly, enjoying pleasant feelings of longing. What it was a longing for I had no idea, and did not even question: it was just a sort of general yearning; but it was very nice. I do not think she felt any of the vibrations of my interest, or even noticed me on the other side of the class. I never attempted to say anything to her about it, indeed would not have known what to say. Actually there was nothing to say. It was not a question of saying. I just loved looking at her. She has been a happy memory for me for the rest of my life. I have no idea what happened to her after the autumn of 1939. She was then between nine and eleven years old, so as I write these words she must be either in her mid-seventies or dead.

She is the only child in that class whose name I remember. But there are several others whom I clearly recall as people. There were identical twin boys whom most of the girls could tell apart but most of the boys – including me – could not. There was a girl who was the same age as the rest of us but more grown-up, more sophisticated, with exciting adult attitudes to everything, interesting to talk to. There was a boy who embarrassed everyone by bringing God, Jesus Christ or the Church into every conversation, no doubt under influence from home. The teacher felt that this was not something he could reprimand a child for, so he let it go on, but was as embarrassed as the rest of us, and we could see him fending off opportunities for it to happen.

The teacher was a Mr Saintey (that spelling may be wrong). He was in his forties, balding and bespectacled, with a heavy limp from a wound acquired in the First World War. He was funny and jolly on the surface, and successful in winning popularity with the class, but hard underneath, ruthless if crossed. Like a clown warming up an audience he would burst beaming into the classroom every day shouting: 'Good morning, boys and girls!' at which we all had to rise to our feet and shout back: 'Good morning, Mr Saintey!' Most of the children enjoyed this, it got them going, but I found myself resenting having to greet somebody in terms laid down by himself. He was, I think, more intelligent than the teachers I was used to: he understood us better, and taught us more, but unlike those others he thought we were a lot of perishers, and felt no real concern for us. I expect his chief need, and problem, was to keep himself interested.

He used a wider range of teaching methods than I was used to, and to good effect. Each morning we would listen to the BBC radio broadcast for schools, programmes of whose existence I had not known. Why our teachers in Hoxton had not seized on them with gratitude I do not know. The impact those programmes had on me is illustrated by the fact that I have remembered some of them ever since – for instance one about Alaric, one about the Crucifixion, and a whole series about Toytown. The first two, and others like them, were my introduction to the treatment of historical characters as if they were recognisable human beings, with credible motivations and ordinary human relationships. It was the first time I thought of Jesus as a person.

In addition to making us listen to these radio programmes, Mr Saintey had us devising our own quizzes, and engaging in debates with one another – all at a childish level, inevitably; but this was the first time I had done any of these things, and I found them mind-opening.

An auburn-haired woman called Mrs Campbell gave us singing lessons. She had a penchant for warlike traditional songs that swung along to zappy marching tunes. A typical verse (which I quote from memory, so there may be inaccuracies) was:

> War we wage
> For freedom's heritage.
> The cause is true
> That urges to
> The conflict's close.
> And peace shall crown
> The warrior's bright renown:
> The fame of him
> Who bore him well
> In front of foes.

The fact that we actually were at war had, I think, nothing to do with her choice of songs. This was her repertoire, and she had been teaching it for years.

However, the fact that Britain was at war seemed to come into most things, including why I was there at all. There was a period of several months at the beginning of the Second World War which has acquired the nickname the Phoney War, when although the country was officially at war it was not actually doing any fighting. The months went by, the expected bombing of Britain's cities failed to occur, and increasing numbers of people who had left them in a hurry drifted back to their abandoned homes – sometimes taking their children with them, though many saw here an opportunity to free themselves from their offspring. A result of this was that quite a few children managed to avoid schooling altogether during the war years; and many of these (including intelligent ones) grew up illiterate. Neither in the cities nor in the countryside could life be said to be carrying on as it had in peacetime. What Britain was really doing during this time was getting ready for war, so the whole character of civilian life was changing. It was not just that the young men were being called up into the armed forces: such things as rationing, the blackout, and the carrying of gas masks made ordinary day-to-day life different for everyone, including children. A general seriousness crept into the atmosphere, a sense of huge events impending, and of individuals and families having to relegate their own concerns to second place. We were developing the mentality of a people at war.

I accepted without thinking that the war required me to be away from my home and parents, in spite of the absence of bombing, because there were no schools left in London – I knew I had to go to school, and at home there would be no school to go to. My sister had left London with her school and was now uneasily billeted with a family of strangers in Huntingdon. Everyone, it seemed, was being moved around the country, sent away, shipped abroad, or whatever, and this was what it was going to be like for a long time. As most children do, I just got on with things, taking them for granted the way they were. In this frame of mind I spent the first Christmas of the war at the family home in Hoxton as someone in transit, no longer feeling that I lived there but seeing myself as being on a visit, passing through on my way to Market Harborough. I must have adapted myself with unusual intensity to each place of long-term stay, which then became my world, for from then on I always felt like a guest at home: my visits lasted only as long as the school holidays, and my actual life was always being lived somewhere else.

Apart from an infant stay in hospital, the opening three and a half months of the Second World War were the first period of more than two weeks that I had spent away from home, not only from my parents but also from Hoxton. After that, each move was one more change, one more way of life, one more world. But Worth was the first of my new worlds. For that reason it has remained a bigger experience than the fifteen or so weeks that it lasted might suggest. At long intervals through the years I have felt the need to go back there and stroll through the village, over the railway bridge to the church; to sit in a pew and contemplate the memorial to Ken Constable, and look at the chandeliers, and wander round the churchyard; and then walk back through the village again and down Pound Hill into Three Bridges, following the route that the gang of us used to take every day to school. Sometimes I would continue into Crawley. I would always, at some point, find myself standing in front of the bungalow, with the oak tree still there in its front garden, and wonder who lived there now, and hope that they were not looking out at me through one of their windows wondering what that stranger was doing standing there staring at their house. Now, alas, the bungalow is no more. A few years ago it was knocked down, and a proper house built in its place. But the oak tree is still there. And Miss Rutland's bungalow is discernible as part of the enlarged house next door.

As things have turned out in my life, my period in Worth was the only time I have lived for more than two weeks in a village. While I was there I expected it to be for as long as the war lasted. Because I had no idea that my stay was going to be so short, my mental adjustment was to being there for ever: I dug in, so to speak, and thought of myself as living there. It is true that among the most pungent aspects of the experience were some negative ones, the chief being that it was not Hoxton, and that I was not living with my father. But there were positive ones too, if sometimes difficult to put into words – things to do with openness and sky, the field outside the kitchen door, the trees, first green and then gold . . . clambering around in trees, sitting in trees, talking endlessly in trees. The feeling that stays with me most keenly is of a close community of people surrounded by nothing at all; and the individual things I recall go right down to the various birds and insects, this goldfinch, that wasp, a particular fly, on a particular occasion.

CHAPTER SIX

Within a day or two of my going to Worth to live with my grand mother, the school I had been at in Hoxton was evacuated to the Midlands. I did not hear accounts of this until some time afterwards, but when I did, I heard it talked about so much that it acquired a life of its own in my imagination. The children – each with a label hanging round his neck with his name and address, and each carrying a suitcase – were delivered by their families to Dalston Junction, a few hundred yards from Hoxton. From there they were taken by train to Euston. At Euston they found themselves checked off as one school among many. Thousands of children were being shepherded by their teachers in that great terminus, while extra-long trains stood waiting at the platforms. Then, school by school, the children were packed into the trains, until the corridors would hold no more, and the trains pulled out to their various destinations, the passengers having no idea where they were going. The train carrying the Edmund Halley school stopped first at Rugby. It let a school off there, and then crawled slowly back down another line, stopping at every station. At each stop a confabulation with local worthies took place on the platform which ended sometimes with a whole school getting off and sometimes with no one getting off. Finally, the Edmund Halley was the only school left on the train – and it now seemed to be heading back to London. Perhaps, they thought, they were going home again, there being no one to take them. But at last they were ordered out at a place called Market Harborough, then a town of fewer than eleven thousand people, of which not even the teachers had heard.

In the concourse outside the station, waiting to receive them, was a crowd of empty horse-drawn carts from surrounding farms. Teachers and children were packed into these, and off they clip-clopped into the centre of town, driving other traffic off the roads as they trotted the better part of a mile to the cattle market. Here the children were drawn up in rows, each standing behind his suitcase, while local people walked up and down picking the ones they wanted. The attitudes of these people differed enormously, I am told. Most were decent people who wanted to do something for the children, but some gave themselves patronising airs and made loud remarks, even jokes, about the poverty-stricken state of the urchins in front of them, while others were sharp-eyed shrewdies to whom small sums of money meant a lot and who had spotted here an opportunity to make some. A system was in place whereby the children's parents in London paid maintenance money into the post office, and the families looking after the children drew it out – so if you could keep a child on less than you were paid, you could make a profit. All chose according to their own values: some opted for the most respectable-looking children, some for those evidently in need, some for those who looked least likely to give trouble – and some, I am sure, on other grounds. It was an open market for paedophiles, some of whose activities were later to come to our astonished ears.

I do not believe many of the host families could have seen slum children before, and the condition of the worst of them must have been a shock – the dirt, the lice, the rags, the bony, desperate white faces. There were some that nobody wanted, and these were taken by churches and other charities who sent representatives. For each child a home of some sort was found, to which he was taken straight away, and from which his new guardian had to write to his parents informing them where he was. In a matter of days the teachers, who themselves were billeted with local teachers, were calling round at the houses checking on the circumstances of their charges, and telling them where and when to go to school. As far as Edmund Halley was concerned, there was a Baptist church in the middle of town with assembly rooms attached, and these rooms were made available to the school as its long-term home. Within days of leaving central London, with no idea where it was going, the school was in operation in rural Leicestershire.

Much the same thing happened all over the country, with countless variations of circumstance. To most of those who experienced it, it remained one of the milestone experiences of life. A small literature has grown up about it. One of the myths perpetuated by a part of that literature is that these working-class children were billeted with middle-class families, with resultant class shock and class conflict on both sides, but this happened in only a tiny minority of cases. In those days more than eighty per cent of the population were categorised as working class, and the overwhelming majority of evacuees were billeted with working-class families. In fact I never heard of one who was not.

My arrival in Market Harborough was nothing like as exciting as the one I have described at second hand. I went with my father, who had made arrangements in advance. London's rail terminus for Market Harborough, St Pancras, was only two tube stops from Hoxton, and I remember the steep stairway up to it from the tube exit; then the station building itself, grander than any I had seen (it was built as a luxury hotel). Train journeys took much longer then than now, and it made their destinations seem farther away, especially to children. It seemed to me that we were in the train for most of the day, stopping at town after town that I had never heard of. I began to think of Market Harborough as being an immense distance from London, beyond all those other worlds that lay between. This assumption stayed with me all the time I was there. Yet in fact it is under a hundred miles from London. The fastest of today's trains manages the journey in an hour.

Perhaps a word about distances and communications might help set the scene. In 1940 all but a small minority of people in Britain had neither a car nor a telephone, so neither the personal mobility nor the instant communication that are now taken for granted existed. People travelled outside their own locality mostly by train, and the whole country was criss-crossed with branch lines served by trains that stopped at every little local station and halt. Journeys often involved changing trains twice, or even three times – and each change could involve a long wait. These journeys were exceedingly cumbersome by today's standards – even one without changing that can now be accomplished in an hour could easily then have taken three, if not more; and wartime conditions made matters worse. The cost, too, was a barrier. Most people were poor by today's standards, which made a train journey something for a special occasion, unless it was done for work. Because of all this, most people moved very little outside the areas in which they lived – only a minority even went on holiday. The only ready form of communication with absent friends was the post, so people in general wrote a lot more letters than they do now. However, few had been to school beyond the age of fourteen, so not all that many were good letter-writers. What all this added up to was that travel and communications were slow, laborious and expensive, and people had far, far less of them in their lives than they do today. They lived in more self-contained communities; and because of all these barriers, the distances between them were felt to be greater. If you had a particularly close friend or relation in another part of the country, an occasional letter would pass between you, and perhaps a visit once every few years, but neither they nor you would expect much more. If someone you knew emigrated to America or Australia you took it for granted that you would see them either never again or not more than

once. In Scotland, as the ship moved off, the friends and relations assembled on the quayside would raise their voices hauntingly in the song 'Will ye no' come back again?' If their loved
ones emigrated to New Zealand, a letter would take several weeks
to reach them – so even a direct exchange by return of post would
take some months. Since all these possibilities were improvements
on what had gone before, the whole framework of assumption
and expectation accepted it in a way that is hard for people to
understand nowadays, when children grow up talking on the telephone from infancy, and go on to master e-mail and fax; when
most families have cars, and there are long-distance bus services,
and super-fast trains, and cheap air travel. During the Second
World War in Market Harborough, literally years would go by
without most of the evacuees being visited more than once by
anyone from London, or receiving more than an occasional letter;
and there was no question of talking on the telephone. For many,
London had become impossibly far away. Market Harborough was
now where their lives were. Many of them remained there when
the war ended. Some are still there.

Market Harborough is a compact town surrounded by rich farm-
land. In the nineteenth century it was described as 'perhaps the
best headquarters in the world for fox-hunting'. But it owes its
existence, its location and its character to the fact that it is halfway between Northampton and Leicester. These two county towns
are two days' ride apart, which meant that in the Middle Ages
there was need for an overnight stopping place somewhere near
the mid-point. In the twelfth century Market Harborough was
deliberately founded to meet this need – it can be thought of as
the medieval equivalent of a New Town – and was planned from
the beginning to be a market town. The open space in the centre
was vast, for the market; but over the generations some of the
market booths became permanent, and were then replaced by
buildings, so there are floating islands of architecture in what is

now the High Street. One of these is a fourteenth-century church with no churchyard, thought to have one of the most beautiful steeples in Britain. Beside it is a tiny grammar school dating from Shakespeare's time. The school was built on stilts to function as an umbrella in wet weather for the butter market underneath. So distinctive is this building, and so picturesque, that it has become the logo of the town. During the stagecoach era the High Street was lined along both sides with coaching inns; some are still there, others have left a legacy of coaching yards which are entered under open archways. In the town's history, travel and trade were always the determining factors. After the stagecoaches came the canal, then the railway; but because the town had been a planned one from the beginning, it remained concentrated on its old centre, which has remained pretty much as it was in pictures made in earlier centuries – and is essentially the same now as it was when I first set eyes on it over sixty-five years ago. It was as different from Worth as it was from Hoxton, and I realised as soon as I saw it that I had entered another world.

My father and I went first to the billeting office in the Town Square, where I was registered, and then to the house where I was to live. We walked up Northampton Road until the house numbers were into the hundreds before we came to a terraced house, smaller than its neighbour, with a minute front garden. Waiting for us was a Mrs Burgess, a small, bony woman in her late twenties, quite good-looking though also hard-looking. She put me in mind of my mother, though unlike my mother she obviously liked my father, as most women seemed to do. Cups of tea were drunk, and I was handed over.

Through the window of the front room where we had been sitting I watched my father's back as he walked up the path alone to the front gate. I was struck by what a beautiful overcoat he was wearing.

The following morning Mrs Burgess showed me how to get to

the Baptist church in Coventry Road, where my school was. After that I was on the loose in Market Harborough. Provided I showed up when a meal had been prepared, and came in at night by the appointed hour, Mrs Burgess and her husband showed no concern about where I was or what I was doing. I was back with the indifference I was used to. And after my experiences with my grandmother in Worth, it was welcome.

CHAPTER SEVEN

Market Harborough was such a little town – I doubt whether in those days it was much bigger than Hoxton – that we London kids treated the whole place as our manor. We overran it and made free with it, the more so as we had little means of venturing beyond it. None of us had bicycles, or money for buses, so we got to know few of the surrounding villages. In the town we played in the streets because that was what we had always done – whereas the local children went out into the fields, or played in the parks, which were (to us) surprisingly ample and close. We played in people's gardens too, helping ourselves to their flowers and whatever we felt like taking from the trees. There were, I have since read, some two thousand London evacuees in a town of just over ten thousand people. For the resident population it must have been an unwelcome culture shock, almost a traumatic experience, but no such thought occurred to me at the time. The truth is – I am ashamed to say this – that we Londoners ever-so-slightly despised the locals, even though they were kind to us. As we saw it, we were from the only place that counted, the big city, London, and they were country bumpkins – well meaning, of course, and nice, but yokels. The grown-ups seemed to us slow-moving and slow-thinking, the children absurdly non-violent, innocent, gullible. Compared with us, I expect all this was true: almost every one of us, having grown up on the streets of Hoxton, was something of an Artful Dodger – always keen-eyed for the main chance, unscrupulous, dishonest, quick to use violence if we thought it would serve our ends and we would get away with it. We lied all the time as a matter of course. To the trusting, peaceable children of Market Harborough we must have seemed horrendous. They stood no chance against us, and we took away from them whatever of their possessions we wanted. During my year and a half there, there was very little friendly mixing between us – they played in their groups and we played in ours – though I gather that this changed as the war went on, as one might expect. We evacuees were an impossible handful for some of the families on whom we were billeted. Many reacted by making no attempt to control us beyond insisting on the basics of mealtimes and bedtime. Their ultimate sanction, which they resorted to frequently (it was happening all the time), was to report to the billeting officer that they were no longer willing to have us.

At school I loved being back in the playground atmosphere I had known in London, with 'release' still the favourite game. The girls had now been mixed in with the boys, but I was used to that from Three Bridges, and anyway the sexes played their games separately. The children in my class were new to me: my last pre-war term in London had been spent in the top class of the boys' school, so when that term ended the other boys had departed from the school altogether. What had been Class Two moved up to become Class One, and these were now my companions – boys I had known by sight in the playground, but otherwise did not know. They were a year or two older than me, but I made good friends among them. Some of their personalities have remained alive in my mind ever since: John King, Alan McGouhan, Bert Grant, Ronnie Gentle, Eric Proud (hardly necessary to say that there was a running joke about Proud and Gentle). The school's two leading lights and brightest sparks, Frank Hawkes and Cyril Mortimer, were too grown-up and sure of themselves to be aware of someone two years younger; but my researches for this book had the surprising consequence of putting me in touch with them again, because they stayed on after the war and made their lives in Market Harborough. (They helped me in checking my memories not only of wartime Market Harborough but also of pre-war Hoxton.)

The Edmund Halley school had been reduced in transition. The youngest children had been hived off and put in another school. Some families had not let their children, especially the girls, leave London at all, or had brought them home for the first Christmas of the war, because there was no bombing, and then kept them there. Others had tried to keep siblings together by evacuating them all to some other place, usually following the oldest, or with the mother accompanying. Two of the six assistant masters at my school had been called up, and two had gone elsewhere, so only two were left, though we still had the same headmaster. The two masters were Mr Hickford and Mr Fink, who had taught Classes Two and Three in Hoxton, and the headmaster was Mr Ogle. There was a nice Miss Engel from the girls' school, who had taught my sister. These four made up the staff for a school of nearly a hundred nine-to-eleven-year-olds which consisted of two mixed classes, each of forty-something children. As usual in those days, the woman took the younger children. My class, Class One, was with Mr Hickford. I had been through its syllabus twice already, but that had been with a different lot of classmates and a different teacher – and there had been a time gap since – so I did not mind going through it again. In any case there was no alternative; and I quite liked Mr Hickford. It was to be a problem, though, after I had been through it a third time, what to do with me next.

The first winter of the Second World War was an unusually harsh one; in fact it was said then to be the coldest in living memory. The canal in Market Harborough froze so solid that the entire town turned out one Sunday and walked along it. This was the idea of the local newspaper, and a good one. From the top of Logan Street to the Wharf there was a mass of people walking in both directions as if the ice were a street. It amazed me to see everybody promenading like this. There were constantly people slithering and falling down, while others whizzed past on skates. Whenever since then I have seen a picture like this in a Dutch painting – and there seem to be a lot of them – I have thought of Market Harborough. I was surprised at how rough and multi-coloured the ice was, though of course I know now that it must have been treated to make it safer. I had expected it to be like glass, completely clear and impossibly slippery. Something about the way the bulrushes on both banks stood out of the ice appealed to me especially, and has remained a powerful image. The weather was still freezing, and our feet became as cold as the ice. But it was immense fun.

That winter, going to and from school every day, there would be snowball fights, and groups of boys building snowmen. All this was new to me. In Hoxton, snow never stayed on the ground. In those London streets, full of pea-soup fog, teeming with humanity, such snow as had fallen during the winters of the late 1930s had turned to black or dark grey slush immediately. Only from comics and Christmas cards did I know about things like white snow, snowball fights and snowmen. Now they were real, and happening all round me, and I loved them. One evening when Joey, the other boy who lived with the Burgesses, came in through the back door covered from head to foot with compacted snow (a gang had captured him and rolled him in a snow bank), I thought he looked wonderful. The next day, just before getting home from school, I did a lot of solo rolling in a snow bank to effect a similar entrance, and was deflated by how much less responsive the audience was.

Most of the boys, including me, wore balaclava helmets and woolly scarves, so we looked very different from our usual selves. There were some who knocked together home-made sleds out of

47

wooden boxes, and dragged them along the ice-covered pavements on lengths of string, or took them to nearby slopes for tobogganing, which then developed into races. Ponds and lakes froze, fish died. We were living in a transformed landscape, dazzling white, exhilarating.

That was the winter of the so-called Winter War, Russia's invasion of Finland, which impinged on me to a surprising extent. In his secret pact with Hitler, Stalin had been promised Latvia, Lithuania and Estonia, as well as half of Poland, and in accordance with this he was to take possession of the three Baltic states the following June. But now, meanwhile, he tried to annexe Finland. The blind courage of the resistance he met with astonished the world, coming as it did from so small a country against so powerful an invader. The Finns inflicted great losses on the Russians, driving them into retreat in some places, even pursuing them back over their own frontier at one point. Phrases like 'plucky little Finland' were used all the time, and given an ironic edge by the fact that no other country was doing anything to help them. The British public followed the war with the attitude of football spectators. Stalin being Hitler's ally, we naturally thought of the Finns as being on the same side as ourselves; and because our war with Hitler was quiescent, the Finns' war against Stalin became our front-page news. The local paper had offices only a few doors away from the school, so I passed and re-passed its display windows every day; and although the Finnish war was not reported in its pages, its windows contained an ever-changing display of news photographs from Finland. These all-white pictures of snow-covered scenes drove home powerfully the subarctic conditions of the war. I followed them with as much fascination as I would have followed a serial in a comic, though with the difference that I knew they were real. It was the first time I interested myself in a public news event unprompted by my father.

I had not yet begun to look at newspapers on my own initiative, but people often pointed things out to me in them, and I would then read with interest. However, there was another way my reading habits developed while I was with the Burgesses. Mrs Burgess used to read magazines that looked to me like a version of my comics but aimed at grown-up women. In exactly the same way, these magazines of hers were printed on newspaper, in a smallish tabloid format, with line illustrations; each issue cost a penny or tuppence, and consisted of instalments of half a dozen serials. Her penny one was called *Silver Star*, her tuppenny one *Golden Star*; and there were copies of both lying around the house. I had always regarded love stories as soppy, and resented the apparently obligatory intrusion of a love interest into otherwise decent films, even cowboy films. But now, when I picked up Mrs Burgess's magazines and started reading the stories, I found myself not just interested but suffused with a peculiar melting feeling. Nothing in my comics had caused me to feel like that. It was the feeling I had had in Three Bridges when I looked at Morag Macdonald. Once I discovered it again here it became a fix that I wanted to repeat; and so I became addicted to reading Mrs Burgess's magazines. The serials were more samey than those in my comics. Each was always a love story, and the man was always a higher-up sort of person than the woman – either she was a nurse and he was a doctor, or she was a secretary and he was her boss, or she was a servant in a big house and he was a son of the family. Only the backgrounds differed, but they were nearly always places of work, and that too made the stories grown-up. Work was the grown-up world. Places of work never figured in my comics.

When Mrs Burgess found I was reading her magazines she was put out, and told me they were not for young boys. When I asked why not, she was unable to think of a reason. So she asked her husband. He reacted in the same way: he began by telling me that it was quite wrong for a boy of my age to read these things, but when I asked him what harm they would do he was unable to think of any. These exchanges left the Burgesses not knowing what to say, and the result was that the matter was left dangling in the air – which in practice meant that I continued reading the magazines.

Contrary to what the Burgesses must have supposed, when I read those stories there was no thought of sex in my mind. In fact, in those days no sex entered the stories either. Although it may be obvious now that I was experiencing the first stirrings of sexual feeling, it was not apparent to me at the time. I enjoyed wallowing in the lovely feelings my reading gave me in the same way as I enjoyed wallowing in the bath: it was a pleasure in itself, and therefore an end in itself. I was distantly aware of not under-standing why I felt as I did, and perhaps of being mildly perplexed by it, but any such awareness was peripheral. By and large, the feelings themselves were enough for me. I identified with the young men in the drawings, always tall and slim, clean-shaven and open-faced, noticeably well dressed. They were decent, well-meaning chaps, and yet always misunderstood, even by the girl herself. They always loved the girl, if only coming round to it at the end; but until that point something always stood between them. For me all this was light years from identifying with figures like cowboys, gangsters, pirates, airmen and explorers, as I had done before. These new chaps were everyday people, not exotic, and certainly not superheroes; yet somehow I relished the thought of being in their shoes.

It was during this period that I went to adult films alone for the first time. Market Harborough had two cinemas, a fleapit on the road to the station called the Oriental, and a bright, modern one, the Ritz, that had just been built in the road I lived in. Both were open only in the evenings, when they showed the main film twice; and both put on two programmes a week. Before the days of television it was common for whole families to go together to the cinema a couple of times a week, and I went as often as the censorship rules would let children of my age go in by themselves. I preferred the Ritz, because at the Oriental the manager walked down the centre aisle halfway through the programme spraying the audience with disinfectant: I did not like that, although it did not stop me going there. I saw a lot of films, and now that I was going on my own they made a greater impact on me. One called *Poison Pen*, in which Flora Robson played a woman in a village who wrote anonymous letters, and ended up hanging herself, gave me nightmares. (It was the first time I had heard of anonymous letters, and this is one of those associations that have recurred ever since.) The opening sequences of *Wuthering Heights* frightened me so much that I had to leave the cinema and miss the rest of the film. These films cut so deep that if I find myself watching one of them now on television, more than sixty-five years later, and not having seen it since or even thought about it, I realise that I remember parts of the dialogue and some of the screen pictures. The memory often takes the form of knowing what words are going to be spoken next, and sometimes I check this by saying the words aloud before the character utters them I am seldom wrong, and when I am, it is usually because something else that I have forgotten happens before the words are spoken: they always come soon. A lot of these films are not even especially good ones. Those I liked best were adventure stories on an epic scale, historical for preference, like *Drums Along the Mohawk*. The bigness of the stories gave me a sense of satisfaction that was also big: I felt satiated after them, as if I had just had a wonderful dinner. There were a couple of films with Ronald Reagan, and I was so intrigued by the formation of his upper lip that the next day I stopped on my way to school to examine it in the still photographs outside the cinema. From then on I knew who he was, and was less shocked than surprised when he became President of the United States.

Each time I went to the cinema there were newsreels and other shorts; and of course my grandmother was no longer there to force me to miss them. For ten minutes or so before the lights went down the management would put on Flanagan and Allen records, to indicate that things would soon be under way. These included 'Underneath the Arches', 'Hometown', 'Umbrella Man', and one that struck me as so sad that I thought it ought not to be a song at all – it made me feel desolate to listen to it. It began, I think:

> *We're always on the outside,*
> *On the outside always looking in.*
> *We're never there when fortunes are made:*
> *When the sun starts to shine*
> *We are caught in the shade*

and ended

> *But we know some day we're going to be on the inside*
> *Instead of the outside always looking in.*

Because I was familiar with the Flanagan and Allen characters, a pair of rough-sleepers, the optimism of this ending came across to me as implausible. The whole spirit of the song struck me as the opposite of what songs were supposed to be for.

Within myself I had a new sense of freedom. For the first time in my life I was not living with any of my family. There was something liberating about not being watched over, as if I were now able to be *me*. I found myself capable of doing many things I had not been able to do before. For instance, my family had tried to teach me to swim on our summer holidays, and also on visits to Pitfield Street swimming baths, but I had seemed incapable of learning. Now, free to go by myself to the local swimming baths whenever I felt like it (I had been forbidden by my parents to go alone, but I found that the baths had periods specially for children, so I went), I learnt to swim almost immediately. The school started organising visits to the baths, and I went on all of them, and loved them.

Behind the swimming pool was my favourite park in Harborough, a square open field surrounded by trees. It was the best place I knew to play release, and was close to where I lived. In fact I liked it so much that after I moved across town I often went back to it. Along the far side of it straggled the village of Little Bowden, once separate but now absorbed into Harborough. And it was in the village school that my Cubs evenings were spent. In London I had belonged to the Lifeboys, the junior division of the Boys' Brigade, but they did not exist in Harborough. Next best were the Cubs, the junior division of the Boy Scouts, so I joined them. And along I went to their weekly meetings, wearing a green-and-gold cap. They read Kipling aloud to us – *The Jungle Book* and *Just So Stories* – and we hopped up and down in a crouching position like little apes, touching the floor with our fingertips and chanting: 'Akela, we'll do our best.' We were sometimes divided into two lots, one of which shouted 'Dib, dib, dib' at the other, and the other shouted back 'We'll dob, dob, dob'. I asked the other boys what this meant, but they had no more idea than I had. It was only when I was grown-up that I discovered that 'dib' and 'dob' were acronyms: 'dib' was really 'dyb' and stood for 'do your best', and of course 'dob' was short for 'do our best'. I enjoyed these evenings because of the Kipling stories. I was spellbound by Rikki-Tikki-Tavi, and characters like the cat who walked by himself. In adult life it has always seemed to me that Kipling is a genius who is underrated because of his imperialist views. At its best his work taps into something that has the capacious significance of myth and legend, in the same sort of way as *King Solomon's Mines* does, and not much other such literature.

CHAPTER EIGHT

Home life with the Burgesses was lacking in warmth, and I cannot say I liked them very much. But I did not spend much time with them, and was not unhappy – life outside the house was too enjoyable for that. Their general way of living was roughly what I was used to: the same sort of space, the same kind of furniture, similar meals at similar times, not much heating, no running hot water, no bathroom, an outdoor lavatory, chamber pots under the beds. Most of the evacuees lived in homes like this, I was to find. At that time most of the homes in Britain were probably like it, for Harborough was a more than averagely prosperous town. In my grandmother's newly built bungalow at Worth I had lived with all mod cons, but did not yet take them for granted.

Outside the Burgesses' home things were more different from what I was used to. The town was uncrowded and easy-going, roads broad and open; there was plenty of space in the streets – plenty of space everywhere – and no families living in single rooms. Every family, it seemed, rented a two-up and two-down house, the chief difference between them being size – some looked almost like dolls' houses. But even though all the families seemed to have houses to themselves, nobody used their street doors. All the houses had little back gardens, with back gates, and everyone went in and out by those. All over Harborough there were gravelled, mossy lanes running behind the houses, into which the back gates led, and this was where you met people coming and going. You never called at anyone's front door. Ours was the last gate in our little lane. At the other end of it, where it ran into a side street, was the butcher's, Gregory's. I would be sent there for sausages, and they would make them on their sausage machine in front of me while I waited.

The other people whose gates gave on to the lane lived neighbourly lives, continually dropping in on one another. The exception was a woman who lived in the house next door – she was, though I did not realise it at the time, mentally ill. She was Mrs Burgess's sister, but the two were not on speaking terms. What the background to their relationship was, and why they were living next door to one another, I do not know. The sister, who lived alone, was nasty to everyone, including us children. Mrs Burgess told me and Joey not to talk to her unless she spoke to us, and then to be polite but keep our distance.

When I went into the centre of town, which I did every day to school, its appearance was dominated by the church. I liked the look of that church, in fact it looked just right, somehow; but it would never have entered my head to go inside it. Having no churchyard, it just stood there naked, big, out of proportion to everything else, and in the middle of the High Street. From wherever you were, in or around the town, it was the focal point. The shopping life of the High Street swarmed around it. I found the High Street as a whole pleasing to be in: it made me feel comfortable – I suppose because I had lived nearly all my life in a market street. These surroundings were what I was used to. The town in general seemed a harmonious one in which everybody had a similar way of life. In the course of playing with other boys I went inside homes in many different parts of town, and they all seemed to share the same mode of living. There was no sign anywhere of the sort of poverty that was widespread in Hoxton. Yet nobody seemed well off either. I was to discover from enquiries made many years later that Harborough was largely a one-class town –

prosperous, respectable working-class – just as Hoxton, in its very much poorer way, had been a one-class area. And in such environments people are seldom prompted to think about social class.

Every now and than Mrs Burgess would draw a contrast between the way we did things and the way 'the gentry' did them. I had never heard that word before. It was not in Hoxton's vocabulary. I asked what it meant. She told me that gentry were people who had servants. She herself had been 'in service', as she expressed it; and she explained to me that this was the commonest thing for girls in the surrounding villages to do between leaving school and getting married. She talked about it at some length, since it had been what her life had consisted of before marriage, and it opened new vistas in my mind. Where I came from, and with only a few exceptions, people neither were servants nor had them, and both ways of life were foreign. The old-style cockney was noted above everything else for his cheekiness to anyone in authority, his lack of deference, his independence of outlook. But here was Mrs Burgess portraying a totally different mentality, that of a servant. If she was to be believed, the great thing about these gentry who employed servants was that they were given to disapproving of things for inscrutable reasons: they disapproved of all kinds of normal behaviour that everyone else took for granted. They wanted things done differently. For example, at the end of each course during a meal they did not pile up the dirty plates at the table and carry them out in a stack to the kitchen. They thought this was morally wrong, and they ticked you off if you did it. Instead they carried each plate away separately. This was obviously a silly thing to do, but it was what they wanted. And it was never any use asking why. If you did that, they got angry and said you didn't know anything, and called you stupid – and then you might lose your job. So what you did was find out how they wanted things done and then just do them, no questions asked. It was dangerous to start thinking for yourself.

I had never seen any of these capricious creatures, these gentry, and I wondered where they were. There were none in Hoxton, that was certain. I had not been aware of any in Worth, and I could think of none in Market Harborough. I asked Mrs Burgess about this, and she told me that they did not live in towns; they lived in the country, in and around villages. They had to do that because there was not room enough for them in a town: not only did they have to have big houses, they had to have a lot of land round their houses, and this was not possible in a town. London chauvinist as I was, I took this to mean that they lived only in inferior places, the middle of nowhere, where no one else really wanted to live.

Domestic life with the Burgesses was lived on the cheap. I think they budgeted to make money out of their evacuees. When they sent us to get our dinner at the fish and chip shop they gave us tuppence, not threepence; so instead of getting a proper fish with our penn'orth of chips we got what was known as 'a penn'orth of smalls', fragments of broken fish deep-fried in batter. Neither of us had seen these in London, and we resented them, because we wanted a real fish. Smalls were mostly balls of batter and air. We considered the Burgesses mean. But I do not think we were undernourished, and I certainly have no memory of being hungry.

However, my personal hygiene was not of the best. I had no awareness of it, but my mother discovered it when she visited me. Her coming was not her idea. The Burgesses felt they ought to meet her – or, more precisely, they felt it would be wrong for her not to see where her child was living, and assumed that she wanted to know – so they wrote and invited her to come for a day. When she did, she took me out for a walk in Welland Park so that we could talk, and there we sat on a bench. Looking at me from the side, she said suddenly: 'You've got something in your ear. What is it?' She peered, then put a finger in, then got out a handkerchief and began poking around. She started muttering things like:

'Good God, this ear is absolutely filthy! What on earth . . . I've never seen anything like it! This is disgusting!' and so on. My ears had not been washed since I was last at home. I was astonished at the amount of gunge that came out of them – and at how black and thick it was. So abundant was the filth she dug out that the only thing to do with her two handkerchiefs was throw them away. She then examined my hair, my neck, and my arms. She made me take my shoes and socks off and looked at my feet. I doubt whether any of me was fragrant, but my ears, fortunately, turned out to be in a class by themselves. What emerged under interrogation was that I had two ways of washing myself: I washed my hands and face every morning when I got up; and when the Burgesses told me to I had a bath, though I could not say how often that was – certainly not once a week. So it was always either 'face' or 'from the neck down', and the ears, being in between, got left out. The thought of washing them had never occurred to me. But I could see her point.

My mother was angry at Mrs Burgess for letting me get into such a state, and said a lot of insulting things about her. But once we got back to the house the two of them discussed it as if the whole thing were my fault, and what I needed was more super-vision. My mother had given me such a talking-to that I actually needed no supervision from then on.

The Burgesses had no experience of looking after children. Both of them were only children themselves, and they tended to address me and Joey as if we were grown-ups – which I liked. Mr Burgess was nervous, and stammered, but in spite of that he was self-confident underneath. He protected himself with little formal-ities of speech and behaviour. He once started speaking to me as I was pouring milk from a jug, and I stopped and looked up, at which he nodded towards the jug and said: 'P-p-proceed.' I knew what the word meant, but no one had used it to me before, and it delighted me. For days I went around saying 'proceed' to my friends, and sometimes even 'p-p-proceed'. Once when we had some people to tea he noticed that I was eating tinned fruit without bread and butter, and ordered me to take some. I found bread and butter boring (I always have) and disliked it in combination with fruit, so I refused. He was adamant. 'You *can't* eat tinned fruit without bread and butter. It's unheard of. Fresh fruit, yes. Tinned fruit, no.'

Of my companion in the house, Joey, I have surprisingly few memories. He and I shared a bed, but we went to different schools, had different friends, and lived separate lives. He was not from Hoxton but another part of London, and was a year or two older than me. He was a bit of a clown, the sort of boy who enjoys making people laugh because this causes them to like him. He was Jewish, and even at that young age had a recognisably Jewish sense of humour: self-deprecating, acute, disconcerting, warm. I found him unusually funny, and admired him, and envied the way people liked him. He had more initiative than I, and was constantly doing things I would not have dared to do – and then, being untroubled by the risk of disapproval, getting away with them. One morning when we were lying in bed awake, talking before getting up, he said: 'Let's not go to school today. Let's say we're too ill to get up. Let's spend the whole day in bed.' Fantastic, I thought. The whole day in bed. But we'll never get away with it. If I had tried that sort of thing at home my mother would have asked a couple of irritated questions, taken a quick look at me, and said: 'Come on, there's nothing wrong with you. Up you get. You'll soon feel better,' and not taken no for an answer. But Joey insisted it would work. So we waited, giggling, for Mrs Burgess to come and wake us. When she did, we put on solemn faces and said our piece. To my amazement she accepted it, with total indifference. 'If you're ill I suppose you'd better stay in bed. But you'll have to stay there all day, in case the school sends somebody round. If they come and find you up I'll be in trouble myself.'

I couldn't believe it. What a pushover. No school. And the whole day in bed. As easy as pie. We had often talked in the mornings about not wanting to get up, wishing we could spend the whole day in bed. Well now we could. This was it.

For an hour we chattered away excitedly about what we had done, laughing uncontrollably, delighted with ourselves. But eventually we exhausted that, and the conversation began to dry up. Now what? The truth began to dawn on us about what we had committed ourselves to. Endless hours of the day stretched ahead of us. And we were going to have to stay in bed for all of them. What were we going to do? I do not remember what the answer to that question was, but I do remember the day as one of unparalleled boredom, the worst I have ever spent. Long before the end of it our only thought, and our only topic of conversation, had become how wonderful it was going to be the next day when we would be able to get up and go to school.

CHAPTER NINE

As virtually all children did in those days, Joey and I went to bed a lot earlier than the grown-ups. We were asleep late one evening when we were woken by some sort of crisis downstairs. Voices were raised in panic, doors slammed, heavy thumping ran along corridors, then more people shouted, adult footsteps scuttled along the path outside. It was fraught, frantic. We expected someone to come into our room and tell us what was going on, but nobody did. It was typical of the way children related to adults then that we stayed where we were, and waited to be told: we would not have dared to go out on to the landing and look, still less go downstairs and ask what was happening. We switched on the light and sat up in bed listening to the hullabaloo, trying to decode it, and discussing it between ourselves in tense voices.

At last our door opened and a woman came in whom neither of us had ever seen. To the two of us sitting up with the light on, gawping at her, she said: 'You must be wondering what's happening.'

'Yes,' we said.

'There's been an accident,' she said. 'But everyone in this house is all right. The best thing you can do is go to sleep. You'll be in the way downstairs. Just stay here in your room. Go to sleep.'

And away she went.

In obedience to instructions we turned off the light and tried to sleep. But soon a weird wailing came from downstairs. It was

Mrs Burgess. She was howling in a way I had never heard anyone howl, groaning, sobbing, gasping for breath and shouting: '*Oh no! No! No! Oh no!*'

There was a low murmur of adult voices trying to console her, but she carried on shouting as if they were not there.

Joey and I sat up in bed again and switched on the light. What could have happened?

Again, after a long time, the unknown woman came back to our room. This time she sat on our bed and talked to us properly. She seemed quite nice.

'It's her sister,' she said.

'What, the lady next door?'

'Yes.'

'Is she dead?'

'Yes.'

'What sort of accident? Was it a car accident?'

'Er, yes.'

The woman stayed with us for as long as the howling went on, which was a long time. When eventually quietness returned she settled us down for the night and left us. I never saw her again, and never knew who she was.

The next day, or the day after, Joey and I were taken away from the Burgesses and billeted with other families. We, too, never saw one another again. I do not think I set eyes on the Burgesses either, except from afar in one of the town's shopping streets.

For years I accepted what the unknown lady had told me, knowing no reason not to. But as a grown man, on a visit to the family I was then sent to live with, I was told what had actually happened. Mrs Burgess's sister had hanged herself in the house next door, and had left a suicide note blaming Mrs Burgess.

I was taken in by a family called Toombs, who lived at 34 Logan Street. They told me I would be there for only a few days before being sent to somewhere more permanent, but this was just a cover story to conceal the fact that I was on probation. I stayed a year and a half. It was my first experience of happy family life, which came as a revelation.

Mr and Mrs Toombs were in their middle or late fifties. They had had six children, all of whom were now grown-up, and five of whom no longer lived with them. Mrs Toombs was later to tell me that she took me in because she missed having children around. Her name was Eva, but she told me to call her 'Auntie' (I had always called Mrs Burgess 'Mrs Burgess'). She was a motherly but no-nonsense woman who lived almost permanently in an apron. Her dead-straight hair had been chopped off halfway down her head in a straight line all the way round, and had an amputated look which I never liked. Her two oldest children were in their mid-thirties now, married, and living in more distant parts of the Midlands. Three others were married and living in Harborough. The youngest, Kath, was seventeen, unmarried and living at home. She worked in a factory that stood almost immediately outside the back gate.

Mr Toombs managed a grocery shop in the High Street, the main grocery shop in town. It was one of a chain called Maypole which I think had branches all over the country, certainly all over the Midlands and the north. He had been with them since leaving school, working his way up from grocer's lad, through jobs in Evesham and Leamington Spa delivering groceries by pony and trap, until finally he came to Market Harborough as a manager. To me he remained distant – I have an idea he had not been enthusiastic about taking a strange child into the house, after having at long last got free of his own. He was not unkind to me, but paid me little attention. He had a tendency to grumble in a humorous, good-natured way that his family teased him about. Typically of this, he told me he had a low opinion of London. He had passed through it as a soldier during the First World War on the way to Flanders, and had seen it all the way from St Pancras station to Waterloo. Upstairs in the attic was a German helmet with a bullet hole in it, a souvenir he had brought back from the trenches. I was curious to know if he had killed the man in the helmet, but he would not tell me – in fact, he would not tell me if he had killed anybody. (I am pretty sure he had.) He still looked like a cartoon of a First World War soldier, with what people used to call an Old Bill moustache; and he had the military virtues of doggedness, integrity, and a willingness to take responsibility. I always thought of him as belonging to the last war.

Kath was obese, owing to some glandular condition that no one knew how to cure. Not tall, she looked as wide as she was high, and therefore globular. As a number of fat people do, she moved with light-toed elegance. I had noticed this when I had seen her, once, before I knew her. I had been with the Burgesses and Joey, and the four of us had been heading up to the top of Logan Street to walk along the frozen canal when we passed Kath walking the dog (whom I now knew to be Flossie). We had made some crude joke among ourselves about her fatness, and then in the very act of laughing I had noticed how gracefully she walked. It disconcerted me, because it made my laugh feel suddenly on the wrong side of my face. For that reason the incident had stayed in my mind. And now here she was. On the day of my arrival – new and awkward, not quite ten years old – I was introduced to her when she came home from work. As she flopped heavily down on the settee in the corner of the living room I said, laughing shyly (by way of a joke meant to hold out a hand of friendship), 'Mind the couch don't bust.'

She scowled at this and said nothing. Seeing her expression, Auntie asked her: 'What did he say?'

'Mind the couch don't bust.'

Auntie rounded on me. 'Don't you be rude to our Kath. If you're going to talk like that you won't be able to stay here.'

I shrank into myself. I had meant well. Never again did I refer to Kath's fatness, though she was to become, for over a year, my closest friend.

The two of them showed me round the house. The family did nearly all its living in what they called the back room, looking down to the garden, eating their meals at a dining table set against one wall, and sitting around the rest of the room on armchairs and the settee. Leading off it in the direction of the garden was a kitchen-cum-scullery, tacked on as an extension, and quite sizeable. At the scullery sink was a cold-water pump, which must at one time have been out of doors. Out of doors still, in the little concrete yard before the garden started, was the lavatory. On the other side of the house, facing the street, was what they referred to as the front room, and here there was an upright piano and a gramophone, and other musical instruments. They showed me a zither, something I had not seen before, and a Hawaiian guitar, which I had seen in films. There was a mouth organ. Auntie told me I must never touch any of the instruments, as they were delicate, easily broken. In one corner was a pile of records. Auntie looked more and more thoughtful. 'I think you'd better always ask me before you come into this room,' she said.

I told her I was used to playing records by myself on the gramophone at home.

'Even so,' she said firmly.

She played me a tune on the zither to show me how it was done – a before-my-time popular song called 'Rainbow Valley'. It was not much of a tune, I thought, but it looked so easy that I thought I could play it myself.

'The trouble with a zither is, the strings break,' she said. 'And when they do you can't replace them.' Then in her firm voice again: 'That's why you mustn't touch it.'

She opened the lid of the piano and plonked her fingers down on a few of the keys at random, to let me hear the sound. Then she said: 'Come on, our Kath. Give us a tune.'

Kath opened the piano seat, which turned out to be full of sheet music, took out a piece, set it on the rest, sat down and played it. It was a popular song I knew. I was mesmerised. It seemed to me indescribably wonderful that she could do this. She played well, with a bounce in the rhythm and a sense of freedom in the style, her podgy fingers rippling over the keyboard with accuracy and assurance. I was so impressed that I was almost speechless, but I did manage to ask her: 'Do you have lessons?'

'Not any more. I used to.'

'Why not?'

'I wasn't getting any better.'

When she finished playing, Auntie said to me – perhaps warned by my reaction – 'You can come in here with our Kath, but you must never, ever touch the piano yourself. Do you hear that? Never touch the piano. If you do, I won't have you here any more.'

The room they gave me was on the first floor, overlooking the garden. It was the first time in my life that I had had a whole room just for me. As well as a wardrobe, a chest of drawers and a bed – the biggest I had had to myself – it contained a table and a chair by the window. The house as a whole was quite big by my standards – only two storeys, but with more rooms than I was used to, and an attic on top of those. They had, of course, needed every square inch of this space when their six children were at home. The Toombses did not own it but, like nearly all house-dwellers at that time, rented it. (The figure of fifteen shillings a week is in my mind, but that could well be wrong.)

A lot of things about the way the Toombses lived were new to me. Whatever the pudding was at dinner, they poured hot custard over it, as they did on tinned or stewed fruit at tea: 'custard with everything' seemed to be their motto. In Hoxton we had used either the top of the milk or nothing at all – real cream only with guests, unless we were broke, in which case we had custard. Instead of eating their Yorkshire pudding with the meat course, they ate it afterwards, as, literally, a pudding, covered with jam. Pots of tea were made at all hours of the day, not only with meals. On Sundays it was as if we drank tea all day, using the same leaves over and over again, gingering them up now and then with a fresh pinch.

Most of our food came from the Maypole. Mr Toombs was strict about not letting his family have more than their rations. I often heard Auntie try to cajole him out of this, but I do not think she succeeded. Even so, we ate well. There was always plenty of unrationed food: vegetables and fruit were never rationed during the war, and nor, until after it was over, was bread. Nor was game: we ate lots of rabbit, which I loved in spite of the agony of biting on bits of shot.

The newspaper that came into the home every day was the *Daily Mirror*. It was new to me, and I took to it immediately. Its big, bold, high-quality photographs would have been better teaching aids for my father than the pictures he had used from the *News Chronicle* to interest me in the news, and they helped me to get interested by myself. The family talked about the *Mirror* as if it were an oracle – 'Have you seen today's *Mirror*? . . . The *Mirror* says . . . According to the *Mirror*' – an attitude to a newspaper I had not encountered before, and one which encouraged me to look at it. I passed straight over what I thought of as women's things, such as cookery and clothes, and devoted the cream of my attention to the strip cartoons and the letters. The letters maintained a fiction, which I took literally, that they were answered by two unbelievably ancient men who referred to themselves as 'the Old Codgers'. They were familiars of my daily life. I read more and more of the news, partly because it pulled me in like a serial; and when real fighting began I was hooked. Every day the paper printed sketch-maps of the battle fronts, with all the names in block capitals, and huge arrows showing where the armies were moving. And every day brought new developments in the story. It was more exciting than a comic. And it was real. As far as the war was concerned, there was never any question of my confusing fiction and reality. I was too much part of the war myself, and it dominated all the most important aspects of my life.

Because I was a child throughout the war – nine when it started, fifteen when it ended – it never occurred to me that England could possibly lose. I took it for granted, as a fact, not a judgement, that however bad things might get, England was bound to win. So when I heard adults expressing a fear of possible defeat – as in 1940 quite a few did, and with reason – I thought they were not just cowards but stupid, because they were failing to grasp the obvious. However, there was no defeatism in the Toombs household. The decisive fact, as far as Mr Toombs was concerned, was that we had beaten the Germans last time, and this proved that we were better than they were, so we could beat them again. We were only having this war at all because they had not learnt their lesson. This time we would teach it to them properly.

There was a collective hedonism about the Toombs family that was new to me. I was used to living in a family in which each one went his own way. My father and grandfather took it for granted that the serious purpose of living was to enjoy oneself, but they also took it for granted that enjoyment was outside the home – for them in such things as horse-racing and theatre. The Toombses shared the first of these assumptions but not the second. Auntie and her husband almost never went out together, but they took it for granted that the chief object of life at home was to enjoy themselves. They played almost every game that could be played in the house. On the table at which we ate they played cards, board games of every kind, dominoes, shove-ha'penny, and goodness knows what else; and there was a miniature snooker table that fitted over it. A dartboard hung on the wall behind the settee. In the garden there was a badminton net and a swing. The use of all these had fallen off a bit after their children had left home, but now a new generation of grandchildren – our Geoff, our Bernice, our Ray – was dropping in to visit their teenage aunt Kath and their grandmother, and getting caught up in these things all over again; and my arrival brought them back to full strength. In my first couple of weeks all the games were hauled out of their cupboards and shown to me, one after another; and if I did not know how to play them I was taught. It put me in my element, because I loved indoor games. My favourite of those new to me was ninepins. The feeling of inner satisfaction I got when I knocked down all nine with a single swing of the ball was indescribable. I felt them go down deep inside my own body.

The Toombses were a games-playing family like no other. I began to suspect that Auntie had taken me in because she wanted someone to play games with. I became quite good at them – that is to say, no better than the others, but no worse. And they gave me great feelings of happiness, which included a hitherto unknown sense of belonging.

Another thing the Toombses did was sing at the piano. Soon I was going into the front room to do this with Kath almost every day. Sometimes she played popular classics as well – Beethoven's 'Für Elise', Schubert's 'Serenade', Brahms's 'Lullaby', Strauss waltzes – most of which I then heard for the first time; but usually she just played the sort of popular songs that are now called 'standards'. In various parts of the room were piles of sheet music that went back through the thirties and earlier. A lot of these songs I knew already, but many I did not. I would stand at the top end of the keyboard beside Kath as she played, and she would tell me when to turn the pages. At first, when she suggested I sing along with her, and pointed out the words printed there on the music, I was too shy to join in; but I soon got over that, and happily stood there singing. She explained the musical notation, and how it related to the keyboard, so that I would be able to turn the pages without having to be told. We made our way through all the music she had, not once but several times. There were our favourites, of course, which we performed over and over, but we constantly tried less familiar songs for a change. Many a whole afternoon or evening was spent in this way. We got quite hooked on it, and would squeeze songs into little bits of time – if, say, the whole family was in the back room, and Auntie announced that she was going to make a pot of tea, either Kath or I would say: 'Time for a song,' and we would slip into the front room and play one while the tea was being made. Sometimes Auntie would come in and sit in an armchair and listen. Because of this I now carry in my head hundreds of those songs. The best of them – by George Gershwin, Jerome Kern, Cole Porter, Irving Berlin – are among the true glories of twentieth-century music, and will last as long as any of it.

Kath and I did more and more things together. She got on well with people, and had good friends among the girls she worked with; but they had boyfriends, while she, because of her obesity, did not. This made her find me a welcome companion. On my side, I had my schoolfriends, and spent a lot of time with them; but I found her more interesting. At first I just enjoyed her company at home, but soon we were doing things out of doors together. Her parents rarely went to the cinema, but she and I took to going together every week. Sometimes we went into the middle of town to shop – not that I personally did any shopping, but I liked going into the music shop when she bought sheet music or a record. I also liked it when we went to the library – it was then that I made the transition from novelettes to books. The dog, Flossie, a Jack Russell terrier who was part of the family (and was seen as often on the tea table as anywhere else), needed to be exercised, so we would walk her in the surrounding streets, or in Welland Park, or on Lubenham Hill. On these walks Kath and I talked nonstop. She was interested in most of the things that interested me. She engaged with daily life at a down-to-earth level in her factory while at the same time loving music, reading books, and being interested in ideas. Nowadays, as a matter of course, she would go to a university, but until after the Second World War this was out of the question for nearly all such people – of whom, inevitably, there were a great number. In spite of the age difference – she seventeen and I ten – there was nothing condescending about her attitude towards me, and we related as equals. What she taught me chiefly had to do with the bringing to bear of intelligence on daily life. None of my schoolboy companions could do this to anything like the same extent. And I could talk to her about thoughts that were going on in my mind unconnected with what we were doing, and she would understand and respond, which almost none of my schoolfriends did.

CHAPTER TEN

Logan Street was near the edge of Harborough, and I thought of myself as living a long way from my school in the centre. Each journey there or back was like an odyssey. I would set out through the garden, going out of the back gate and down the lane into Highfield Street. In walking the length of Highfield Street I might pick up a friend or two. We would turn right into East Street; and there almost immediately in front of us, on the next corner, was the shop that sold the things that mattered. If any of us had any money we would go in and buy sweets or a comic. In the same shop there was a post office, where Auntie drew out the money to keep me, and where later I was to start spending some of my pocket money on savings stamps to help win the war. We would encounter schoolmates in the shop, so an enlarged gang of us would emerge, and then, perhaps, start arguing in the street over sweets or comics, or something that had happened the previous day. We might have a fight there and then, or two boys would go at it while the rest of us formed a ring round them and watched; or the general argy-bargy might carry us round the corner into Nelson Street. Here the space widened, so we would forget about the fight and start a game. But we had to keep moving towards school, so our game would carry us on past the Catholic church and down towards Coventry Road. There on the pavement we would encounter local children about to go to their own school, beside the church, so we would set on them and terrorise them for a bit, perhaps chasing them into school. Finally we would arrive at our own school, behind the Baptist church, and carry on our games and fights in the playground until the bell rang.

I did this journey in one direction or the other four times a day, and each time it was crammed with incident. In or alongside the central flow of events all sorts of other things would be going on – two boys would be playing a running game of conkers, or swapping cigarette pictures, or telling dirty jokes, or one would nip across to the other side of the road to barge into somebody else's game of hopscotch. These four journeys were often the best things in the day, and still bulk huge in my memory, like sea voyages. Among the most disconcerting experiences I have ever had was returning to Market Harborough as an adult and finding that each such journey covered only a few hundred yards, and is now no more than ten minutes' walk, if that.

I remember boasting to one of the local children, on the pavement outside the Catholic church, how much bigger London was than Market Harborough. 'It's not just twice as big, or even three times as big, it's twenty times as big.' While I was saying this I thought: I'm overdoing things here. This isn't true. He won't believe it. And he did not believe it. But the truth is that London was several hundred times bigger than Market Harborough, and I myself had not the remotest conception of the fact.

I had little idea where Harborough was. On my daily way to school, when living with the Burgesses, I had passed signposts with names like Kettering, Wellingborough and Corby, but I had never heard of any of them, and had no idea what sort of places they were, or where they were. I never went to any of them. London, of course, was unmanageably distant. It was the common experience among us evacuees that almost no one in any of the families we lived with had been to London. Apart from Mr Toombs's journey between St Pancras and Waterloo, none of the Toombs family had – nor, so far as I discovered, had any of their neighbours or friends. What they thought of as the big city was the county town, Leicester. Once a year the Toombs family organised a day outing there, a mammoth and magical shopping expedition which was preceded by weeks of planning and discussion, and great excitement. Because it was such a special occasion they returned home loaded with presents for those of the family who had not been with them. It was the nearest thing they ever had to a holiday. All this caused me to think of Leicester as so far away as to be beyond my ken. There was never any question of my going there myself, and indeed I never did. It was fourteen miles away.

The only places I went to outside Harborough during the year and a half I was there were some of the nearby villages, and not even many of those. While I was with the Burgesses, Joey and I had walked a couple of times to Braybrooke, three miles away. On one of these walks we had carried on to the little town of Desborough, a couple of miles further. Night began to fall as we were walking back, and we were afraid it would get pitch-dark while we were on the road and in open country. By the last stretch of the way we were jogging. When we got home we were angrily told off for being so late; and naturally, when we were asked where we had been, we said, 'Desborough.' We were not believed. It was considered too far away for us to have been there.

From the Toombses', the village I went to more than any other was Lubenham, two miles away. I liked the walk that took you there, over the hill. It was on Lubenham Hill one night that I first registered that some of the stars were in patterns. It was a lucidly clear night, the sky amazingly full, and I tried to trace some of the patterns. I knew that stars, like aeroplanes, were actually big, and looked small only because they were a long way away. In fact I knew that they were bigger than the world, but looked even smaller than aeroplanes because they were zillions of miles away. And I stood there transfixed, gazing at hundreds of them,

lost in wonderment at them for the first time. I felt an unspeci-
fiable, disturbing intimation that since there were all that many
of them, and they were all that big, our earth and we people on
it could not really be what we . . .

Harborough was my whole world while I lived there, except for
brief trips to London during some of the school holidays. In my
letters to my parents I told them how much happier I was at the
Toombses' than I had been with the Burgesses, and they arranged
to come and see me. I looked forward to showing my father off
to the Toombses, but I puffed him up in such extravagant terms
that Auntie began to wonder whether my parents might not be
too grand for them. She became quite agitated about this. 'Are
you sure they ain't swanky?' she said more than once. 'I can't bear
swanky folks. I do hope they ain't swanky.' I did not know what
swanky meant, and although I asked her I could not get out of
her any explanation that I could understand. To me now it is
fairly obvious that she was afraid of being patronised, perhaps
because my family owned a shop, and had a car, but above all
because they were Londoners. She would have found it intolerable; and it could have ruined her relationship with me. But she
need not have worried. When my parents arrived she found my
father delightful – full of charm, but unassuming and likeable. It
commended him especially to the Toombs family that he was good
at both cards and snooker. It is so much easier to play snooker
on a miniature table than on a full-sized one that he made enormous breaks, breaks of which they had never seen the like. They
were as excited as I was. They were impressed, too, by his sight-
reading at the piano. Knowing from me that he liked opera, they
had dug out from their collection the score of *The Merry Widow*,
which Kath rarely played because parts of it were difficult. The
rest of us stood round the piano while he sight-read it with ease.
I was ravished by 'Vilya's Song', and the way his right hand floated
up the keyboard with the tune: I thought I had never heard

anything more beautiful. The hair on the nape of my neck bristled up harshly, and my skin went cold all over my body, and then stood out in goose pimples. I was transported to a degree I do not think I had ever been before, not even by other music.

The whole visit was a success. It created bonds between the two families, and made me all the happier to be where I was. After my parents had left, Auntie said to me: 'I like your dad. He ain't at all swanky, is he? Funny, you'd've thought he'd be swanky. But he ain't.'

I am not sure about the sequence of events, but I know that after going to Market Harborough in January 1940 I made a couple of visits to London during the remainder of that year. On the first I went for the first time to an opera. It must have been during the school Easter holidays, because it was a birthday treat for me, and the performance was at Sadler's Wells Theatre, which closed in the spring of 1940 for the rest of the war.

The opera, in this case operetta, was *Die Fledermaus*. As people did in those days when they went to the theatre, I wore my best suit, whose conker colour I still remember. I was with my father, mother and sister. We sat in the upper circle on the same level as the chandelier that hung in the centre of the auditorium. I remember my father saying to me: 'Each sheet of glass in that chandelier is as tall as you are,' which was his way of getting me to look at it with interest and curiosity. He had told me beforehand what the story was going to be, and already I knew the overture from his recording of it; but nothing could have prepared me for my reaction after curtain-up. It was as if the music was taking the cover off the stage action and letting me see the real thoughts and feelings that were going on inside the characters. It was what a play or film would have been if you had seen the characters' insides instead of their outsides. And I knew it was the music doing this. It was telling you what was *really* going on. And what music! Occasionally a character would sing a bit from the overture that I recognised, but most of the time they were singing other things; but either way, it was one super tune after another.

In the first interval I asked my father: 'Are other operas like this?'

'Yes. Only a lot of them are better.'

'*Better?*'

'Yes.'

'How?'

'Well, there's no talking. In this one there's lots of talking. But in most of the others it's music all the time. And with some of them it's better music.'

Gosh. In spite of all the listening I had done to his records, I had not realised that opera was like this. I had heard it as music only. I knew there were stories and characters, because he had told me about them, but I had not understood how basic they were to the whole thing, or how connected they were with the music. I had, I suppose, unthinkingly assumed that opera was like what a film would be like if it were all soundtrack music. A new world opened.

The performance must have been on my last day in London, because in the next few days I was walking around Market Harborough singing bits of *Die Fledermaus*, and reliving the fact that with this bit three characters each suddenly shoved the same foot forward, and with that bit one tore his wig off and shouted: 'I am Eisenstein!' I went through it in my mind over and over, the stage action alongside the music, hugging myself about the way they mingled, not having realised that they *could* mingle.

From then on I went to opera nearly every time I went to London. After Sadler's Wells closed, its opera and ballet companies shifted their base to the north of England for a couple of years, but revisited on tour during that time, and then moved back to London. Meanwhile there was a surprising amount of one-off opera in London during the war, even miniature seasons of it. Also there was the Carl Rosa touring company. All of them concentrated on the most popular operas – such as *La Bohème, Madame Butterfly, Tosca, La Traviata* – so these, luckily for me, were the ones I saw first. My special favourite was *La Bohème*, which by my mid-teens I had seen three or four times. Puccini was my first love with staged opera. I have particularly sharp memories of seeing my first *Tosca* at the King's Theatre, Hammersmith, with Joan Hammond in the title role and Otakar Kraus as Scarpia. When I saw *Madame Butterfly* my father described the plot as tawdry (the first time I heard the word, which has ever since been associated in my mind with Pinkerton) and said that as far as the music was concerned we might just as well go home after the first act.

I was older now, and getting to be a better companion for him. Because I was living away from home, and was seldom around, he treated me as if I were on holiday when I was at home, and took me out a great deal, to theatre and concerts as well as opera. It gave him an excuse to see more of the things he wanted to see himself. Like most of the population, he was becoming much better off financially as the war went on. He was also launching me on a way of life that became habitual to me during the school holidays, and which was quite different from the one I lived for the rest of the year – going to live performances in central London once or twice every week. And because I was seeing most things for the first time, they had an impact on me such as few performances have equalled since.

It was either at the end of 1940 or in the following year that my father took me to my first Shakespeare play. This was *Richard III*, with Donald Wolfit. It affected me in some of the ways *Die Fledermaus* had: it seemed, somehow, to be all expression. Never had I been so swept up and carried along by a play. The sheer driving force of it was phenomenal. Wolfit's powerful and explicit style of acting, unsubtle but good, was just right for a child. The play itself came across to me as something like a gangster story set in historical times. What a brilliant idea, I thought, if you were the severalth in line to a throne, to bump off those in between so that you became king. I clamoured to see it again; and the second time I became aware of all sorts of things I had not noticed first time round. About the play as a whole there was something huge as well as marvellous, something that filled every space. It was like seeing the whole world in a play. People had always said that Shakespeare was the best writer of plays, and now I could see what they meant.

What with opera and Shakespeare, on top of the shows I already loved, I developed a passion for theatre in general – perhaps I had had it from the start – that has given it a special place throughout my life. Already, while the older members of my family had been going to grown-up theatre without me, and talking about it afterwards with lots of 'you should have seen this' and 'what a pity you weren't there', I had been revelling in the music halls, the variety shows and pantomimes that I was taken to, and thinking them more fun than anything else I did. When my sister Joan was considered old enough to go to straight plays but I was not, she confirmed my excited imaginings about what I was missing, and I was deeply envious. But now, at last, at *long* last, here I was, going. I was like a starving man let loose on food. The combination of love and greed was lustful. I went whenever I got the chance, and saw whatever came my way, to some extent indiscriminately, though there was always this special love of opera and Shakespeare. Jonathan Miller has remarked to me that Shakespeare's plays are in such a different class from everyone else's that if we call those others 'plays' we ought to have a different word for Shakespeare's; and that is how they came across to me from the beginning. They spoke to me directly in a way that only music did otherwise; and this was not, I think, something primarily to do with the use of language, still less the poetry. It had no more to do with concepts than music does. I was not sitting there listening to people saying words, I was sitting there watching people doing things; I was watching things happen. And for years, whenever I saw a Shakespeare play, for the first few minutes I would have little idea what was going on (or, for that matter, what some of the words meant); but soon it all began to fall into place, and I would be taken up into it in a state of luminous absorption. It became not just clear to me but compellingly interesting who was doing what, and why. I would be lost in it. From then on I would be unaware of not understanding anything, though I am sure that if you had stopped the play at almost any point and said to me: 'What does this unfamiliar word here mean, or that condensed metaphor?' I would not have been able to tell you. It was the play itself that had got me, and was sweeping me along; and I would have seen the words as dangling from its outside, with the same sort of relationship to it as a recipe (which I would also not have understood) to a delicious meal (which I would have eaten with joy). A play is not its words, it is something else, something intangible, that stands behind the words – though the language is needed for us to make contact with it.

CHAPTER ELEVEN

At some time in 1940 an offer came for Joan and me to be evacuated to the United States. Quite a lot of British children were sent there during the war. Our offer came from relations so distant that neither Joan nor I knew of their existence. I think one of my grandfather's siblings, or perhaps a cousin, had emigrated to the United States and eventually acquired a family in the Midwest; and the invitation now came from a younger generation of that family, a couple roughly my parents' age, with children. None of us had met them.

My mother was for sending us, but my father held back. The war had been going on for nearly a year now, and it had become obvious that it was going to last for some years more; so, if we went, it would be a long time before they saw us again, and before we saw England again. Also, getting to the United States meant crossing the Atlantic on a ship that ran the gauntlet of German submarines, so it was not a risk-free option. In fact, the crossings were stopped after one of the boats was torpedoed and seventy-three children drowned. My father was so undecided that he came to the conclusion that we ourselves should make the decision. Joan was nearly fourteen now, and in a better position than I to make a rational choice, which I think she probably did. I was adamant that I did not want to go. Fortunately, Joan did not want to go either, so that was that. But for the rest of the war our father was prey to a feeling that if either of us should be killed or injured, as so many children he knew were, the fault would be his.

Although I did not have the adventure of going to the United States, I did a lot of very good growing-up in Market Harborough, opening out in all sorts of directions. Some of this had to do with the age I was reaching anyway, but some with living away from my family, and some with being for the first time in a happy home. I began to feel a kind of security I had not felt before. In Hoxton I had always been free to wander outside the home, explore, go my own way, do my own thing; but within the home I had felt unwanted, in the way, a nuisance, always having to watch my step so as not to bring down explosions of anger, or get a smack in the face. But the Toombses actually wanted me there, and enjoyed having me, and told me so. Inexplicably, they had chosen to have me. For the first time I *felt* wanted. And this meant I no longer had to get away from home to be myself.

But my very happiness, combined with a deeply ingrained insecurity, gave me an irrational fear of doing something that would bring it to an end by causing the Toombses to send me away. And there was, I was firmly convinced, such a something. On my first day, Auntie had told me, not once but three times, that if I touched any of the musical instruments I would not be allowed to stay. So I developed what can only be described as a phobic terror of being suspected of having touched a musical instrument. The problem was that music was becoming, if it had not already become, my ruling passion, and I longed to immerse myself in it, and learn to play all the instruments, especially the piano. But I did not dare to reveal this to the family, for fear of being thrown out. It is obvious now that they would have helped me in every way they could, but it was not obvious to me then. I suppose it was itself part of my insecurity that I thought the complete rejection of me was something that could happen at any instant. When I stood beside Kath at the piano, singing, I never, ever touched the piano.

I am sure she did not even notice this, and would have laughed me out of the inhibition if she had. When she and I listened to records on the tinny old gramophone, I left her to do everything, I never touched anything myself. And I never allowed myself to be left in the front room alone – until, that is to say, one day.

I was in the house by myself, and I knew that the others would not be back for a long time, so – thrilling with excitement and terror – I went into the front room and started trying to play the piano. I found it impossibly difficult. I could get no music out of it at all, only sounds. I knew there would be no more chances, so I had a go at the zither instead – when I had seen Auntie play it, I had been struck by how simple it looked. I searched on it for the tune she had played, 'Rainbow Valley', and discovered it with an ease that amazed me. It excited me, too, and I played it over and over, first to get it up to speed and then at different volumes – loudly, softly, and then as loud as I possibly . . . *Choi-oinggg-gggg!!* A string broke. My heart stopped. My blood froze. Auntie's words came back to me, and I heard her voice inside my head as if she were there. There could be no doubt about it. As soon as she knew what I had done she would throw me out, and I would never see the Toombses again.

My only thought now was to delay her finding out for as long as possible. The next person to play the zither would see what had happened, but the instrument was not played often, so it might be weeks before it was discovered. I fiddled the broken string into being as unnoticeable as I could make it, and put the instrument back in as unobtrusive a position in the room as I could find.

Ever since then I have had inner knowledge of what it is like to have a guilty secret. For several weeks I lived in permanent terror, almost unable to think of anything else. It dominated my life. Every time anyone went into the front room my throat tightened as if I were being strangled.

The person who discovered the broken string in the end was Kath. She asked me secretly if I had done it, and I said I had – by now she and I were heart-to-heart friends, and in any case she would know it had to be me. 'Better not tell our mam,' she said ominously. Several more weeks went by. Then, at last, Auntie saw it. 'Ooh look, our Kath, one of the strings's broke. Damn nuisance. We'll have to try and get a new one. What a bother.' Then nothing more was said. My relief was indescribable, not least because I was so incredulous. When I finally got used to the situation, and realised that I was not going to be destroyed by it, I came to feel that if that incident did not take me away from the Toombses, nothing was going to.

My closeness to Kath educated me as much as my school did. Not the least part of it had to do with sex – which no older person had ever talked to me about. She told me that the girls in the factory spent most of their time discussing boys, and sex, in very frank terms. She passed on to me, as being the only person she could talk to about it, the juiciest things they said. So I became especially well informed about such things, or so I imagined. I asked her all the secret questions that I had about sex, and she answered them to the best of her ability. I also confided to her my extravagant but secret ambitions about what I was going to do when I grew up, and years later she told me that these changed all the time but were always 'very grand'.

My life with the Toombses fitted in happily with my life outside. I roamed around Harborough with gangs of cockney kids who would call to collect me at the back gate. We extended our wanderings further afield, as we became overfamiliar with our old pursuits, and more adventurous. In the end we were playing in woods and fields, building huts, and climbing trees. Some of the more enterprising boys began to catch rabbits, though I never did. We were becoming, without realising it, countrified. We even started gathering wild flowers, and taking them back to our homes to keep in water, a pursuit which in Hoxton would have been considered cissy. One of our hunting grounds for these was Dingley Dell, which contained standing pools of wild violets. We still, as we always had, fought over territory; and there was once a pitched battle between two gangs of boys over who was to have the violets.

A few days after this battle my parents came up from London to visit me, and the moment they arrived they jumped on me with inquisitorial harshness. I had, they said, just caused them the most appalling embarrassment. They had given a lift to a couple from Hoxton who also wanted to visit their son in Market Harborough, a couple they scarcely knew. No sooner had the car entered the town than a group of boys appeared ahead of them, playing in the street, and the couple shouted: 'There he is! That's him! Stop the car!' My father pulled over, and his passengers called out to their son. The boy came across to the car with the most enormous black eye, a fruity one.

'Good God!' said his mother. 'How on earth did you get that?'

'Somebody hit me.'

'Who?'

'A boy called Bryan Magee.'

Paralysed silence inside the car. My parents, they told me, did not know where to look. The other parents could not think what to say. When my father eventually set them down, he promised to give me a giant-sized telling-off – which he was now doing.

'You must have copped him a real fourpenny one to give him a black eye like that.'

'Yes,' I said with satisfaction. 'I did.'

'Why?'

''E pinched me violets.'

And so he had. After I had gone to all the trouble to gather a really big pile, and was cradling them in my arms, he tried to hijack them by hitting me in the face as hard as he could while my hands were full, grabbing the flowers out of my arms, and running away with them. I was after him like a greyhound, and caught him.

Another way in which we evacuees adapted our old ways to our new circumstances was by taking up competitive games that had not been available to us in London. The one I became most devoted to was conkers. A conker is a horse chestnut, and what you did was thread one on a piece of string and hold it dangling while another boy swung his against it, like a ball on a demolition crane, and tried to smash it. It was then your turn to try to smash his. Each tried to destroy the other's. If you succeeded first, you added to the number yours had broken not only his but also the number his had broken too; so if yours was a twoer and his a fourer, yours became a sevener. We reached amazing figures. Boys not only went to obsessional lengths to find conkers that were unusually compact and hard, they specially looked for misshapen ones that had something like a cutting edge that could split an opponent's conker; and they secretly baked these to make them harder. (This was illegal.) We often went climbing trees for conkers, and knew where the best ones were. Even if you weren't in need of any at the moment, a good one was a valuable commodity that could be traded for something else.

My special friend for a good deal of this time was a boy called George Hall, not from Hoxton but from New Cross, though he had somehow arrived at the Edmund Halley. I had never heard of New Cross, and George told me that it was in south London, which I had been conditioned to regard as a place not to be taken seriously. To this day, whenever I see or hear New Cross mentioned there is a microsecond during which the thought of George Hall crosses my mind. I do not know if everyone's mind works in this way, but there are scores, if not hundreds, of instances in which the connotations of a word have never freed themselves entirely from the circumstances in which I first encountered it; and a large number of these derive from this period of my life. Whenever I hear the word 'tawdry' I think of my father with me at *Madame Butterfly*; and the word 'proceed' brings back the sight and sound of Mr Burgess saying 'p-p-proceed'.

George was a tough boy with a long, pointed, unusually determined nose and chin. His school cap (we were not required to wear them, but a lot of us did) was invariably askew, because when he put it on he picked it up by the peak and swung it up on to his head with a sideways sweep of the arm and then left it where it landed, so the peak was always sticking out to one side. He told me his father was a heavy for hire who worked the south London dog tracks, and he entertained me with funny stories about his old man's adventures. We all, in our different ways, boasted about our fathers, and much of what we said was either made up or exaggerated: no doubt George was the same, but his basic story about what his father did rang true, and George certainly knew a great deal about it all. My father had taken me to greyhound racing tracks innumerable times, and had pointed out to me people like George's father, and explained to me what they did, and the tricks the criminal fraternity got up to; so I was already familiar in quite a bit of detail with the setting of George's stories, and much in them fitted what I knew. I envied him for having these stories; and this led me to invent colourful ones of my own, about my own father, to tell to him in exchange. Although my father could do no wrong in my eyes, and I loved him and my grandfather with unconditional love, I had always felt that working in a shop was an un-macho thing for them to be doing – though I did not regard them personally as unmanly – so I now fitted them out with a few semi-criminal adventures.

I missed George when his family took him back to London, and I never heard of him again. None of us were letter-writers at that age, not even the girls, and none of us had telephones; so when childhood friends were separated there was no more contact. George's place was taken for the remainder of my period in Market Harborough by a boy called Stanley, who lived in Coventry Road, not far from the school. He explained to me that he was Jewish Orthodox and therefore had to be billeted with an Orthodox Jewish family, but at first no one had known how to find one in Market Harborough, and his seemed to be the only one. I asked him what was different about being Jewish Orthodox, and he tried to explain their ways of eating and drinking; but he did not really understand them himself, and got in such a muddle that I never understood.

The war had a great effect on anti-Semitism in Britain. Before it, I had been used, as a normal thing, to hearing people make anti-Semitic remarks, even though there was no trace of this in my family. But once we were at war with the Nazis it became taboo – as someone put it, Hitler gave anti-Semitism a bad name. So whereas in Hoxton there had been a certain amount of anti-Semitism all around, the only time I heard an anti-Semitic-sounding remark in Market Harborough was from Auntie, who was the soul of kindness, and had probably never met a Jew. There was a visiting funfair in one of the fields, and I was there with some other boys when the man running one of the stalls cheated me over my change and then brushed all my protests aside. As a child I was powerless to do anything about it. When I got home I told Auntie, and she said: 'He jewed you.' Each time she told the story, the word came up again. 'Did you hear, our Kath? Bryan got jewed at the fair . . . Yes, they jewed him out of sixpence' . . . and so on. I had never heard the expression, but somehow knew it was not right. This must have been due to my father's teaching, plus perhaps wartime propaganda beginning to have its effect. The massive public indictment of the Nazis that went on throughout the war concerning their treatment of Jews had the incidental effect of driving anti-Semitism very largely, though never entirely, underground in Britain.

In fact the war changed everything, and children adapted to it as if war conditions were normal – which for them they soon were: the blackout (a total absence of any light at all showing out of doors during the hours of darkness, not even chinks of light from windows), rationing of nearly all the basic goods of life, shortages of nearly everything else, queues, regulations, the fact that there were almost no young men around, so that you only ever saw middle-aged and old ones not in uniform. Because social activity was so focused on what everyone called 'the war effort', most other things went by the board, and were either underprovided for or ceased to exist. No services seemed to work as they should, and none could be relied on. If you complained, the reply was: 'Don't you know there's a war on?' You were expected to put up with things no matter how badly they turned out; and on the whole people did: if a train departed two hours late the passengers made a joke of it, and if it then went to a destination different from its advertised one they coped with the consequences of that too with a lot of jokey grumbling. Such things were expected to happen during a war, and it was considered unpatriotic to complain. As government slowly took over responsibility for everything, the inefficiency and muddle that are natural to bureaucracy became a normal part of everyday life.

On the other hand there grew up, alongside that, a community of purpose such as has never existed in Britain before or since. We were all in the same boat, each one doing his bit. 'Doing your bit' became a dominating idea in daily life, and it affected everyone's behaviour. These sentiments grew more powerful as the war proceeded, but they were already strong enough by the end of 1940 to be obvious. When the government appealed to the population to hand over all the metal it could for the manufacture of armaments, people voluntarily gave up the railings in front of their houses, the fences from their back gardens, and all the pots and pans they could do without. I was not surprised that other families should give up theirs, but I did not expect us to give up ours. Kettles and pots that had not been used for years were winkled out of remote corners and piled up in the back room, and even stranger metal objects made their way down from the attic. When Auntie and Kath could think of nothing further they could spare they took up hammers and, to my astonishment, started bashing holes and dents in all the objects. When I asked why they were doing this they said it was so that no unofficial person would steal them and take them home to use himself. This was too good an opportunity to miss, so I grabbed a hammer and laid into the pots and pans with ecstasy.

The peak occasions of our lives were those when Winston Churchill spoke to us on the wireless. Everyone – family, neighbours, teachers at school, other children – would talk excitedly in anticipation beforehand, so there was a great buzz and build-up. When the moment came, the whole family would be seated round the radio, waiting. I remember staring at the set as that voice tromboned out of it. The language was direct and clear: even I understood every word. But the articulation was peculiar to this man: a bit of snarl, a bit of bark, a lot of bray, sometimes a rising inflection as if delivering orders under protest, sometimes a melancholic, throwaway fall – I became familiar with its musical patterns. The message was always the same: defiance. We were not going to give in, ever, in any circumstances: we were going to win this war, whatever it cost. In each speech there would be a sentence or phrase that no one afterwards forgot. But for days people would be discussing the whole speech animatedly, quoting extensively and approvingly, while phrases from it crept into other conversations. Churchill was visibly taking people over, galvanising them, putting backbone into them. And that was how I too reacted. I regarded this man as speaking for me. No other speeches I was ever to hear matched these in the significance they had for me at the time they were made.

I think I was in London, visiting my parents, when the Blitz began – there is often a problem with memory of knowing whether something was itself a beginning, or whether it was just new to me. I was there for part of it, and I think I was there when it started. It evoked surprise and yet not surprise: surprise because of the shock of its happening, and not surprise because it had been expected for a year. I found it hugely exciting: the whistling and screaming of the bombs as they came down, the sound of each one growing louder and louder as it fell, culminating in the satisfying explosion; the fact that, loud as they were, you could not see them falling but only hear them; the weirdly earth-shifting crunch of the anti-aircraft guns; the lordly search lights sweeping the sky, occasionally picking up a plane and clinging to it, chasing it as it veered and ducked, and suddenly being joined by another searchlight that crossed it at the point where the plane was; the elephantine barrage balloons appearing and disappearing in their beams. I would nip out of doors to look at it all whenever I got the chance, with my mother chasing after me to shove me back in. I took it for granted that the bombs would not hit me. I knew I was untouchable. Later in the war, as I grew older and more self-aware, I became terrified during bombing raids. But at the age of ten I found them exhilarating, as if each night was Bonfire Night on an unsurpassable scale.

On the first couple of nights I was asleep in bed when the air-raid warning sounded. My parents dug me out of sleep and bundled me downstairs to the kitchen, where we bedded down. On subsequent evenings they tried to delay my going to bed in case there should be an air raid. In fact, once the Blitz began, London was bombed every night for several months; but at the time people did not know that this was going to happen, so to begin with they looked on it as a separate question each night. If the raid was late in coming, people would start to think there was not going to be one. I would become sleepy and fractious, and complain about being kept out of bed. This drew bitterly ironic comments from my parents to the effect that whenever they had wanted me to go to bed I had wanted to stay up, but now that they wanted me to stay up I was insisting on going to bed.

My father arranged for us to spend our nights in a beer cellar in one of the local pubs, a few hundred yards away. It stood by the bridge over the Regent's Canal, at the bottom of Southgate Road, and was called the Prince of Wales. (Its sign was a head of the boy-king Edward VI, who, as a matter of fact, was never Prince of Wales.) Over the coming years I got to know the publican, Percy Buckhurst, well. He had a full moustache and a deep, carrying voice, and was fully in charge of whatever was going on – every inch the host: hail-fellow-well-met, firm, but genuinely friendly. He liked people, but had no illusions about them. Years later I discovered that his pub was one of two beside the canal in which recruiting was done every evening for jobs that might not be legal. I do not think he felt a need to break any laws himself – apart from the licensing laws, naturally – but he had a good idea what the people in his pub were up to. In this he resembled my father, who was an appreciative observer of life, and knew every trick of the trade, but was honest himself. The two were good friends.

When we left home to spend the night in Percy's cellar we changed into our oldest clothes, and took armfuls of blankets. All my life I have found it unpleasant, bordering on the painful, to have wool next to my skin – I have some sort of allergic reaction to it – and this was when I discovered that fact. The cellar was big, the size of the whole ground floor of the pub, but we and the Buckhursts were the only occupants. We were kept company by gigantic vats of beer, and the pub's entire stock of bottles, empty as well as full. The alcoholic atmosphere, so heavy as to be almost tangible, was thick with the heady, pungent reek of stale beer. I quite liked it, though it may have had something to do with the fact that we were all frowzy and red-eyed when we woke up in the morning. In this state, dirty and dishevelled, still wearing the old clothes we had slept in – and probably smelling of stale beer – we made our way home for a wash and change, and a longed-for breakfast. By this age I had been so indoctrinated with the idea that it was important for us as a family – running a clothes shop as we did – to appear in the streets well dressed that I was acutely self-conscious on these walks home. For the whole family to appear so scruffy together in public felt to me an infringement of the right order of things, as if we were making exhibitions of ourselves. But I did not experience it for long. Either because I had to go back to school anyway, or because it was now looking as if raids were going to happen every night, I was sent back to Market Harborough.

Harborough was never bombed, though Coventry, twenty-five miles away, was, in one of the most famous air raids of the war. I watched it with the Toombses from their attic window. Logan Street runs up a hill, and from the top floor of number 34 Coventry is visible on the horizon – or at least the German air raid on it was. Actually, the scene was as if a volcano were erupting beyond the horizon, so that what we were seeing were the glow and the tops of the flames, and sudden circles of light from explosions, all coming from a conflagration whose main body was out of sight. For me it was like the Blitz again, though the familiar sounds of aeroplanes and exploding bombs were farther away. And the mere fact of having been got out of bed to watch it was enough to make it exciting. Auntie kept muttering things like 'Oh, those poor people!'; and for the first time it crossed my mind that it might not be fun to be in the middle of what I was looking at. In the ensuing days the newspapers and the wireless seemed to be about nothing else, talking up the destruction of Coventry

93

as a war crime. The people of Market Harborough, living so near, discussed nothing else either. And I found myself profoundly moved by it, simply because I had seen it and it was now being talked about.

CHAPTER TWELVE

What to do with me became a problem for my school. When a new year began in September 1940 I was ten and a half, and had another year to go before sitting the scholarship that was later to become known as the eleven-plus. This was an exam that everyone took, and it decided whether you went on to a grammar school or an ordinary school. I had already been through the syllabus of the top class three times, twice in London and once in Market Harborough. (A class existed for half a year.) There was obviously no point in going through it twice more. Yet what else was there for me to do?

The decision was made that I should go along with the rest of the class in all subject matter that was new to me – a new book, a new dictation, anything I had not done before – plus all those activities in which repetition was of value, such as singing and Bible-reading; but for the rest of the time the headmaster would teach me separately. This seemed a good idea. The headmaster, Mr Ogle, said he would introduce me to the next level of mathematics, called algebra. The trouble turned out to be that he could not remember it himself. He had never had occasion to teach it. Algebra was not part of the junior-school curriculum, and in any case he had done no teaching throughout the years I had known him. I would find it impossible to say what he had been doing with all the hours of his day in Market Harborough, where he had three assistant

95

teachers in a school consisting of two classes. There can have been little administration.

The Baptist assembly rooms that had offered us a home were ample for our needs, and the building had an open, wall-enclosed space at the back that served as a playground. Virtually the whole of the first floor was an assembly hall. It could be divided into two by a sliding, folding partition, which we used to create the spaces for our two classes. At the back of my bit was a dais which had been the hall's platform, and was to become my personal territory. To one side of this was the door by which we entered, to the other a tiny room which was the headmaster's study. Although that was so small that it was difficult for more than three people to get into it at the same time, the headmaster spent all his day in it, and was seldom seen. If a boy was sent to him to be punished, the two of them would have to come out into the classroom to have enough space for the swing of the cane. Mr Ogle was given to periodic explosions of anger, and he had a huge voice, so occasionally a lion-like roar would come from that miniature room. The most volcanic eruption ever to be heard was not against a boy but against a boy's mother, who had gone in to talk to him privately. What she said I shall never know, but his voice came from behind the closed door in an unbelievable shout. 'How *dare* you! How *DARE* you! Get out! Get out this minute.' The door crashed open and a good-looking woman was pursued by him into our classroom. To say that his eyes were blazing is not a cliché: it looked as if fire was coming out of them. The woman hurtled into the room and stopped, bewildered, not knowing which way to run. He guided her by chasing her towards the exit door, still shouting: 'How dare you say a thing like that to me! Don't ever show your face in here again.'

At the time I was unable to imagine what she could have said to provoke such a reaction. The only thing I could think of was something obscene, yet somehow she did not look like that kind

of woman. Today the thought occurs to me that she might have
offered him sexual favours in return for help to a son in serious
trouble with the police, or with the courts. That was the way things
were sometimes done in pre-war Hoxton. Be that as it may, the
class, which at the time was under Mr Hickford, reacted in a typically British way by carrying on as if nothing were happening. The
incident was never referred to. When I asked Mr Hickford a day
or two later why it had happened, he said he did not know, though
I could see from his eyes that he did.

Mr Hickford was a broad man with a broad face and an over-
balancing aquiline nose. At the time there was an actor called
Frank Cellier, still to be seen in old British films, who reminded
me of him. Hickford's trouser legs ended several inches above his
shoes, and people's attention was drawn to this by his habit of
moving up on his toes as he walked. His nickname was Jumpy.
He spoke with a regional accent which was neither London nor
Wales: I think it was from somewhere in the Midlands, though
not the part we were in. He was a good teacher, full of common
sense, effortlessly able to keep order without menace. A lot of
what I now think of as level-headed attitudes – liberal yet realistic, down-to-earth yet tolerant – were inculcated by him, and it
was the first time I heard some of them expressed. In this respect
he was like my father; but being a schoolmaster he was in the
habit of addressing us impersonally, about life in general, people
in general, society, religion, politics, the past. He had fought in
the First World War, and this had scarred him. He believed that
war against Hitler was necessary, but discouraged in us any chau-
vinistic or romantic attitudes towards it.

At the beginning of the new year I was given a desk all alone
on the dais at the back of the class, looking at Mr Hickford over
the heads of the other children. This enabled him to include me
in what was going on whenever he wanted to, while leaving me
free at other times to get on with my own work. It was the first

time the school had treated me differently from other children, and Mr Hickford tried to ease this with humour, referring to me jokingly as 'the Professor'. Actually, the fact that I was behind the other children meant that they did not see me during lessons, and were unaware of me for most of the time, so my separate and elevated position – far from causing antagonism, as he had feared – scarcely impinged on them. It was my situation outside the class-room that changed with the new year. For the first time since I had gone to school at the age of three I was the same age as most of my classmates, and this resulted in my being not just a leader but the leading leader, a sort of informal head boy, which I had never been before. I was tall for my age, aggressive, and still quite given to fighting, provided I was sure of winning; and now I could beat anyone in the school. These were the things that really counted with the other children; and it was in those terms that they now saw me – and I came to see myself – as top dog.

The biggest gang in the playground formed itself round me. Mine was the main voice in deciding what we played, and who did what in the game. I made rapid strides in learning how to handle people. But I led them only in what they had always done and expected to do. I lacked the confidence to innovate – with the result that the free and enquiring spirits detached themselves and went off to do their own thing, while the run-of-the-mill majority remained with me. I was a popular conservative leader, but not an exciting or radical one, and certainly not a pioneering or innovative one.

For me, those hours in the playground were marvellously fulfilling. I had, so to speak, come into my own. Having been one of the pack all my life, I was now its leader. The ethos of the pack remained as it had always been. We pursued our ends by any means we could get away with: violence, lying, breaking promises, stealing. The rules, the ways we were *supposed* to behave, were used by us chiefly as a cloak for deception: they represented what others, usefully to us, expected us to do, and we pretended we were doing, but actually did only in so far as we had to: they were our mask, our alibi. Our word was worth nothing, and we looked on anyone who accepted it as a fool. Basically, we were tribal. Our most brutal punishments were meted out to those of our own members who let us down. These got what we called 'torture' – arm-twisting, knuckle-rubbing, Chinese burns – before being cast into outer darkness, or let back in under caution. There is something basic to the human psyche in all this, and in adult life I have found myself recalling it when I have had to concern myself with criminal organisations, especially criminal governments and regimes. They have helped me to understand how naturally and deeply rooted these practices are in a universal and primitive human psychology.

Like all boys of that age who are looked up to as authorities by their mates (I am tempted to say like all authorities), I was a source of much misinformation. The most egregious example I now remember concerned the anatomy of girls. We had had some introductory lessons on anatomy from Mr Fink, during which he told us that every part of the human body served a necessary purpose except for our appendix, which had no function at all but merely gave us appendicitis. Apart from that, he said, every-thing we had was there because we needed it. I was much taken by this, and gave it a lot of thought. I did not see any problem in girls not having cocks, because what they had and cocks were meant to fit one another for an obvious purpose. What about balls, though? You weren't supposed to put those inside a girl; in fact you couldn't. So the reciprocity thing didn't apply to them. I had no idea what they were for, but according to Finky it had to be an indispensable function, whatever it was; and this meant that girls had to have them. Since they did not have them hanging outside their bodies in the ways boys did, this could only mean that they had them inside. The conclusion was logically inescapable; and it provided a neat explanation of why girls looked the way they did: what boys had outside, girls had inside. So I informed my followers that girls had balls, only you couldn't see them, because they were inside. To do my followers justice, there were some who said '*Garn!*' But I continued to believe that women had internal balls until I made the discovery of what balls were for. I must, I suppose, have been already an intellectual in the making.

It would not be fair to attribute the blame for that misunderstanding entirely to Finky; but I suffered for a much longer time from one other for which he was directly responsible. He was taking a Bible class in which we were reading the marvellous lament of David that comes near the beginning of the second book of Samuel, and starts with the words: 'The beauty of Israel is slain upon thy high places. How are the mighty fallen. Tell it not in Gath. Publish it not in the streets of Askelon. Lest the daughters of the Philistines rejoice. Lest the daughters of the uncircumcised triumph.' I put up my hand and said: 'Please, sir, what does "uncircumcised" mean?'

'Well, er,' said Finky, 'the point of what it means here is "unclean". The Israelites thought all people other than themselves were unclean. So what David is really saying here is that the Philistines are unclean.' For years after that I thought I knew that 'uncircumcised' meant 'unclean' because I had been told so in class by a schoolteacher. This meant I also knew that 'circumcised' meant 'clean'.

Among the treasures I carried away with me from what was then truly a bog-standard state school was not just a solid grounding in the three Rs but also a familiarity with many parts of the Bible in the King James version. We read the Old Testament with Finky, the New with Hickford. With Finky we picked out the best of the short stories from the books of Judges, Kings, Samuel and Chronicles, and with Hickford we read the teachings of Jesus, especially the parables, and the key incidents in his life and death. We also learnt by heart the thirteenth chapter of Paul's first letter to the Corinthians, the one beginning 'Though I speak with the tongues of men and of angels . . .' Although I never believed any of it as religion, I thought it terrific stuff. The stories were simply great stories: and pervading all of it there was something hauntingly memorable, unforgettable. It would not have occurred to me to give any conscious consideration to the quality of the language – I would not have known what that meant – but it might have had something to do with my response, because I have always found alternative translations uninteresting, impossible to re-read, however much more accurate they might be. Some of it affects me in the way music does – and there is very little language that does that.

The purveyor of this priceless material, at least as far as the Old Testament was concerned, was not a nice man at all. Finky's stick was never out of his hand, and he enjoyed hitting us. At the same time he tried to curry favour with us by being foul-mouthed in our idiom, but this made us think less of him. He was broad and red-faced, with a thin moustache, and eyes that glittered behind gold-rimmed glasses. On one occasion I was standing alone with him between periods, about to tell him a dirty joke (I got a kick out of doing this to a master, though it would have to be a master I did not respect), when the headmaster came up out of nowhere and joined us. To tell a dirty joke in front of the headmaster was unthinkable, so I tried to make an excuse and slip away, but they both said no, no, stay here and go on with whatever it was you were going to say. That was out of the question. I was covered with confusion. I was not sufficiently master of the situation to come up with something else on the spur of the moment. I became tongue-tied, and went bright red. I have an idea that the headmaster may have interpreted this aright, and that Finky also realised that he did, because both at once became embarrassed and told me to run along.

Years later, when I was a young adult on a visit to Mr Ogle, he told me that Finky had been a 'twister'. He regularly collected money from the other teachers on behalf of an insurance company that offered to top up their pensions, and more of this went into his own pocket than should have done. He was endlessly fiddling with his accounts, and did it at his desk in class while making the children get on with work of their own.

At the beginning of my last school year, Ogle used to have me in his kiosk of a study every day to work on algebra, the two of us filling the room by sitting side by side at his desk. He explained to me what an equation was, and how it could be either valid or invalid, and then set me some simple ones to solve. Unfortunately he omitted to tell me how to do it. I failed completely to get the hang of it by myself. I kept eliminating x from both sides and ending up with $0 = 0$. When he tried to show me where I had gone wrong, and what I ought to have done, he found he could not. For a while he hoped I might somehow hit on it for myself, if I went on trying long enough, and he encouraged me to struggle, but eventually he decided that there was no point in this, so I gave up. He was perfectly happy about that. 'You'll be doing algebra next year anyway,' he said contentedly, as if nothing we had been doing had been of any consequence.

From then on I was left to my own devices whenever the rest of the class was doing something I had done before. Provided I could be seen seated at my solitary desk in the middle of an otherwise empty platform, apparently occupied, it made no difference to anyone else what I did. Occasionally a teacher would wander up and enquire, but he always wandered off again and left me to it.

At first I read. Sparked by Finky's introduction to anatomy, I read a book called *Wonders of the Human Body*, which I found engrossing. It taught me most of whatever anatomy I have ever

known. This was followed by *Lorna Doone* and *Hereward the Wake*
– I think they must have been abridged editions. They transported
me completely away from my surroundings. Since my favourite
film was, and had been for years, *Captain Blood* – I had seen it
four times – I read the novel it was based on, by Rafael Sabatini.
So excited was I by the book and the film together that I felt
impelled to write the book myself – not to copy out Sabatini's,
but not just to tell the story either: to write my own whole book.
By this time I had had enough of reading anyway, and wanted a
change of activity. So I helped myself to a pristine exercise book,
wrote

CAPTAIN BLOOD
by
Bryan Magee

on the first page, and carried on writing. After a week or two of
real effort I grew increasingly surprised and dismayed at how
slowly I was progressing. I kept contrasting the amount I had
written with the bulk of Sabatini's book. Something was obviously
wrong with my assumption that it would take the same length of
time to write a book as to read it. The truth dawned on me that
it was going to need several months of writing every day. And I
began to think that if *that* was what was involved, it was silly to
give all that time and effort to writing a book that someone else
had already written. Only if I wrote a book that was mine and no
one else's would it be worth it. So I abandoned *Captain Blood* and
set to work on an original book.

I had started to write books before, but never persisted beyond
the first few pages. I would begin in a rush of enthusiasm for the
story I had to tell, and then peter out after a couple of days. If
later, after months or a year, I came across what I had written, it
would look shamingly childish to me: I would cringe at the thought

of anyone else seeing it, and tear it up. But now, with my newly gained experience, I approached the task in a more realistic frame of mind.

In the kind of stories I enjoyed reading most, the hero was a crook, or at least some sort of rascal, just as the films I liked most were those in which the hero was a pirate, or an outlaw, or a gangster. I was in thrall to the idea of the baddie as hero. I was still reading pulp novelettes, but also now a few proper books, presumably written for adults, about people like the Saint, Raffles, and Bulldog Drummond. I decided to write a book about a gangster who always wore a mask, and whose identity was a mystery to everyone, friend as well as foe, to be revealed only on the last page. I called it – and him – *The Masked Mystery*. I had no plan for it, I simply made it up as I went along. The whole thing brims with absurdities that are revealing of my ten-year-old self. The sort of thing I would do would be to have gangsters burst ferociously into a nightclub and, at gunpoint, demand ice creams from a terrified management. But I wrote it with my whole self, and meant it with the utmost seriousness.

The moment I began writing, I realised that I did not want anyone to look at it while I was doing it. But this meant I could not write it at school, where teachers would want to inspect whatever I was doing. So, after the first day or two, I worked on it at home, during spare evenings with the Toombses. It took months to finish, but finish it I did, filling two exercise books down to the bottom of the last page.

Because it took so long, I did not embark on the writing of another book until I was grown-up. This one, my first, unexpectedly survives, because it fell into the hands of my sister, and was therefore not destroyed by me in the way I destroyed my other writings. I cannot help toying with the idea of publishing it one day. If I do, I shall not change a single word, but merely paragraph and punctuate it. I would like it to be illustrated by pictures which I see in my mind's eye as not unlike those drawn by Nicolas Bentley for the Damon Runyon stories.

My writing showed the way to my reading. Having started to write books, I now began reading them to the exclusion of novelettes and comics. I had long been in the habit of going to the library with Kath, and now I invariably got her to take out a book for me as well. When people asked me what I wanted for Christmas, or for my birthday, I would ask for a book; and it was those books, books that were mine, books I kept, that made most impact on me. Not surprisingly, people gave me books that were intended for children. One I considered wonderful was *A Buccaneer's Log*, but I cannot remember who wrote it. I discovered school stories, and through them the existence of schools of a different sort from mine – schools where the boys actually lived all the time, and had fun. How marvellous, I thought, to be at a school like that. As I read about the intensity of the friendships that were brought about by living together, and the equally intense hostilities, the high drama of games on proper cricket fields and football pitches, the ragging of unpopular masters, the hushed excitement of secret midnight feasts in dormitories, the forbidden sorties out of bounds, the common life and practical jokes of the dayroom, boys having their own individual studies, and over and above everything else the sheer fun that everyone seemed to be having most of the time, I developed a nostalgia for a world I assumed would never be mine. What so held me about the stories was that it was boys just like me, not grown-up men, who were having the adventures, and that schools like this did actually exist, so that these things were going on in the real world. There was one writer who seemed in a different class from the others, a man called P. G. Wodehouse. He wrote several of these books, but his masterpiece, I thought, was *Mike*.

CHAPTER THIRTEEN

Into my Garden of Eden came my mother. Unexpectedly, she announced a visit to me, by herself, for a weekend. She travelled by rail, and I went with Kath to the station to meet her. She stepped down from the train in a hat that made me think of Errol Flynn in *The Adventures of Robin Hood*. Her suitcase was as big as she could manage. I did not twig, but Kath did immediately. Afterwards, she observed scoffingly, 'You don't take a suitcase that size for a weekend.' As soon as we got back to Logan Street, and polite preliminaries had been gone through, my mother raised with Auntie the question of her staying with us permanently.

Now that London was being bombed nightly, a lot of evacuees' mothers were turning up in Market Harborough to join their offspring, but it had never occurred to me that mine might. Many years later, I learnt from other members of my family that during the air raids she had become terrified to the point of near-hysteria. Hoxton was being bombed to smithereens, and night after night someone known to my parents would be killed, perhaps a whole family. Mine stopped sleeping at the Prince of Wales because of the danger of a direct hit, and travelled by tube every evening out to Southgate, where my aunt Peggy lived with her husband Bill. My grandparents did the same, so all six of them were sleeping every night in one of the northernmost suburbs of London, though they went on working in the centre during the day. That meant they were still, at night, on the edge of the danger area, and they heard the bombs coming down and exploding, and also the aeroplanes, and the anti-aircraft guns. Sometimes a stray bomb would fall not far away. So my mother carried on being terrified, with a fear that was not wholly within her control. The others began to be seriously concerned that she might have a break-down. Some of them looked on her behaviour with compassion, others with contempt, but all agreed that the only sensible thing for her to do was to get away from the bombing altogether. My sister and I had been sent out of London for this purpose, so it occurred naturally to them to think of her joining one of us. That is how it came about that she came to see me 'for a weekend' and asked to stay for good.

Auntie was not keen. She put forward the obvious objections, the chief being that there was not a spare room for my mother to have – there had been once, but I now occupied it, and I was too old to share it with her. Auntie also pointed out gingerly that my mother did not know Market Harborough, and did not know any people there; and she would almost certainly not enjoy living in such a small town, because she was used to London. The Toombses would feel they were letting her down, were not giving her what she expected. And so on and so forth. The discussions went on a long time, with Auntie only too obviously not wanting her to stay. The crucial phase of the talks took place outside my hearing, and I do not know what decided them, but the outcome was that my mother moved in as a paying guest, sharing Kath's room, and her bed. (It was common practice in those days for members of the same sex to share a bed, not least on visits away from home, for instance on holidays.)

It was easy to find a job in wartime, and my mother soon got one as a waitress at the Three Swans, which was then, as it is now, the best of Harborough's hotels. The hours were always long, though variable. To be there in time to help prepare breakfast she had to get up at six in the morning; and although she might be free for two awkward periods during the day, she was not usually able to leave work for home at night until after the last dinner guest had left the dining room. As a healthy woman in her late thirties, living with a happy family, she could still have gained a lot of pleasure from life if her temperament had been different. As things were, she grumbled perpetually. The rest of us became fed up with this – repeated complaint is irksome even when justified. She went on feeling, as she had in London, that she was working hard all the time without ever having much money; and she remained a doggedly lonely person who never came to terms with her situation.

I was aghast at the whole turn of events. Getting away from my mother had been a motive with me ever since I could remember. When I left London to live with my grandmother in Worth, and then again with the Burgesses in Market Harborough, I may have encountered domestic unhappiness in new forms, but it had never entered my head to want to go back to my mother. With the Toombses, for the first time in my life, I had a happy family and a happy home. And now, like a bomb out of an empty sky, my mother had dropped in and was wrecking things. The destruction began immediately. For instance, it had always been accepted by the Toombses that, if a discussion of general interest got under way, I would take part in it on equal terms with everyone else; but on the first or second day after my mother's arrival, she and Auntie were talking about something that was in the newspaper, and I started to speak, getting as far as the words 'in my opinion', when she rounded on me angrily and spat: 'Shut up. You're not old enough to have an opinion.' She felt that the Toombses had let me get above myself, and that I needed to be put in my place.

She felt the same about the dog, Flossie, and objected to her being on the table during meals. In fact she objected, and said so, to a great many things that were taken for granted in the household, from having custard on everything to reading the *Daily*

Mirror. For herself she ordered the *Daily Telegraph*, which she had never read before and which I found nothing like as interesting – when your eye fell on the *Mirror* it was drawn in to pictures, but when it fell on the *Telegraph* it smacked into a solid wall of print. She upbraided me for leaving letters from my father lying around. Other people would read them, she said. I did not think they would, and in any case what difference would it make? She told me to tear them up after I had read them. 'Never let other people know your business' was one of her reiterated lessons to me, which she would enlarge on. 'If you tell one bit of your business to this person over here, and another bit to that person over there, they will both tell other people, and then before you know where you are the whole of your business is known to everybody.' I struggled to understand what this business could possibly be that it was essential nobody should know, and supposed it must be more or less anything personal. Actually I now think that that is precisely what it did mean. My grandmother was the same. In both cases, I believe the attitude had been created by prolonged experience of deprivation and desperation, which produced the feeling that survival depended on rolling your private self into an enclosed ball like a hedgehog.

But I did as I was told. When a letter from my father came I would stand beside the fire reading it and then tear it up and throw it into the flames. One day Auntie asked Kath in my presence, with pointed heaviness, if she had noticed that I always did this, and asked why it should be, and wondered if I thought that other people were going to read my letters, and said nobody would dream of doing any such thing, would they, our Kath? Shamefacedly, I said I did not think so either, but I did it because I had been told to by my mother. This evoked a lot of heavy harrumphing but no further comment.

I had worn glasses for reading since I was five, and my mother decided it was time to have my eyes tested again, so she took me to a clinic in the centre of town, where tests for children were free. When we arrived we found a row of broad-backed wooden chairs on which mothers and their children sat waiting, and we took our places. Someone explained to me that the doctor would need to be able to look inside my eyes, so to make this possible I was going to be given eyedrops that would make the pupils dilate, and it would take a little time for this to have its effect. The drops were put in, with me still sitting there on the straight-backed chair, and I was told to close my eyes and sit quietly. I did. I seemed to drift into some sort of internal confusion, and the next thing I knew, *Crash!*, an almighty smash that I was in the middle of, as if I had exploded. I had to struggle out of uncon-sciousness as if I were deep underwater, fighting desperately to get to the surface. When I came to, I was lying on my back on the floor, looking up at people bending over me, all of them talking at once. My vision was very blurred, which made the whole experience dream-like, but that was actually the effect of the drops in my eyes. I had fainted. I was helped to my feet, and was then violently sick. There was something especially horrible about the whole experience, something traumatic. And although I had never fainted before, I was soon to do so again.

A couple of weeks later, at school, when we were all standing during morning assembly, Mr Ogle said he was going to tell us something of unusual interest that he had just been reading, about how the inner ear worked. I listened in a normal frame of mind, and with interest, until he started talking about cones, and then rods floating in fluids, and my thoughts changed to something like 'Ugh, how horrible, how disgusting!' and then everything went blurred, and *Crash!*, I fainted. I had been standing behind my chair, and a corner of it caught my cheekbone, or the bone above my eye, as I went down. Mr Hickford, who had been standing to one side, bustled over, swept me up in his arms and carried me out of the classroom, then down the stairs to the open doorway, where there was fresh air. I was then grossly sick. He stayed with me. He asked if I had had any breakfast, and when I said I had, he said I must have fainted because of the heat. I knew with certainty that I had fainted because of what the headmaster had been saying about the rods and cones in the inner ear, but for some reason I was not able to say this, so I reacted as if I accepted his explanation. It was the same when I got home at the end of the day. I knew why I had fainted, but was not able to tell anyone. By this time the biggest black eye of my life had puffed up like a purple doughnut which had my eyeball as its hole, so I said I had got this in a fight. It did not occur to anyone to disbelieve me. As the days went by, and the doughnut modulated through all the colours of the rainbow, becoming an object of admiration and wonderment to everyone, I even started to boast about it, as if getting it was an achievement I was cocky about.

Another couple of weeks after that, there was a mass inoculation at school against diphtheria. We queued up at the front of the classroom to get our injections, and then went back to our seats. After I got mine I began to feel peculiar, alarmingly detached from everything. It got so bad that I went up to the front of the class to tell Mr Hickford. While I was talking to him I began to shake all over. He led me to the side of the room, where some wooden benches were set against the wall, and got me to lie down full length on one of them. My whole body and all my limbs were now trembling uncontrollably. It was a terrifying experience. After a while the class carried on with its work, with me lying there to one side shaking violently. No one took any notice of me, and indeed I did not want them to. Eventually I calmed down, and began to feel normal again.

These three incidents, coming close together, were the only ones that were so extreme, but they were a milestone in my life. They brought something into it that has never left, and that I have had to live with ever since. I have phobic reactions to descriptions of the internal operations of our bodies, and to injections, and to medical procedures generally. I have found other people uncomprehending about this, and unsympathetic rather than sympathetic. It is not the case, unfortunately, that by exercising self-control I can master these reactions. Their chain of cause and effect does not pass through my conscious mind, and they have happened before I know they have happened. As far as control is concerned, it is like being in the driving seat of a car whose steering wheel comes off – one is simply carried along, unable to make any connection with the causes of what is happening. Most people seem to find this impossible to understand and therefore to believe. They think I ought to take a grip on myself, and they say things like: 'But an injection is a mere pinprick, it doesn't hurt' – as if pain, which is something they understand, were the point. ('Well if it isn't the pain, what is it?') To this day, if someone starts to describe an operation, I feel faint, and this is not something I can prevent from happening. I change the subject, rudely if necessary, or just tell the person to stop, or else I leave the room. If I did not do one or other of these things I would pass out. Before a visit to the dentist, and before any kind of medical test, I take a tranquilliser – the only occasions when I do. To people with this sort of affliction it comes as a godsend that modern pharmacology has given us the means of defence. Phobic reactions have one thing in common with severe seasickness, in that although they are hideous to experience, to the point where you might start to think that even death would be preferable, a couple of hours later you can feel normal again. But while they are going on there is no question of your thinking about anything else.

It is obvious to me when I look back that this sudden onset of serious disturbance was connected with my mother's crashing into my life. At the time, though, no such connection occurred to me. Just as I had always regarded my nightmares as aberrations unconnected with waking life, so I looked on these new terrors as if they were nightmares that happened during the day, bolts out of the blue, not tied to anything. At about the same time, I started doing some peculiar things. I counted the cracks in the pavement as I walked along: some days I would have to step always on a crack, other days never on a crack. I had to count everything twice; and when I closed a door I had to open it again and close it a second time. When I was beckoned up to the front of the class I believed that my body was being turned round in space as I went, and would therefore need to be turned back again on my way back, so on the return journey I did a reverse spin like a ballroom dancer. Ronnie Gentle noticed this and remarked on it, but I pretended to be surprised, and said I didn't know I was doing it.

Although I did not believe in God, and had never supposed that I did, I started to say prayers in bed at night. There were three or four of these. I made them up myself, and they were interminably long. It was essential that I say the exactly identical words every night, twice. They expressed all my wishes and fears. I remember wanting to pray that I would live for ever, but realising that this was not going to happen, prayer or no prayer, and wondering what the maximum time would be that I could hope for – obviously it would be longer than any individual had so far lived – and settling in the end for two hundred. So every night I prayed, twice, to live to be two hundred. The fact that I would still have to die all the same gave me a feeling of insecurity in the dimension of time, as if I were balanced on a narrow strip of it, and was inevitably going to fall off sooner or later, no matter what happened. There had been no me at all before I was born, and there was going to be no me after I died, so I existed only on this strip in between; and although two hundred years seemed an endlessly long time, I knew it would in fact come to an end, and then I would be dead for ever and ever and ever. Given that I was in time right now, I wanted to stay there. But I knew this was impossible.

This started me thinking about time. How had I got into it? Before today there was yesterday, of course, and there had been a day before yesterday, and a day before that, and so on, back to the day I was born. But there was also a day before the day I was born. And a day before that. Before every day there was a day before. And that meant that there could never have been a beginning – which seemed impossible. Going back for *ever* was just somehow meaningless, it disappeared into nothingness. It was impossible to see how its actually happening could be a fact. Anyway, if there had needed to be an infinite time before getting to now, we would never have reached now. So it must have started at some point. On the other hand, if there was a beginning, what had happened before that? If *anything* had happened before that, it wasn't a beginning. I was stumped. The more I thought about it, the more stumped I became. I didn't see how there could have been a beginning, and I didn't see how there could not have been a beginning. One or the other had to be true, and both were impossible. I became obsessed with the problem.

At some point in all this it occurred to me that the same must be as true going forward as backward. There would be a day after tomorrow, and a day after that; and after every day there would be another day. And either time would just stop or else it would go on for ever and ever. It was impossible to imagine it stopping. How could it stop? And what would happen after that? If anything happened after that, time had not stopped, and was still going on. But how could it go on for ever and ever and *ever*, without *ever* stopping? Such a thing could not actually *be*, surely? Not stopping was as unthinkable as stopping.

The place where I spent most time turning these thoughts over was in bed at night. However, it was in the park behind the swimming baths that I made the discovery that the same thing was true of space as of time. I was lying on my back in the grass gazing up deep into a fathomless sky and wondering what was up there. What would happen, I thought, if I just went up like a firework rocket and kept on going? Could I keep going for ever and ever? Or would I eventually have to stop somewhere? There stole over me the creepy realisation that I had stumbled across another version of the same problem as with time. It was impossible to imagine going on for ever and ever and ever. The endlessness of it meant it could never happen in actuality. But if I came up against something that brought me to a halt, it would have to be something in space, and then what would be on the other side of it? There couldn't be *nothing*, not if it was in space; there would have to be more space. But if there was more space, then whatever it was wasn't at the end of space. I was baffled again, and it was the same bafflement.

In the opening pages of my book *Confessions of a Philosopher* I have gone at length into these childhood musings, and their connection with questions that came up later in my life, so I will not repeat it here. In any case, to do so would unbalance the present book, in which they are no more central than other aspects of my life. I know from experience that most people are not interested in them. Those who are can turn to the other book. The perplexities I am talking of – which admittedly I pondered for part of every day – did not dominate my life: all the other things I have been writing about were going on at the same time. The child who every day puzzled over whether or not time had a beginning also loved singing popular songs at the piano, and spending hours playing games like conkers and release.

Another of my favourite places for spending time in metaphysical thinkings was the lavatory. No one had ever taught me to pay my longer visits regularly, or indeed every day, nor did it occur to me to do so. I went when I felt like it. This was usually every two or three days. Without realising it, and without noticing that I went less frequently than other people, I may well have lived in a permanent state of slight constipation. This had the consequence that my sessions in the lavatory lasted between twenty minutes and half an hour. But they were never a physical problem for me. Something always happened immediately, and then I knew from the way I felt that I needed to wait for a second instalment. People often grumbled at me for occupying the lavatory for so long, but I thought there was nothing I could do about this, any more than I could sleep faster. That was how long it took. And if they could do it quicker, good luck to them. In any case, I quite enjoyed it: I would sit there undisturbed, in peace and tranquillity, lost in all sorts of thoughts and daydreams. On one such occasion, when I had been there even longer than usual, and two other members of the family had been waiting to go with increasing exasperation, there was an outburst of protest when I got back indoors. 'What on earth do you *do* in there all this time?' they chorused; to which I replied, with simple truth: 'Think.' They considered this hilarious, and there were great shouts of laughter. It was taken up into the family's private language, and 'thinking' or 'having a think' became accepted terms for going to the lavatory.

Because my puzzlement about time so occupied my mind, I found myself talking about it to other people – to Kath and Auntie, to three or four of the boys at school, and on one occasion to Mr Hickford. I suppose I expected some sort of *Gosh, isn't that interesting* response, followed by animated talk, but that is not what happened. Some said they could not see what I was talking about – which foxed me, because it seemed to me as clear as daylight. Kath said she could see what I meant, but could not think of anything to say. Mr Hickford said I ought not to trouble myself with thoughts of that kind because they might upset me: better not to think about it, he said. He may already have been worried about me because of my fainting and getting the shakes. None of them showed any inclination to think about the issue: having disposed of it with me they then, obviously, forgot about it. This puzzled me profoundly. How could they not be interested, I thought, if they had no solution to the problem? Why did they not engage in excited discussion with me? I just could not understand it. But there it was. They didn't. After a while I came to the conclusion that there was no point in going on trying, so I carried on thinking about these things by myself.

Mr Hickford's idea that I might find it upsetting proved to be true. That reaction started from a football match that was due to take place the next day. One side or the other was bound to win, I thought, or else there would be a draw. And there was bound to be a particular score, even if it was nil–nil. Whatever the result, that result, and that one result only, was what was going to happen. I had no way of knowing what it was until the following day, but whatever it was, for the rest of time it would be true that that was what it was. And it was true now, already. In fact it had always been true, from the beginning of time, that that was what it was going to be; only I didn't know yet, that's all. With the force of a sledgehammer it hit me that this applied to everything. Just as, in the past, there had been one set of events and no others, so in the future there would be one set of events and no others; and it was true already that they were going to be whatever it was they were going to be. But if this was so, I thought, I could not have any freedom. I was trapped in my life, and nothing I could do would change anything. A feeling of nausea swept over me, followed by feelings of panic. It was claustrophobia. I was terrified. I wanted to run away. But of course there was nowhere to run to. I could not run out of my life. Nothing I could do would make any difference.

When Mr Hickford warned me that my thoughts might upset me I had not understood what he meant. I had always found this kind of thinking absorbing. It was frustrating, admittedly, because

I did not seem able to find any answers to the simplest and most obvious questions; but this very fact made the questions interesting, kept me thinking about them, and held me in thrall to them. Out of that I got some sort of satisfaction alongside the frustration. But now I was frightened. I tried to stop myself from thinking about the future in this particular way. It was too terrifying to face. It became a taboo subject for me within myself, and I shied away from it every time it hove up on the horizon of my thoughts.

CHAPTER FOURTEEN

At the end of 1940 the Magees and the Toombses spent Christmas together in Market Harborough. My mother was there already, my father came up from London, and my sister Joan, now fourteen, came over from Huntingdon.

My father arrived with a pile of records and our old wind-up gramophone. It was obvious to him that my passion for music was developing at an express rate, and he was concerned that I was not getting the best stuff, which in his mind was orchestral music and opera. The only classical music I was hearing was the little salon piano pieces that Kath played. If I had been living at home, he would be taking me to concerts by now, but in any case there were no concerts in Market Harborough. Nor, of course, was there any opera. So he brought records of these things to leave behind. On his previous visit he had noted the tinniness of the Toombses' old gramophone, so he brought our much better one, which he no longer needed because he had his electric radiogram.

He also brought a Monopoly set, which the rest of us seized on and played addictively throughout the Christmas holiday. As a game it still possessed an aura of novelty. I had watched it being played in London before the war, but had never been allowed to join in, if only because the grown-ups played for real money. They had told me that first-class passengers on the transatlantic liners played not just for real money but for the sums specified in the game. I grew to love it in a way I have loved no other board game, in fact few games altogether – billiards and snooker some time later, and then poker.

For a child, I became quite good at Monopoly. The top hat was always my talisman. My favourite game plan, if the fall of the dice gave me any chance of following it, was to make a determined effort early on to buy up the property sets with Whitechapel and the Angel, because the cheapest properties were the easiest to get control of, and if you could do it quickly enough you could build up a winning position earlier than other players. The game is very educative in how to conduct negotiations, which is what it mostly hinges on.

It was a glorious Christmas, with an abundance of whatever were the unrationed foods, and music in such intervals as we allowed ourselves between marathons of Monopoly. My sister Joan kept herself a little apart from it all. I discovered when I talked to her alone that she had a different attitude from the rest of us. The girls of Highbury Hill High School were would-be sophisticated young ladies who had been ejected against their will from the capital city just before they expected to inherit it. They looked down their noses at the country folk with whom they had been billeted in Huntingdon. They were much worse in this respect than us younger boys, and Joan, then embarking on a perfectly normal phase of teenage awkwardness and self-consciousness, arrived in Market Harborough with attitudes of this kind towards the Toombses – who, of course, objected to them, just as the people of Huntingdon must have done. The result was a silent stand-off between the two parties. But the Toombses showed themselves very understanding about it, and did not allow it to impair their relationship with me.

After my father had gone back to London I found myself the keeper of some of his records, and able to play them whenever I liked. There was Wagner, of course, but all of it (I am sure by design) straightforwardly tuneful, none of it slitheringly chromatic or 'advanced': some of the more lyrical parts of Act III of *Lohengrin*, for example, and Act I of *The Mastersingers*. One oddity was a transcription for solo violin and orchestra of one of Wagner's rare piano pieces, 'Album Leaf', a fill-up to the overture to *Tannhäuser*. There were excerpts from stage works by other composers too, for instance duets for tenor and baritone from Verdi and Puccini, and my old friend the ballet music from *The Bartered Bride*. The purely orchestral pieces were short – for instance Beethoven's *Egmont* overture, and Mendelssohn's overture to *Ruy Blas*. The nearest thing to a contemporary piece was *Rhapsody in Blue*. I realise now, thinking about it, that there were not all that many more records than I have named; but at the time it seemed like a cornucopia. I played them until I knew them by heart – and then went on playing them. Often, if I was by myself and had only a few minutes, I would pop into the front room just to play one side, which lasted about four minutes. The fact that these records were now 'mine', and the gramophone too, and I could play them whenever I wanted to, and listen to them by myself, made a huge difference to me. I felt I had begun my first free voyage out on to the open sea of music.

My mother, who must have been given a record token by my father at Christmas, bought a couple of records to add to this collection. Both were highlights from operas she had seen with him and enjoyed, *Madame Butterfly* and *The Tales of Hoffmann*, in each case a potpourri of some of the best tunes strung together for orchestra – or rather, in the case of *Hoffmann*, for military band. The Toombses were surprised at how much better their own records sounded on this new gramophone, so we all went through a honeymoon period of record-playing.

I was hearing again, after a long time, the sound of a symphony orchestra. And again, as before, it spoke to me in a unique way. My skin prickled into gooseflesh at the sound of the violins: the sound itself was beautiful, regardless of what they were playing. I formed a passionate desire to learn the instrument, and started badgering my mother about it. She kept saying no, it was too expensive: first of all you had to buy the violin, then you had to pay for lessons. But I went on and on about it, and in the end she said all right, when April came she would buy me a cheap second-hand violin for my birthday – not a good one, mind. 'Do you promise?' I persisted. 'Yes,' she said. 'What about lessons?' I asked. She laughed and said: 'There wouldn't be much point in giving you a violin if you didn't learn how to play it, would there?' This reply made me tingle all over.

For weeks and months I lived for the violin I was going to get, thinking about it several times a day, and in bed at night. I peppered my mother with questions. 'Where are you going to buy it? Who are you going to get to give me lessons?' – and to these she always gave wait-and-see answers, accompanied by looks and body language indicating what a wonderful surprise it was all going to be. I ticked off the agonisingly slow days to my birthday, and feared they would never pass. During the night before, I hardly slept. I went down to breakfast in the morning almost uncontrollable with excitement, my heart in my mouth, expecting to see the violin on the table, and wondering whether it would be packaged or naked. I found a different present there. Still the penny did not drop. As I started opening the present I looked up at my mother and said: 'Haven't you managed to get the violin yet?'

'What violin?'

I naturally assumed she was joking. 'The violin you're giving me for my birthday.'

'I'm not giving you any violin.'

She was serious. I stopped unwrapping the present. I could not take in what she was saying.

'But you promised,' I said.

'I was joking.'

This was flagrantly a lie, at odds with everything that had been going on for weeks. 'No you weren't,' I said. 'You promised.'

She laughed, snortingly and derisively. 'Now you're the one who's joking. How on earth could I afford a violin? Where would I get the money from? Be serious.' She laughed again, as if it had been obviously a joke all along.

I was reeling. Everything started moving away from me. 'Why did you promise?'

'To keep you quiet.'

In that moment it was as if the world stopped. She had straightforwardly lied to me, betrayed me, in what mattered to me more than anything else in the world. I was completely incredulous, except that I knew it had happened. But I could not come to terms with it. I went into a state of shock.

I had never liked my mother, but this was a historic turning point in our relationship. Before, I had thought of her as indifferent to me. Now she was behaving like an enemy. And so she was to prove at other points in the future. Only a few months later she put all her energy and determination into preventing me from being given piano lessons which my father wanted to pay for. And she was successful in that, too, for a time.

My relationship with Kath became closer, no doubt because of all this. I was growing up fast at this age, and becoming more of a companion for her. In music she had a special love for the operettas of Sigmund Romberg and Rudolf Friml, songs from which had been popular hits between the wars – 'Indian Love Call', 'The Desert Song', 'The Donkey Serenade' and the rest. She had the piano scores of some of them, and I sang from these to her accompaniment. The most popular of the operettas had been, and were still being, made into films, all of which she had seen. The leading stars were usually Nelson Eddy and Jeanette MacDonald, and Kath had decided that Nelson Eddy was her pin-up boy. He was a good-looking baritone with a fine, if hard and unvarying, voice. I went with her to the Oriental to see the films *Balalaika* and *New Moon*, and became hooked on the songs in *New Moon*. I had been given some money for my birthday, so I decided to buy the records from the soundtrack. When I told my mother this she forbade me to do it. I was taken aback – it was my money, and I thought I could do what I liked with it. She said the songs were rubbish, and that I wanted to buy them only because of the influence of Kath. It was too much money to spend on records, she said – and records were far too expensive, anyway. I knew that my wanting to buy the records had nothing to do with Kath, and I insisted that it was my money to spend as I liked. We ended with a compromise: I could buy two ten-inch records, but no more.

When I told Kath and Auntie what had happened, Auntie said: 'Why does she say the songs are rubbish?'

'She says they're about nothing else but love. And all that stuff about love is a lot of silly nonsense.'

Auntie looked personally affronted. 'But it's love that makes the world go round, isn't it, our Kath?'

At about the same time, my mother did a parallel thing over books. There was a lending library just off the main square, near my school, and Kath asked me one day if I would change her books there for her, giving me a note about what she wanted. When I was in the library the thought came into my head that it might be time I had a go at one of these grown-up novels myself, so I picked out two or three extra and persuaded the librarian to let me take them. There was nothing saucy about any of them, as I recall: they were standard middle-brow commercial fiction, the usual lending-library fodder, which was positively demure by today's standards. But when I got them home my mother was scandalised.

'You can't read those,' she said. 'They're much too old for you.'

She was rattled and angry, and I was puzzled as to why. I could understand that I might try the books and find them boring, but I did not see how they could do me any harm.

She exclaimed about how wrong it was of the librarian to let me have the books. 'What can she have been thinking of? It's disgraceful. She ought to be ashamed of herself,' and a lot more in that vein.

Next day she marched down to the library, with me reluctantly in tow, the books held savagely under one arm, and berated the librarian in front of everybody else there. I could see that the poor librarian was as much at sea about what she was supposed to have done wrong as I was. In retrospect, my guess is that my mother was rattled by the fact that I was growing up, perhaps even beginning to overtake her in some respects, and she wanted me to stay in my place. Also, I think, I was getting the backwash of years of resentment at the money my father spent on books and records which were of no interest to her, while the family was living in poor circumstances. She had come to look on such things (plus theatre, opera, and above all concerts) not as feasts that enriched our lives but as follies that were ruining them, and she viewed them with implacable hostility. I was to come damagingly up against this attitude for the rest of her life, which lasted until my mid-twenties.

The most immediate result, in the Market Harborough library, was that the librarian was ordered to allow me to take out children's books only. Kath was to be left to change her own books in future, and I was to be kept on a diet of *Just William* and the like.

I had, myself, no sense of books or music being in any sort of hierarchy. The only thing that seemed to me to matter about any such thing was whether you liked it or not, or at least whether you found it interesting. I was constantly having the experience of finding myself suddenly liking something that I had not liked before, so I never thought of taste as fixed. When I played records,

I played Beethoven and Wagner interspersed with music-hall songs and jazz, whatever I felt like playing. That unmistakable inner feeling that you got in response to some things but not others was the only thing that mattered; and you could get it in response to anything. You got it to differing degrees, of course; but even so, you either got it or you didn't: no one could *talk* you into having it, nor could you talk yourself into having it. If someone else got it and you didn't, that might persuade you that there was something you were missing, and you might give it another try. Lots of music of every kind gave me the feeling, and plenty of every kind did not, and as far as I was concerned, any of the former was better than any of the latter. Taken all in all, there was no shortage of good stuff.

If I knew a piece of music, I took it for granted that all well-informed grown-ups were bound to know it too. Once, in a bout of enthusiasm for a tenor–baritone duet from a Verdi opera, I asked Finky and Ogle what they thought of the singers Heinrich Schlusnus and Koloman von Pataky, and if they could tell me what else they had recorded. The two teachers responded in an amused way, asked me how I came to know the record, and exchanged approving little glances as I explained. I could see perfectly well that they were jollying me along, but I thought it was because this was ABC to them, even though they happened not to know the answer to this particular question. It would never have occurred to me that they had not the remotest idea what I was talking about, and that this was the joke between them. It was a long time before I realised that most people were not acquainted with, and did not even particularly like, the kind of music I found myself loving most. And when I did, I found it hard to understand, and even harder to come to terms with.

In 1941 we were all getting deeper and deeper into the war. One morning Kath came into my bedroom and woke me up to tell me that Germany had invaded Russia. After that I followed Hitler's drive into Russia in the *Mirror* every day with such intensity of interest that I can still remember some of the cartoons and maps. Our government told us to grow as much food as we could, and even advised us what to grow – for instance rhubarb. Everyone grew rhubarb, and we ate rhubarb jam ad infinitum, not to mention rhubarb tart, rhubarb pie and just plain rhubarb (with custard). Unused land in and near the town was turned into allotments to grow food, and most families acquired an allotment in addition to their garden. The school had one, and my class had to spend an afternoon every week working on it. That was where I learnt to use a spade, fork, rake and hoe. I got a certain satisfaction out of digging up potatoes with a fork, but for the rest I found it intolerably boring. So I leant on my spade and chatted instead – to the exasperation of Mr Hickford, who supervised us. He made me work next to him so that he could inhibit me. Once, when he and I were digging, he asked if my name was Irish, and I said I didn't think it was. It was the first time I had heard this mentioned, and it was a blank to me. He said he had fought his way through the First World War without acquiring any grievances against anybody except for one person, an Irishman who had done the dirty on him. This had given him a permanent prejudice against Irishmen; so he was pleased I wasn't one.

The fact that all of us, the whole of society, even children, were working together in a joint war effort created a bond that I can still recall. It was a marvellous feeling of common purpose and social warmth. Self-evidently, we had to win the war, whatever it cost, so everything must be subordinated to that; and we all had this feeling of being an essential part of it. To many individuals it gave a sense of purpose and fulfilment that they never had at any other time, and after the war one often heard people say that the war years had been the happiest of their lives.

This warmth of comradeship flourished in a daily life that was physically deprived. There was no investment in the social fabric, so the look and quality of everything declined, became run-down and grey, tatty. The world out of doors was totally blacked out from sunset to sunrise. Basic foods were rationed; so was clothing. Everything else was scarce, so you had to queue to get most things. Long, silently waiting queues were part of everyday life, and many people spent several hours a week in them, especially women with large families. Children were often sent to do the queuing, or part of it. Factories kept their output up round the clock by changing over to shift work through the twenty-four hours. My mother and Kath were like the rest of the population, or most of it, in getting out of bed in the dark to go to work in the morning.

The factory in which Kath worked was a few yards beyond the end of our garden, its chimney visible to someone sitting in our back room. Previously it had manufactured swimming costumes, but now it was packing parachutes. Its chimney emitted not just smoke but noise: about every five seconds it gave a loud, vibrant belch that was a nerve-racking nuisance for everyone living near it. At one level of my mind I got used to it, and ceased to notice it, yet at another I was conscious of it all the time. The people in the neighbourhood complained to the local authority, but were told that nothing could be done: the chimney had once had a silencer, but this no longer worked, and a replacement was unobtainable in wartime. The factory had to carry on because it was involved in essential war work. So the people living round it would have to put up with it. ('Don't you know there's a war on?')

Because Kath started work early she got home at about the time I got back from school. We would then do something together while Auntie prepared the tea – play darts or skittles, or sing a few songs, or listen to records. After tea I would go out and play with my friends most evenings; but sometimes I would stay in and play a game with members of the family, or listen to the wireless; or there would be a musical evening. The radio programmes we listened to were mostly variety shows, of which there were a great many, and which we loved. Radio then had the place in people's lives that television was later to acquire: its stars were known to everyone, and their catchphrases came into everyday conversation. At school we would fling around jokes we had picked up from them, and would sing their songs – between us we could usually piece the words and tunes together. One of the comics we read was *Radio Fun*, the characters in whose strip cartoons were the radio personalities.

Some evenings, depending on the hours my mother was working, I would pick her up at the Three Swans and we would go to the pictures. Sometimes I had to hang around till she was free, and then I would chat to the other people behind the scenes in the hotel. The staff got to know me; and it was on these occasions that I met the owner, John Fothergill. What impressed me about him more than I can express was that he had written one of the books we had at home, *An Innkeeper's Diary*. He must have been the first author I met. Needless to say, I had not read the book, but I was familiar with it as an object, and knew that it was about the job I was seeing him doing, namely running a hotel. He must have been the best-known hotelier in Britain at that time, because his book had been a best-seller in the thirties and was currently in Penguin Books at a time when Penguins were the only mass-circulation paperbacks. I saw him as an outlandish figure. He wore his hair to his shoulders, and buckle shoes, and went out of doors in a cape, none of which I had seen a man do before. Yet he was not effeminate. He had a wife and two sons, and was very much the boss, both of his family and of the hotel. He spoke to everyone in a direct way that I found disconcerting. He was simply saying what he thought and felt, but I had never heard anyone do that. If he thought you had an ugly face he told you so. Sometimes you could scarcely believe your ears. Most of his staff took little offence, having learnt from experience to let it brush off them. ('Oh, you don't want to take any notice of him. That's just his way. He's all right.') Some could not cope with it, and left. My mother was impervious to his candour. She would probably have talked that way herself if she could have done so and survived.

I still possess two copies of *An Innkeeper's Diary* that he inscribed to her, in one of which he had stuck that day's menu, not even the size of a postage stamp. It is written in his own hand in black ink on a piece of orange card:

```
3 Swans
soup
lamb
stk & kid pie
rabbit
jam roll
treacle pud
cheese
```

Underneath, on the flyleaf of the book, he had added: 'paper-saving device 12.12.40'. All this was his way of protesting against wartime shortages of food as well as paper, and disclaiming responsibility for their effects. All his menus were like this, and he wrote new ones each day, with great care (he had been an art student). My mother felt a fool when she handed this menu to a guest, who often could not read it because it was so small, which meant she had to tell him what it said. Not that Fothergill cared what guests thought – if he did not like one he told him so, and told him not to come again. My mother had many good stories to tell along these lines. But some of the most interesting things about him were things I did not know, and would not have understood. He had been a close friend of Robert Ross, who in turn was the closest and most loyal friend of Oscar Wilde. After Wilde's imprisonment and exile, Fothergill visited him in France and stayed with him there. A mere eight or nine years after I knew Fothergill, the opportunity of asking him about all this would have been valuable beyond price, but it was wasted on me when I was ten.

CHAPTER FIFTEEN

I was in Market Harborough when a bomb destroyed my old school in London, completely, and made the rooms over our shop uninhabitable. This happened in a night raid, when my family and the neighbours were sleeping somewhere safer, so no one that I knew was hurt. The shop itself remained undamaged. It continued in business throughout the war, and for several years after. Eventually it was swept away as part of a slum-clearance programme. Today there is nothing there, just a small empty space.

After the bombing, my father had no choice but to move. Since he was already spending nights at his sister Peggy's in Southgate, and his parents now lived in that area, it seemed natural to look for a place near there. A huge number of families left London during the Blitz – many thousands of rented homes were simply abandoned – so house prices and rentals tumbled, and he found he could hire a roomy modern flat at a low rent. The one he chose was in a block only five or six years old, built in the mid-thirties almost opposite Arnos Grove tube station, which is the station before Southgate on the Piccadilly Line. The address I now wrote to was 22 Arnos Grove Court, London N11. It conveyed nothing to me at all – I had never heard of Arnos Grove, and was not to go there until I left Market Harborough for good in the summer of 1941.

In the spring of that year the so-called Battle of Britain took place. This was a battle between two air forces, Germany's and Britain's, for control of the sky over southern England. The Germans wanted it because the invasion they were intending was guaranteed of success only if they had air control. The outcome was touch-and-go: the British came within a hair's-breadth of losing. If they had, they would certainly have lost the war, which would then have been over altogether, with the Germans the victors – neither Russia nor America was yet in it at that point. As it was, the British air force – few in numbers and inadequately serviced, the pilots flying themselves to exhaustion – snatched the victory by the skin of their teeth. It is a heroic story, immortalised in one of Churchill's most quoted sentences: 'Never in the field of human conflict was so much owed by so many to so few.' Those pilots are still sometimes referred to as 'the few', and rightly so. They achieved the cessation of the nightly bombing of London, and far beyond that the fact that Britain remained in the war, to become three years later an indispensable launching pad for the invasion of western Europe by, chiefly, the Americans. This was true liberation for the whole of western Europe, which, without it, would have faced 'liberation' and domination by Stalin as the only alternative to Nazi occupation.

To me at the time, the most important consequence of the Battle of Britain was that my mother returned to London because the bombing had stopped, and left me at the Toombses to become happy again.

At the end of the school year, that summer, I sat for the scholarship, as did my classmates. It was a school from which rarely more than one child a year would be expected to pass. The previous year it had been a boy called John King, but his parents would not let him go to a grammar school, for fear he might 'get above himself', as they put it – might think he was too good for them. The year before, in London, it had been a boy called Bourne, very clever – I do not know what became of him. This year it turned out to be me. That surprised me, because I knew of at least one serious mistake I had made in the examination. This had been invigilated by the headmaster, Mr Ogle, who walked round the room from boy to boy, gazing down thoughtfully but silently at their answers as they wrote. Afterwards he explained to me a mistake I had made in the arithmetic paper, resulting in a wrong answer. When I heard this I thought: Well that's it, then. No grammar school for me.

But I was passed, the only pass in the school. There seemed to be some question about what school I should go to next – not, apparently, the grammar school in Market Harborough. Grammar schools in those days still charged fees, and for children who got scholarships these were paid by local government; and the local authority in Market Harborough was willing to pay only for local children. I would have to go to a school which was contributed to by the London County Council. So it looked as if I would be sent to a London grammar school that had been evacuated some-where else, in the way my sister's had to Huntingdon. I waited to be told which one.

Meanwhile, knowing I would not be coming back to Market Harborough, I went to London for the summer and stayed in my parents' flat for the first time. Never having been there before, and knowing that I was not going to stay for long, I found I no longer thought of my parents' home as my home. In fact it was with reluctance that I had left Market Harborough. I had been happier there than anywhere else in my life. To this day I have a special affection for it.

My regret increased when I looked around in Arnos Grove. This was unknown territory. I was not acquainted with a soul there, did not know even such shops as there were, or the streets, or the names of the streets – rows and rows of anonymous houses that were there only because railway and tube stations were nearby. It was unrecognisably different from any environment I had known, and it felt like a desert. To a degree that was almost disturbing I found it empty and alien. There was, so to speak, nothing there, no oxygen for me to breathe. To do anything, even fairly basic shopping, one had to go somewhere else. From that time onward I paid three visits a year to it until I joined the army, but only for brief stays, and never got to know it properly. I never felt it belonged to me or to my life, as I had felt so strongly about Hoxton and Market Harborough. That experience implanted in me a dislike of suburbs, an active hostility to them that has remained with me ever since, though I am belatedly coming to realise the occasional unfairness of this.

Being at Arnos Grove was at its most interesting at the beginning of the experience, when everything was new. The two nearest shopping centres were Southgate and Palmers Green, both of them a journey away. These were typical suburban shopping centres, but I had never made use of such things before, and the novelty was stimulating. To Palmers Green we went on a bus, or, if we wanted to save ourselves a long walk, two buses. We preferred it to Southgate: there was a greater variety of shops, including a bookshop; two cinemas (one calling itself the Palmadium) as against Southgate's one; and, not least, a theatre. All London's theatres (except for the Windmill, which afterwards proclaimed 'We never closed!') shut down at the outbreak of war, and this one had been the first to reopen. It was small, called The Intimate Theatre, and had been founded in the mid-thirties by a very young John Clements, now a famous actor. He directed weekly repertory there, appearing in many of the plays himself. We went as a family quite often, though our primary allegiance remained with West End theatre. This had now got going again, bomb-damaged and blacked out – one or two of the theatres had been totally destroyed – but with a new spirit that was sparkling and alive with the defiant vitality of wartime. To get to the West End from our flat, all we needed to do was walk across the road and get on a tube that took us to Piccadilly Circus in twenty-five minutes – which was about the same time as it took us to get to Palmers Green.

We went to the West End for other things too: on Sundays at leisure, as we had in the past, but also, now that there were two earners in the family, on shopping expeditions. One of these remains a treasured memory. My father felt he could at last afford a complete recording of a symphony or a concerto. Most of the symphonies he wanted occupied six discs, the concertos four or five. Long public consideration was given to what it should be. The choice came down to Tchaikovsky's Fifth Symphony or Rachmaninov's Second Piano Concerto. But still he could not make up his mind. So evenly attractive were they for him that he decided to buy whichever the rest of us preferred. So, with much prior discussion and a sense of family occasion, we went together to Imhof's in New Oxford Street and spent an afternoon crowded together into one of the tiny booths listening to different recordings of both works. In the end we took a vote. The winner was Tchaikovsky, in the performance by the Philadelphia Orchestra under Stokowski. We carried it home in triumph – metaphorically, you might say, brandishing it over our heads – and I got to know that symphony note for note before I heard most other symphonies at all. However, my father's appetite for the Rachmaninov had been intolerably whetted, and before long he bought some of that too, though only the last movement, and in a cheaper recording: so I got to know that movement by heart before hearing any of the rest of the concerto.

He was now acquiring so many records that storing them became a problem. He got a cabinet-maker in Hoxton to make a piece of furniture to his specification, with drawers just the right size for records, and designed to stand in a particular corner of our living room. There would have been no space for such a thing in our old home. Our new flat was preferable in every way, except for where it was. It possessed not only an indoor lavatory but a bathroom, and a modern kitchen. There were four other rooms, two of them quite sizeable: one of those was our living room and the other my parents' bedroom. There was a middling-sized but still comfortable room for Joan, and a smallish one for me. The flat was in a corner of the building, on the second floor, and protruded in such a way that it had windows on three sides. This gave it a lot of light. It lacked amenities which today might be taken for granted – there was no central heating, and no lift – but in those days few people had either of these, and it did not occur to us that we should have them. In fact we thought of ourselves as well housed – except that my mother did not regard a flat, any flat, as a proper home. She thought of us as camping, albeit comfortably, after having been bombed out. In her view, only when we had a whole house, like Peggy and my grandparents, or the Toombses, would we have a real home.

My grandparents having moved too, to Southgate, it was a journey of only a single stop on the tube for us to visit both them and Peggy. Family visits became a ritual Sunday activity. During the week my father and grandfather commuted by tube and bus to the family's shop in Hoxton; and all of us went to the theatre by tube; so the tube was our lifeline. I thought of us as travelling on it by day to wherever our lives were, and coming back on it at night to sleep in a dormitory called Arnos Grove.

My father, though he still worked in the shop, was no longer able to go there every day. He had been conscripted into ARP – Air Raid Precautions – by the branch called Heavy Rescue. Its job was to dig people out of the rubble of bombed buildings. In addition to the digging, he drove one of the trucks that carried away the injured and the dead, as well as the rubble. Carrying wounded in these circumstances called for driving with sensitive care for the injured in the middle of an air raid, usually over rubble, which was sometimes burning. The rescuers had found that if they waited until an air raid finished before they started doing their work, the death and suffering among the victims were appallingly increased, so they started at once, with the air raid going on around them. It meant digging in the dark, or in only such light as the raid itself provided. This rendered all the more grisly some of the things they uncovered – severed limbs, legless corpses, an eyeball, a tongue. My father worked at this throughout the Blitz, and the fact that his contribution to the war was humanitarian mattered a great deal to him, but he found it horrifying – not enough to make him ill, but enough to give him nightmares. He found it almost impossible to talk about.

Because the work was so stressful, and nearly all of it at night, the rescuers were not on duty permanently but worked in shifts – twenty-four hours on, twenty-four hours off. This enabled my father to be in the shop in Hoxton every other day. This had been going on for months while my mother and I had been in Market Harborough, but he had said nothing about it in his letters.

When I came back to London in the early summer of 1941 the nightly raids had stopped, but no one could be sure of that at the time, so rescue workers, like pilots, had to stay at their posts. On my father's invitation I sometimes dropped in on him at his ARP depot during the day. And I sometimes went with him to Hoxton, which was now in a pitiful state. A third of it had been physically destroyed. East London in general got the worst of the bombing, because the chief target was the docks, and the docks were in east London. Much of the slum housing of which it largely consisted was so flimsy that a building did not need a direct hit to be destroyed: it could all too easily be swept away by blast. Thus a well-placed bomb would demolish a whole street. In Hoxton several streets had simply disappeared. There were bomb sites everywhere, on which only the most rough-and-ready beginnings had been made to clear up. There were far fewer people around than before the war: the children had been evacuated, the young men called into the armed forces, and as many of the rest as could do so had left. A lot had been killed. Everyone knew people who had been killed – my family, being shopkeepers, knew more than most. For years afterwards I would still be hearing: 'Don't you remember So-and-So? He was killed in an air raid.' The victim that I knew best was my grandfather's favourite sister, known to us all as Aunt Rose – an almost picture-book sweet old lady, especially good with children.

Because of all these things, Hoxton was something of a ghost town. But new figures were beginning to appear in it. The head villains of the razor gang that had lived in Hoxton before 1936 were coming out of prison. For years in the early thirties they had terrorised the racecourses of southern England, until their activities became a national scandal and they were lured into the notorious Battle of Brighton and swept off to gaol. Penal servitude 'with hard labour' meant what it said in those days, and the men, still young, came back fitter than they had ever been, hardened in muscle and mind, re-educated in crime by experience of prison, and impatient to resume their activities. The armed forces were determined not to have them, so for reasons that were never stated they were not called up – though my father thought that some of them would have made good Special Operations commandos. Officialdom handed Hoxton back to them. They resumed most of their former activities, but without the racecourse terror. Rationing and shortages opened new worlds of possibility. The serious operators moved into the black market, and organised large-scale robberies, chiefly from the docks, but also elsewhere. Once they had secured control of both supply and the market their thefts were tailor-made to meet demand. They became rich beyond anything they would have dreamt of before the war. When rationing ended, some of them moved into legitimate business, usually out of concern for their families, especially their growing-up children.

At first, before they became too rich to want our clothes, they came to our shop for their made-to-measure suits, as they had before. I met some of them, and found them unusually interesting: they seemed to think differently from other people, more independently. Being impressed by this, I was impressed all the more by the respect they showed to my father and grandfather, whom they addressed as 'guv', the accepted term of deference. This was because the shop had become known among them for not having allowed the children of local men in prison to go in rags. The respect this induced was real, and had nothing to do with smart suits. And it had a happy side-effect for us, in that it meant we were never burgled.

The leader of the gang was now out too: Jimmy Spinks, known to everyone as Spinky. This was when I got to know him. I would lay a bet that he never in his life heard of Graham Greene, or knew that while he had been in prison a novel prompted by the Battle of Brighton had been published with the title *Brighton Rock*, and a leading character, Pinkie, with a version of his name. All this was unknown to me too, of course. In any case, Spinky's actual character could not have been more different from Pinkie's. He was the champion bare-knuckle fighter of the age, and the strongest-looking man I have ever seen: of only average height, but wide and hugely muscular. One of his colleagues described him as 'built like a brick shit-house'. This exceptional body was always elegantly suited, and there was something soft and easy about his walk, like a cat's, so that you could see just by looking at him that he could move very fast. His eyes surveyed you in a detached way, gleaming with low cunning. But the most striking thing about him, more than any of these, was the skin on his face. No one who saw it forgot it. It contained more razor scars than you would have believed could fit on to one face. It captured the story of pre-war Hoxton as no chronicle inscribed in any other medium could have done.

I have no more to relate about Spinky than I have told in *Clouds of Glory*. I do not remember anything he said: people paid attention to his every word, not because he was a conversationalist but because what he said mattered. Even so, I do remember perceiving that – although he was back with us once more, richer and more powerful than ever – he was a figure of the past. His world was no more. And I think he knew it. But there was nowhere else for him to be, or perhaps, more importantly, nothing else that he could be.

For me, too, Hoxton had lost its meaning. We no longer lived there. None of my friends were there, and I could find nothing to do. I was too young to help in the shop. No customer wanted to be waited on by an eleven-year-old, even an eleven-year-old who knew what to do. So I just hung around chatting to my father and grandfather when they were not busy, and shrank out of notice when they were. Eventually I became so bored that I asked my father if I could stop going. When he asked why, and I said it was because I was bored, he reacted as if stung. 'It's a good thing not all of us are bored,' he said. 'It's not clever to say you're bored.' It had hurt him, I think, because I could opt out and he could not. Deep down he had always found being in the shop boring, but felt trapped in it and had to make the best of it. What hurt *me* was the implication that I was adopting a superior attitude, giving myself airs, when no such thought was in my mind. Even so, I stopped going to the shop, and this meant that I stopped going to Hoxton.

Instead I hung around in Palmers Green and Southgate, waiting to be told where I was to go next. My parents would go off to their jobs in the morning leaving me in bed. Once I was up, the first thing I would do, usually, was play some records. Then I would read the paper, the *News Chronicle*. I got to know Palmers Green for the first time, and went to the cinema there a lot in the afternoons. In the evenings my father taught me poker and chess, and took me to some memorable concerts. And the time passed.

When, at last, the news came about what I was to do, it took a form that was as unexpected as the prospect had been of going to America.

Perhaps surprisingly, some of the best public schools in Britain are in London itself – Westminster, St Paul's, Harrow – and there are several others that are very good, including Mill Hill, Dulwich, Highgate and Merchant Taylors'. At most of these the London County Council maintained a small number of assisted places for boys from state schools who, it was thought, might benefit. A list of them arrived in the post for my father, with a letter inviting him to apply for me to go to one of them. Harrow, I believe, was not on the list, but all the others I have mentioned were, and several more. Typically of him, he showed the list to me and said: 'Which of these would you like to go to?' Typically of me, I had not heard of any of them, except for one. Typically of any eleven-year-old who has to choose a name from a list on which there is only one name that he recognises, I chose the one I recognised.

In the streets of central London I had occasionally seen a boy wearing a dark blue coat from his throat to his ankles that was open at the front from the hips down, so that, visible beneath it, was a pair of grey knee breeches with silver buttons at the knee, and below those a pair of bright yellow stockings disappearing into the shoes. It was an amazing sight, I thought. The first time I saw it I asked what it was, and was told it was a boy from a school called Christ's Hospital, where they wore this uniform, because of which the school was known as the Bluecoat School, and boys like this as bluecoat boys. Years later my family swore that when I was told this I said: 'I'm going to go there.' I find it not at all difficult to believe this, but I do not remember it. Anyway, I went there.

In 1941 Christ's Hospital was no longer in London, but it had been a conspicuous feature of the City of London's life for three and a half centuries, and still retained extensive property there. It also preserved a special relationship with the City fathers, which is why it was part of the London County Council's assisted places scheme. Its beginnings were unique. When Henry VIII dissolved the monasteries in the 1530s the question arose of what to do with the buildings. Some of these were enormous, for instance Greyfriars monastery in the City of London. At that time, when most adults died at quite a young age, a number of children without families lived like animals on the streets of London (as they do today in some other parts of the world). This became a social scandal, if only because of the child crime and prostitution to which it gave rise. The Mayor and the Bishop of London persuaded the King to approve a plan to sweep these children off the streets and into the now empty Greyfriars monastery, there to house, feed, clothe and educate them. The scheme went ahead, and the new school began in 1552 in vast, already old buildings, financed by City money. By this time Henry VIII had died, so it was his son, Edward VI, who signed the royal charter that officially founded the school in 1553. Although it was always thought of, rightly, as a school, it was launched with a full complement not only of teachers but also of beadles, caterers, nurses, a surgeon, and so on and so forth – a total institution, grand and imposing. It took in girls as well as boys, and gave them the best education by the lights of the day. When the children left they went out into widely differing social circumstances, depending on their sex and abilities. Among the boys the scholars went on to Oxford and Cambridge, still helped by the school, while many of the otherwise clever ones, being well educated, and already living in the City, got jobs there, again helped by the school and its benefactors. Quite a number became rich, and helped the school in their turn. The less able were apprenticed to skilled trades. With the girls the future depended more on marriage, but on this side of marriage the abler ones became teachers of some kind, usually governesses, and the others companions or housekeepers.

Many of the more ancient public schools began as charities, but only Christ's Hospital remained true to the spirit of its original purpose. Because the others were such good schools the socially privileged wanted to send their children to them, and this had the paradoxical effect of turning charity schools into bastions of privilege. But with Christ's Hospital 'need' remained the talisman word: unlike the others, it never took in the children of the well-to-do. Clearing the streets of a London teeming with abandoned children was a job that could be carried out only once, but the school continued to take in children in need of care and education, and became a godsend to families in the middle and even upper classes who had become impoverished. It gave their children first-rate schooling which they could not have afforded to pay for. Once established, it took in such children from all over the country, and from English families abroad. At each stage of its development it attracted the involvement of remarkable people. When most of the buildings were burnt down in the Great Fire of London in 1666, the reconstruction was supervised by Wren and Hawksmoor. At one point Wren, Pepys and Newton were governors together. Pepys persuaded King Charles II to found a new school-within-the-school, the Royal Mathematical School, to train navigators for his navy; and Newton wrote a textbook for it. More than a hundred years after this, Coleridge and Charles Lamb were boys at the school together (and were lifelong friends as a result). Soon after them came Leigh Hunt, who joined their circle. All three of these wrote about the school, and all spoke of its remarkable classlessness. As Leigh Hunt said: 'More boys are to be found in it, who issue from a greater variety of ranks, than in any other school in the kingdom . . . the boys themselves (at least it was so in my time) had no sort of feeling of the difference of one another's ranks out of doors.'

Until the late nineteenth century it was standard practice for masters, including the headmaster, to take in private pupils, so there were boys who were taught in the school's buildings by its masters but were not members of the school. One of these was Warren Hastings, who became a governor. Others included Camden and Pugin – and one who possesses my favourite name in the English language, Sir Cloudesley Shovell.

In 1784 the girls were separated from the boys and given their own school in Hertford, thus becoming the first girls' public school in England. At the end of the nineteenth century the boys' school, in search of space for playing fields, bought a vast twelve-hundred-acre site in the Sussex countryside, built a new school there on the largest scale for eight hundred and fifty boys, and moved into it in 1902. However, it remained a 'London school' in its conception of itself and, since universal education had now come in, it tried to recruit the more promising boys from the London state schools – hence its involvement in the LCC scheme for assisted places. When I went there the great majority of boys had come from private schools, but the state-school minority was big enough, and sufficiently long-entrenched in the school's history, to be taken for granted, so there was as little class aware-ness among us as there had been in Leigh Hunt's day.

One did not need to be poor to go to Christ's Hospital, merely not well-off enough to belong to the five per cent or less of the population who went to the other public schools. In fact, most of the families were of above-average prosperity. I have since discovered things about this that I did not know at the time. The bulk of the boys were children of professional people who were not well paid – doctors, teachers, army officers, clergymen and the rest – or were from families like this in which the father had fallen ill, or had died. Some came from poor branches of grand families, or from families that had once been well-off and had now fallen on hard times. Others were from working-class

backgrounds. In the England of that day it was almost ostentatiously true that we came from all social classes.

People often suppose, because Christ's Hospital is a charity
school, that it must be a poor one, but the opposite is the case.
Because it provides free, or at minimal cost, what at other boarding
schools has to be fully paid for by parents, the school needs to
be rich, and is very rich. At the time I write these words it is by
a long way the richest school in Britain, in the size of its endow-
ment – more than twice that of Eton, for example. Its money
comes chiefly from land, large amounts of it in the City, but also
elsewhere – a great deal in Sussex, for instance. Some of its possessions are surprising: when I was there it was the ground landlord
of two of Shaftesbury Avenue's theatres, the Queen's and what is
now called the Gielgud.

The school assessed my parents' means and decided that they
should pay £6 a term – £18 a year – towards the total cost of
keeping me in every way, including all my clothing, sport and
entertainment, for the nine months of every year that I would be
living there. It also suggested that they send ten shillings a term
to my housemaster to be doled out to me in instalments as pocket
money. Among the information it sent was the fact that piano
lessons could be provided as an optional extra, for a small fee. I
asked if I could have them. My father said yes, my mother said
no. My father pointed out that if I had gone to any other school
I would have been a day boy and continued to live at home, and
this would have cost a great deal more than sending me to Christ's
Hospital, so they were saving money by sending me there, and
could afford the lessons. My mother said they were having to kit
me out with all sorts of things for my new school (I asked her
what things, and she was unable to say – Christ's Hospital provided
everything, and these 'things' were imaginary: she thought kitting
a child out for school was something you did) and they could not
afford more expense. The argument became heated. It began in

the living room, but when the two of them started to get angry my father ordered me to go to my room and stay there until they decided.

I went off to my room and perched on the edge of the bed, my face in my hands. Usually in a dispute between my parents I could put money on my father to win, but not always, and something made me unsure this time. There was something deeply rooted about my mother's opposition to my learning music. It was beginning to create in me a kind of depression. I could hear their clamant voices through two closed doors, but not what they said. Then the anger seemed to subside, and all I could hear were mumbles. But I still went on having to wait a long time. At last my father came into my room, with a sympathetic look on his face, and put one hand on my shoulder as I looked up at him. 'We've reached a compromise,' he said. 'You won't have lessons straight away, but you can start a year from now.'

A year was an endless time. To me this answer sounded like no. If it had come from my mother it would have been no. But at least I knew my father would keep his word.

The school asked him to bring me on a particular train from Victoria station, and to have with him an empty suitcase to take my clothes away in. We found an unoccupied compartment and took possession of it, he almost as nervous as I was, though showing it less. When the train got under way I stuck my head out of the window, as I always did in trains, and saw the face of a boy of my own age at almost every other window. When the train went into a curve I could see a row of little white faces along its whole length, each one poking out separately, like horses' heads from stable doors. I asked my father to have a look, and it made him laugh. The phrase we used ever after to evoke that journey was 'little white faces'.

We disembarked at a station called, I could scarcely believe it, Christ's Hospital. In those pre-Beeching days it was a substantial building in red brick, with three covered platforms and a comfortable waiting room – all of it since demolished, so that it is now just a halt, though still with frequent trains. Most of the other passengers got off too, the grown-ups carrying suitcases. In the station's large concourse we were gathered together by those waiting to receive us, and led away in a long winding line up a slope that passed successively alongside the school's gymnasium, swimming pool, armoury and post office to one of its gates, at which point playing fields opened up beside us and we could see large buildings filling the view ahead. There was a row of turrets against the sky, and beside them a square tower that overtopped them. We were led round a free-standing shop to the other side of the tower, where we found ourselves in what I was later to be told was the biggest quadrangle in England except for the Great Court of Trinity College, Cambridge. Enclosing the lawn were the dining hall, the chapel, the main assembly hall (called Big School) and the Old Science School – all in bright red brick, and all looking to my eye gigantic. Embedded in the sides of the buildings were life-sized statues of people, some of whom seemed to be kings; and in the centre of the quadrangle was a statue of another king. Cloisters ran along two of the quadrangle's sides. The quadrangle itself opened off an avenue that ran away into the distance under grey stone arches in the cloisters, through which we could see school houses one beyond another. From the expression on my father's face I could see that he, like me, was too impressed to say anything. Neither of us had realised that a school could be like this.

We were ushered into the dining hall – big enough, my father was to be told later while waiting for me to change, to contain Nelson's flagship HMS *Victory*, its ceiling the largest unsupported wooden ceiling in England. Along one wall was what remains the biggest oil painting I have ever seen, a canvas, not a mural, representing the ceremony at which King Charles II founded the Royal

Mathematical School, painted at the time by Antonio Verrio. It was eighty-seven feet long and sixteen feet high. On other walls were life-size equestrian portraits of Queen Victoria and Prince Albert. By this time the impression I had above all others was of size, sheer size, a scale that had been inconceivable to me in relation to a school. And first impressions are notoriously important. Although this school was to be my world for several years to come, and to become as familiar to me as the skin on my hands, there was a small part of me that never ceased to be impressed by it, to see it as magnificent. And the detail that always impressed me most remained the very first one I had encountered, the fact that a school in the middle of the countryside should have its own railway station with frequent trains to and from Victoria.

Boys wearing the famous uniform came to lead us new arrivals to go and get ours. Our parents gave them the empty suitcases, and we were taken away. We were led to one of the school houses and up some stairs into a dormitory. There, against rows of beds, stood several queues of boys in front of people carrying out fittings on them. Next to me in my queue was one of the few boys taller than me, the first new boy I talked to. An affable fellow, he told me his name was Morrison. Smiling cheerfully, he said: 'D'you suppose either of us'll become head boy?' Then, surveying the others without looking impressed: 'One of us'll have to.' Seven years later he did.

Eventually it was my turn to be transformed. First the knee breeches, the silver buttons surprisingly loose and clunky. Then an open-fronted white shirt with no buttons and wide three-quarter-length sleeves. Then came the tricky bit: how to tie the separate white bands round the neck and safety-pin them to the shirt so that they did not drift askew. I had to have it done for me, and was told it would take a few days to learn. Then I rolled on the mustard-coloured stockings, and finally elbowed my way in to the big, billowing coat – more silver buttons on the sleeves and down the front, ending with an extra big one at the bottom. And there I stood, just like the boys I had seen in the London streets. I was given a leather girdle to hang round my waist, and for a moment I just stood there with my thumbs stuck in it, trying to take myself in. Then my minder, who had packed my former clothes into the suitcase, led me back to my father, who by this time was standing outside the dining hall gazing at the view. When I emerged from under the cloister a look of astonishment crossed his face, followed by a repressed radiation of pride. I knew what his emotions were, and basked in them. As I walked towards him I was overcome with shyness because of my clothes. I could feel them on me in a way I never did again, and my stride was self-consciously long.

The next thing we did was go to my house and meet the house-master. The sixteen houses were in eight blocks, each named after an Old Blue – worthies such as Middleton, first Bishop of India, and Peele, a poet and playwright contemporary with Shakespeare (he was Shakespeare's collaborator on *Titus Andronicus*) – so each house had that name plus the suffix A or B. Mine was Barnes A. This, I was told – erroneously, it happens, but I believed it throughout the time I was at the school – was after Thomas Barnes, the outstanding journalist of the nineteenth century, the editor of *The Times* who earned it the nickname 'The Thunderer'. So we went past Lamb to Barnes (the two had been friends) and were shown into the senior housemaster's study.

There sat Douglas Burleigh, known to his boys as either Dougs or Snugs. He and my father got on famously, with an ease and warmth that I found unexpected. I suppose I thought my father would be a little overawed, for no better reason than that I was. But now I began to feel left out of the conversation – they were not even talking about me. I remember my father using the phrase 'in this democratic age' in a sentence the rest of which eluded me. They seemed not to want to end their conversation; but another parent was waiting at the door, so I was taken away.

My minder was waiting outside for us, and showed us the rest of the house, which was home to fifty-something boys: dayroom, with separate studies at the far end for the nobs; tuck cupboard outside it, where he said any food of my own would have to be put away, to be unlocked for only a couple of hours each afternoon; changing rooms, a forest of clothes on hooks and pegs, ankle deep in rugby boots; washrooms, including a row of showers over a trough big enough for a whole rugger team to sit and bath in at the same time; shoe room, pairs of slippers in pigeonholes all round the walls; lavatories at the back on the other side of an air passage. Doing a turn round the back of the house we saw a swarthy eighteen-year-old, the skirts of his coat tucked up into his girdle, pumping a bicycle tyre. 'That's Neighbour,' murmured the minder with admiration. 'He's the house captain.' All the way down the front of his coat, so close as to be almost touching, were big silver buttons of the sort that I had only one of; he had a stand-up black velvet collar, which I did not have, and at the end of his sleeves were half-drooping black velvet cuffs, again with silver buttons – very elegant. I asked why his coat was so different from mine, and was told: 'He's a Grecian. Grecians all have coats like that. They're the top boys of the school.' Taking a leaf out of Morrison's book I said: 'I'm going to be a Grecian,' at which the minder said: 'I expect you will be one day.'

There came a seemingly natural point when my father left us, as he was meant to, and went to the station to catch the next train back. I was so full of my new surroundings that I did not mind him going.

That night I was taken down to 'the tube' to sleep. German bombers had been flying over Christ's Hospital on their way to and from London, and a few had been shot down nearby, so the whole school had taken to sleeping underground. This was made possible by an ingenious feature of the school's construction. The houses, thickly laid along a central avenue for half a mile, contained the usual tangle of wiring and piping; and so that their underground supply connections could be got at without digging up the surface outside, these ran along a tunnel that could be accessed from inside any of the buildings, a tunnel big enough for several men to walk along abreast. This was known as the tube. In downpours of rain, or when the school was snowed up, it was a walkway for everyone's use. And during the Blitz it became a mass dormitory with beds along the whole of its length.

The houses kept their separate identities in the tube, and slept in that part of it that was under their own house. In the Barnes A section we junior boys were supervised by a house monitor called Morgans, a six-footer from South Africa. There were six house monitors, all of whom looked to me like giants. I had never been in a school where the oldest boys were eighteen, and fully grown. For me there was conceptual dissonance in the fact that these adults were 'boys' in my house. I looked up at them with awe. They seemed to me even bigger than ordinary people; and their differentness was emphasised by the Christ's Hospital clothes, which made them seem like creatures from elsewhere.

In those days the monitorial system was exceedingly powerful. Almost every aspect of life in the school outside the classroom was organised by the older boys. They had what felt like total power over us, including the power of punishment. We saw it as them, not the masters, who ran our day-to-day lives. When they left the school they went straight into the army, where they arrived ready-trained in exercising authority over their fellows – with the result that in wartime conditions they sprinted up the ladder of promotion. We became used to the sight of uniformed captains and majors around the place who were young Old Blues revisiting the school.

Next morning the first thing to do was to find my class. A notice-board in the dayroom told me which one it was. All new boys were in two forms, it said, the third form and the lower fourth –

LF for short. This LF was divided into five streams, from A to E, and I was in LFA. All clear up to this point. The notice announced what time this class was supposed to meet, but did not say where. I turned from the board to a biggish boy who was passing, and said: 'Excuse me, can you tell me where the LFA are supposed to meet?'

'No such form,' he said, not slowing down.

'Yes there is. It says so here.'

'There isn't,' he said, sweeping on. I looked at the notice again. There it was: LFA.

Across the room was one of the monitors, so I went over and put the question to him.

His manner was kindly. 'You must have made a mistake,' he said. 'There isn't such a form.'

'But it says so on the notice.'

'It can't do.'

'It does.'

'Show me.'

He came across to the noticeboard with me and I pointed it out. Understanding spread across his face.

'Oh, you mean LF*A*,' he said. 'You were saying LF*I*.' And he told me where to go.

I was foxed for a while. But that day, as it went on, I made the discovery that I had a cockney accent, a realisation that had never entered my head. As a new boy I was constantly being asked what form I was on (everyone said on, not in), and when I answered, everyone thought I was saying LFI. I came to realise, though with extreme difficulty, that I must be. It was a milestone discovery. All my life I had assumed that the way I talked was normal. The only people who had ever had any problem understanding me were country people, and that was because *they* were different. They had an accent, not me. Country people had remarked on what they called my London accent, but that was because they spoke country, and weren't used to hearing London people talk. In this, as in everything else, I took it for granted that London was the touchstone. London set the standard that others followed, unless they did not know any better. But now it was unquestionably I who was different. Yet I could not *hear* the difference. I was being made aware of it only from outside. I suppose, looking back, I must have been familiar with the way the other boys were talking because I had been hearing it all my life on the radio – indeed it was often referred to, until well after the Second World War, as BBC English. As a broadcaster myself, many years later, I became used to the fact that when people with regional accents hear themselves on the air for the first time they are astonished and taken aback by their own accents, which they were previously unaware of. But at school, of course, I had no such way of hearing myself.

I started trying to speak clearly, to avoid misunderstanding, so that when I said 'A' people would actually hear it as 'A' and not as 'I'. Beyond that, I did not try to change my accent – I would not have known how to, not being able to hear it. Nevertheless, over the next couple of years, and without being conscious it was happening, I came to talk like the other boys. My musical ear probably had something to do with this. I did not know that the change had occurred until people elsewhere began to remark on it – and then again I was surprised, because at every point during the transition I had been talking spontaneously. The nearest thing to this situation that I have encountered in adult life is with the children of friends who emigrate to the United States: after a couple of years they are talking like American children, yet they have not made a conscious effort to change. Before the age of puberty such a change involves no act of will on the child's part: on the contrary, it would require a strong effort of will *not* to change.

In my house there were seven other new boys, six of whom came from prep schools and already talked like the older boys.

This was when I first heard of prep schools. I had not known such schools existed, and looked with wonderment on boys of my own age who had already, for years, been learning Latin and French, not to mention algebra. The only other state-school boy was from Berkshire, and he had a rich country burr. Like me, he was talking like the others within a couple of years.

After my first two days, my recollection of my own newness no longer contains many individual memories. There was so much that was new, so much to learn and come to terms with all at once, that it blurs into one. It was like starting life all over again in a new world. This was what the schools I had read about in school stories had been like, and at first I saw it as glamorous, though really of course it was no such thing, not glamorous at all. Among the boys, the prevailing atmosphere was one of rough good humour and a basic decency. This made things easy for a newcomer. In any case, my most immediate fellows were new too; and I had been used all my life to being in a motley gang of boys, and also to joining new gangs. Having grown up on the streets of Hoxton I felt myself to be streetwise in a way that the others were not; and as an inner-city child, still very much a London chauvinist, I thought of myself as metropolitan in a way they were not. As a typical cockney kid I was cocky, I know. But for all my follies and foibles the others accepted me as I was, and took the rough with the smooth. The school in general prided itself on its attitude towards the individual: it liked to claim that whereas other public schools tried to mould you into a standardised product, at Christ's Hospital they tried to find out what your potential was and help you develop it. And there was some truth in that.

CHAPTER SIXTEEN

People in a war take it for granted that the war will bring upheaval into their personal lives, and children can usually adapt to this more easily than adults. As a nine-year-old on the outbreak of war I had accepted without question the need to leave my parents and my home in the East End of London to live in a village in Sussex; and then again, after a while, to go and live in a town in the Midlands. Even within that town I had lived first with one family of strangers and then another. Meanwhile my parents had been bombed out of our old home in London and gone to live in a suburb I had never heard of. I was repeatedly being plucked out of my existing environment and plunged into a strange one. I got used to this as the pattern of my life. As far as I was concerned, when I went to Christ's Hospital it was another such change, my third or fourth in two years.

Actually, though, unrealised by me, it was a turning point of a different order from the others. From then on, my life was to be lived in a world of well-educated people, and it never had been before. I was now on an escalator that, without any further effort or movement on my part, was going to take me to one of the best *lycées* in France and then the University of Oxford. And that was not all. I had entered a moral universe quite different from any I had known before. Up to then I had lived, in my little-boy way, by the laws of the jungle. All small boys are wild animals, and I do not want to exaggerate the difference between me and others, but I had grown up in circumstances more primitive than most. If I wanted something that I could get by theft or violence, I took it. If I felt that telling a lie would help, I lied. I thought nothing of cheating at games, or breaking a promise. I had no feelings of loyalty to anyone except those closest to me, and with them I behaved myself only because I needed them. I had no guilt about any of this. I thought that anyone who behaved otherwise was a fool, and so was anyone who got himself into trouble by telling the truth. I was like an animal intent on satisfying its needs.

The most basic thing Christ's Hospital did for me (and perhaps against me too) was to socialise me. It imbued me with a different value system: telling the truth, keeping my word, being loyal to friends and also, amazingly, behaving decently to everyone else, never cheating or taking what did not belong to me. The surprising thing is that I took to it and liked it. If anything, I carried the change to excess, as converts tend to do. Looking back, I think I embraced it with such intensity because, unconsciously, I saw it as the only way of being secure and at home in this new environment, which gave me such an exciting way of life – for, from the time I arrived at Christ's Hospital, I loved being there, and would not have wished to be anywhere else. Being an all-boarding school, it was a closed world, more structured and ordered than anything I had known before; and it could be that I needed something like that. Even when I rebelled against it, as I was later to do, I liked having it there to rebel against. Underneath everything, I was happy with it until I left six and a half years later to join the army.

And of course, life there was very much a communal affair. Only the house captain and his deputy – who seemed to me Olympian figures, remote – had studies of their own; the rest of us milled around in the dayroom, which was the focus of our lives. It contained four long tables, each seating six a side on its backless wooden benches, though only in the evening were we all sitting down, doing prep. During the day the tables were used in a haphazard way for games – ping-pong, chess, cards and the rest – or as workbenches by boys engrossed in various hobbies, and by scattered individuals writing letters or reading – there was nowhere else to sit. When the newspapers arrived after breakfast they were pounced on, dismembered, and the separate sheets spread out across the tables so that each could be read simultaneously by a bundle of boys bunched up like a rugger scrum.

Banked against two of the walls were rows of lockers. Each boy had one, and it was his private space. They could not be locked, but the taboo against opening another boy's locker was absolute, so he could keep anything in it he wanted to, however private (except food or drink, which had to be kept in the tuck cupboard). The number on his locker distinguished him for all purposes: it was the laundry mark on his clothes, and the number on his peg in the changing rooms, and on his pigeonhole in the shoe room; and he himself would put it on anything he wanted to mark as his own. Mine was 29. If I lost anything I could be fairly sure that sooner or later I would hear a voice yelling over the hubbub in the dayroom: 'Who's 29?' and I would shout: 'Me!' and then what I had lost would return. I have thought of 29 as me ever since.

Among themselves the boys had an acute sense of status, and this was determined by seniority. This seniority thing was new on me. It was automatic, and went by year of entry to the house. In any organised activity, the senior boy in a group was automatically its leader, regardless of his suitability to be so, as if he were the ranking officer among soldiers. And you accorded respect to this rank, simply as rank – you never cheeked a boy 'above' you: for instance you never called him by his nickname, even though he called you by yours. As a way for people to relate to one another it had the advantage that every boy knew exactly where he stood in every situation, and what he could do, and not do; but the disadvantage was that this bore only an accidental relationship to

his capacities. It also made it hard to have a free-and-easy relationship with anyone on a higher or lower level. I never ingested
this sense of hierarchy, and have never had it at any time in my
life, but it is something I learnt about at school, and I became,
perforce, an accurate if cynical assessor of it.

In various ways all the separate little aspects of our lives seemed
to be governed by rules. We had to clean our shoes at a certain
time each day, and when we had cleaned them they were inspected
by a monitor. After the juniors had washed at night, before going
to bed, we trooped along in our pyjamas to the matron's room
and queued up to have our cleanliness inspected. She looked
especially at our feet, our fingernails and our ears, and might
send one or two of us back to have another go. (By this time I
was keeping my ears clean, at least.) We had to get up very early
in the morning when the school bell rang, and were marched in
columns of four to the dining hall for breakfast. We marched to
all our meals, though not away from them; and the same went
for daily chapel services. There was much complaint about this,
and the authorities maintained defensively that it was the only
way they could be sure of getting eight hundred and fifty boys to
the same place at the same time. The weakness of their argument
was that we were not marched to classes, yet we got *there* on time.
I disliked all this marching about, and avoided it whenever I could.

On weekday mornings there were four classroom periods.
During the break between numbers two and three we had to go
back to our houses, change into gym clothes, and do ten minutes
of organised physical exercise. After lunch, which we called
dinner, there were compulsory sporting activities – rugger and
other outdoor games, cross-country runs, swimming, gym and the
rest – which at least were highly diversified. Then more lessons.
Then the evening meal, which we called tea. Then compulsory
prep in the dayroom. Then bed. In amongst all this there were
two lots of prayers at opposite ends of the day, one in the dayroom

and one in chapel. The only period we could rely on having to ourselves – and very precious that made it – was the three-quarters of an hour between the end of morning school and lunch, the period we called 'twelve fifteen', because that was when it started.

Such was our day. This mass of organised activities in different places (it has to be remembered that the school spread out across twelve hundred acres) confronted the new boy like a maze, so for his first term he had another boy to guide him through it. This other boy was called a nursemaid, and was in his second year. Mine was Jennings. His initials were L.H.C., which stood for Lancelot Hereward Cedric. He was chipper, sparky, with a touch of the Artful Dodger about him, just the right sort to teach me how to be streetwise in my new environment. In my first few days he had to help me dress by tying my bands for me, and to tell me which classroom or playing field was where; but as time went on his teachings grew more arcane. He taught me the nicknames of all the masters, as well as of other boys, and amusingly mimicked their personal characteristics. He explained not only the rules but how to get round them, and which of them could be ignored. For him the distinction between morality and the rules was clear-cut, and I imbibed it straight away: the demands of morality were absolute, but we could play ducks and drakes with the rules. There could not have been a better guide.

The seven other new boys with whom I was learning and doing all this, my only equals in seniority in the house, were a congenial bunch. Some had the sort of names I was used to – Hudson, Griffiths, Mercer, Batts – but not all. There was Piers Hector Erskine-Tulloch, for instance. I knew about double-barrelled names from books and comics, but here was my first one; and there were lots more in the school. From a military family, he was destined for the army from the day he arrived, and was a tough, no-nonsense extrovert even at eleven. He was more thickly built than the rest of us and seemed armour-plated, like a tank. We liked him, but viewed him as a good-natured thug. The one of us most friendly with him was entirely different from him in personality: Richard Cavendish, son of a West Country village parson. He thought differently from the rest of us too, partly because he half lived in the world of the books he read, supposing that world to be real. However, he coped with our world as well, even if he found it disappointing, and was good enough at whatever we had to do, so he was reasonably well integrated. His conversation was characterised by pleasing and appropriate turns of phrase from his books, and was always interesting. The quietest one among us, Graham Courtier, a doe-eyed, olive-skinned boy, flowed along with the stream without being passive or negligible. Peter Batts was small and bucolic, a country boy from a state school, and a little at sea at first – though when he found his feet, what emerged was a competent and reliable person, a future house captain – as also was Chris Griffiths. Mercer (his first names were Sebastian Andrew, but we called him Sam because of his initials) was the odd one out, a problem child who could be goaded into uncontrollable, hysterical, foot-stamping, screaming rages. I am ashamed to say that the rest of us experimented in finding new ways of doing this, and he had to be removed from the school after a couple of years. My skin crawls when I think of it – I was no worse than the others in tormenting him, but no better. Lionel Hudson had just arrived from a prep school in Horsham and spoke in a high-pitched, highly affected way. On my third or fourth day I overheard one of the monitors say to another: 'I'd rather have Magee's cockney than Hudson's ridiculous haw-haw.' Hudson and I both immediately acquired nicknames based on the way we spoke. Neither of these survived much beyond our first year, but for our first three or four terms he was known as Lady Hudson and I as Blimey Magee.

The set-up in the school kept our year in the house together.

The sense of hierarchy set a small but real distance between us and the boys in the years above us. And it was difficult to make friends in other houses, because we were not allowed to go into them, nor they to visit us. Only in classrooms did we mix freely with the other boys of our own year. So the basic grouping in the house stayed always in the background as we moved on up through the school. Within this group, different friendships formed and re-formed over time. To begin with, Batts and I, as the only two who were new to this whole business of boarding-school education, befriended each other: a little, stocky, taciturn country boy and a tall, skinny, garrulous cockney kid – we must have made a disparate pair. Then Hudson decided that I, a real-life East Ender, was a tough guy to be admired, and attached himself to me. At that time he was reading a book by Sapper called *Jim Maitland* about a character who did ridiculously adventurous things, so he identified that character with me and addressed me as Jim. Most of us were reading books of this kind, the most popular being those by Leslie Charteris, about a romantic criminal called the Saint. In direct imitation of him, Hudson and I started committing 'crimes' and leaving our trademark

at the scene – apple-pie beds, sewn-up rugger shorts, hidden tuck and the rest. Our success exceeded our daydreams. 'Who is the Saint?' became the talking point among the juniors. To our incredulous astonishment no one suspected us. It was delicious. But then, by sheer bad luck, we were blundered across one day by our housemaster, Snugs Burleigh, at the scene of a crime we were committing. Our secret was out. He said with an admirably straight face that he would not punish us or reveal the secret if we would promise not to commit any more crimes. And that was the end of the Saint's career.

Except for our relations with Mercer, who was our butt, the whole group of us got on well together. Our foibles as individuals could be a subject of teasing, but such teasing was always good-natured. Griffiths, known as Griff, a Welshman and a Christian from an unusually strait-laced background, was a stickler for doing everything according to the rules, and was relentlessly judgemental from a conventional point of view, so we teased him for that. I talked all the time, and was teased for that. A lot of my talk made fun of convention, and this could get up Griff's nose. Cavendish talked too, but his talk was like a rather good book and paid little regard to what the rest of us thought. At that stage of his life he had enormous cheeks that seemed to be permanently puffed-up, like a cherub blowing a trumpet, and he was known as Cheeks Cavendish: people would puff out their cheeks when he came on the scene. Actually, he was the boy with whom I had most in common, and it turned out that he and I were to become lifelong friends, but that was not evident to begin with. Hudson was giggly and camp, a bit pseudo-posh, and had a piercing laugh, all of which we mimicked. Tulloch eyed the rest of us as if he was itching to sort us out with a group of the Gurkhas he was later to command, and we were wary of him. There was plenty of physical rough-and-tumble among us, wrestling for possession of things, and pushing one another out of the way; but fist-fighting, to which I had been so accustomed, was taboo. Our aggression found its outlet in games, and perhaps also in a certain verbal bluntness that was without malice, and was taken for granted among us – a necessary outlet for people living in such close proximity. The whole experience was a training over many years in getting on day after day at very close quarters with people who were of astonishingly different characters, while remaining on good terms with each of them, and being one of the group while retaining one's individuality.

All this was a permanent background to life in the house. But

in my form I was the only boy from Barnes A. We were even more
of a mixed bunch there because there were more of us, a couple
of dozen, from an even wider range of family backgrounds and
parts of the country. There were more double-barrelled names
(one of whom, a boy called Urquhart-Pullen, was to be killed in
the Suez fiasco of 1956). Our form master, who welded us
together with experienced ease, was the outstanding personality
on the staff, the school's icon figure, Teddy Edwards. He had
taught at Christ's Hospital all his adult life, except for service in
the trenches during the First World War, and would have been
retired by now had it not been for the Second World War. He
took us for three years in two subjects, English and history. His
method was highly entertaining. One of the things that came across
pungently in his teaching of history was the self-importance
of whoever wielded power in any place or time. His derisive
attitude to this was rooted in a conservative, not a radical, view
of things. His descriptions of the doings of the mighty included
so often the Latin tag *magna cum pompa* – or its English equivalent, 'with great pomp' – that he had only to utter the words
'*Magna cum*', and then pause, for the entire form to shout delightedly, in perfect unison, '*Pompa!*'

We had other masters for biology (which we called bilge) and
geography (which we called jogger); and we were streamed separately for mathematics, Latin and modern languages; so in each
of those last three subjects I was with a different lot of classmates.
One peculiarity of the school was that German was its main
modern language: only the top stream learnt French, the other
four German. When this was explained to me I asked if I could
learn German – my reason being, though I did not say so, that I
was hooked on some of my father's Wagner records and wanted
to understand the words – but I was told no, my name had already
been placed in the top stream, and this could not now be changed.
So I started on French. Most of the other boys had been learning

it in their prep schools already, so I found myself at, or very near, the bottom of the class. The same thing happened in Latin.

Our French master, Mr Bazeley, was an Englishman who had grown up in France, and lived there until the outbreak of war, speaking English so seldom that he had a slight French accent. He was a weak man, unable to keep order. Apparently he was a good teacher for older boys, who did not need discipline, but to us he was of little use. Our Latin master, Mr Tidmarsh, was so notorious for picayune meticulousness that his name had become a word in the school's slang to mean precisely that. Once, when we were supposed to have our heads down, I saw him spend a long time contemplating the classroom clock with his chin in his hand, then finally get up, go to the back of the room, pick up an empty chair, carry it to the front, set it down under the clock, step up on to the chair, open the glass case and with great delicacy of touch put the minute hand back by half a minute, then go through all the same operations in reverse. That was tidmarsh. His appearance, too, was tidmarsh: small, neat, precise, smoothly brushed, everything in place and correct. The people least likely to think well of such a characteristic were schoolboys, and their use of his name was always disapproving, in sentences like: 'For God's sake don't be so tidmarsh.' Even so, he was a good teacher. Not only did he set the basics of Latin grammar before us with unparalleled lucidity, he gave what for me were the only lessons I ever received in English grammar. He explained what a verb was, and a noun, and an adjective. He explained what the subject of a sentence was, and its object. His lessons, unlike those of Teddy Edwards, were humourless, but they were of such clarity that they compelled interest by that fact alone.

Our mathematics teacher, Mr Humphrey, introduced us to the Socratic method. If a boy asked a question, Humph, instead of answering it, would ask the boy a question in return, and then another, and then another, so that after three or four steps the boy would find himself answering his own initial question. And Humph would then cry: 'There you are. I didn't tell you, you see. You knew the answer yourself all along.' What we knew all along was that we could not have reached the answer without Humph, because we did not know what questions to ask. But that was the most valuable lesson of all – that the acquisition of useful knowledge depends on asking the right questions.

The teaching I got at Christ's Hospital was of an altogether different standard from anything I had previously received. All the classroom staff were Oxbridge graduates, and the best of them were exceptionally good teachers. I had never met such people before. Up to now I had been taught by men who had themselves left school at fifteen or sixteen and then done a two-year training course, which was the only extension of their own education that was open to them. The difference was brought home to me towards the end of my first term, when I received letters of congratulation from Mr Hickford and Mr Howell (my best teachers in Hoxton) on being at Christ's Hospital – the news had just reached them. Being used to my new environment, I realised as I read these letters that their syntax and idiom could not have come from my present teachers. They were moving letters, the more so because they were not wholly idiomatic or well educated: they were written by men I respected, and owed something to, who were now taking pleasure and pride in the fact that I was enjoying a level of opportunity that had been denied to them.

My process of adaptation to Christ's Hospital was seamless. It must, of course, have been largely unconscious. Time did its work. At that age a child adapts to more or less anything, and the school was so used to absorbing children from unusual backgrounds that it was a process taken for granted. I knew that other people were conscious of the way I spoke, but they were good-humoured about it, and I was never able to hear my own accent. As a lively, quick-talking kid I must have been a real-life cockney sparrow, the myth made flesh. When I talked, people looked at me open-eyed, incredulous, delighted; and when they bumped into me unexpectedly they beamed and said things like 'Wotcher, cock', ''Allo, mate', and 'Blimey, 'ow goes it?' To them it was all a great joke. To me it was, if anything, a cheap success, because all I had to do was talk normally for them to think it was wonderful. I could not quite make out why they had never heard anyone talk like me before, and thought they must have led narrow lives, but at least it had the effect of making me a character. However, they eventually got used to it. And so did I. The joke wore out and faded away: they stopped being aware of how I spoke, and stopped reacting to it; and I stopped being aware of their reaction. But in all that time no one had ever, not once, been unkind to me about it. The remarkableness of that did not dawn on me until many years later.

My first winter at the school was a harsh one. Sussex was covered with snow, and our normal outdoor games became impossible. Out of some deep, dark recess of the house came two giant toboggans, steel-rimmed juggernauts, each big enough to carry an unbelievable number of boys. We went whooping off with them to nearby hills, where we organised pitched snowball battles between teams each of which had its own toboggan as well as its foot soldiers – an even more cunning and fluid form of warfare than release. I had never done anything like this, or been in this kind of landscape, and was made very happy by it. Because we had to spend so much of our time indoors, the school organised a great deal of entertainment for us. There were film shows – I remember *The Good Companions*, *Boys Will Be Boys*, *The Ghost Goes West* and *The Lady Vanishes*. There were debates, onc led by two Grecians whom I got to know in adult life, Bob Pitman and Ted Kenney. There were visiting lecturers whose job was to amuse as well as instruct us. There were recitals in the Prep Hall, and gramophone concerts in Big School. These things all carried on after the snow had cleared.

But then, too, rugger came back into its regal position in the school's life. The boys cared immeasurably more about sport than about classroom work, and to most of them the king of sports was rugby. The members of the First XV were the royal family of the school – not the house captains, nor the school monitors, nor the Oxbridge scholarship boys, nor the stars of any other game. The entire eight hundred and something of us would turn out to watch them whenever they played at home against a neighbouring school: Dulwich, Tonbridge, Whitgift, Brighton and the rest. We would crowd several deep along the touchline yelling 'Housey! Housey!' (our name for the school, the 's' voiced like a 'z'). I was quickly disappointed with rugger as a spectator sport. About every thirty seconds the game came to a dead stop for a scrum, a kick or a throw-in, and this killed the continuity. I considered soccer more interesting to watch; but when I said this I was shouted down. Soccer was despised, a namby-pamby game in which it was almost impossible to get hurt, they said: a weed's game. People laughed at the idea of playing it. But during a later winter the ground froze so hard that it was like playing on asphalt; bones were broken; rugger was suspended; and soccer was brought in as a temporary expedient – but then as a game played in gym shoes.

The playing fields of Christ's Hospital were unusually extensive; altogether the school covered a larger area than any I have seen since (and I have seen most of the famous ones). This mere fact of space was important to me, because although we were confined to the school, and not supposed to go out of bounds, I still had the feeling of inhabiting a capacious environment. If I wanted to be by myself I could go off somewhere and have a range of choices, not only of open country but of copses and woodland. And if I slipped out of bounds I was still on school land. Not far from the station lay the school's farm, the biggest in West Sussex, providing us with seemingly unlimited quantities of thick, ivory-coloured milk. A couple of miles in the opposite direction lay its reservoir on Sharpenhurst Hill, still on school land. (The redbrick tower that was the tallest of the school's buildings was its water tower, built to the height of Sharpenhurst.) One could roam far and wide and still be in the school's hinterland, with most of the houses inhabited by people who worked for it.

There were non-academic sub-worlds within the school. Throughout the war there was the Home Guard, and organised fire-watching every night to protect the school's buildings (luckily it was bombed only once). I was never old enough to take part in that. The school infirmary – again surprisingly big, run by Dr Friend and his staff of nurses – was a purpose-built hospital, kept continually supplied with fractures and infectious diseases. I did a couple of stretches there as an in-patient. Its morning surgery was always crowded, and its dentist and optician served the whole community. The market garden was run by a man whose name, incredibly, was Mr Seed, and it was each boy's wartime duty to work there for one afternoon a week. The Manual School, a large separate building, contained an iron foundry, carpenters' workshops and a bookbindery, and these skills were taught to the younger boys: I learnt carpentry and bookbinding, though I was never any good at either. Another large building was the Art School, where each boy was required to study art for a couple of years – I was hopeless at that too. Another was the Music School, with its many practice rooms and teachers, and a bandmaster who would teach any wind instrument free to any boy who wanted to learn. Christ's Hospital was at that time barred from entering the annual public schools' band competition because it had invariably won when it did. The Officers' Training Corps (OTC), nominally run by masters who had fought in the First World War, was actually run by a real-life sergeant major who controlled the armoury and the shooting range. In a position corresponding to his were the sports professionals, retired now from the real thing and teaching teenagers instead. There was a Scout Hall. There were little staffs, like those in the tuck shop and the post office, and big staffs, like that in the kitchens behind the dining hall. When to all these were added the domestic servants in the houses, and the estate workers out of doors, they made up a large and highly variegated population. Christ's Hospital may have been an enclosed world, but it was a big one, and any realistic consideration of its staff had to include not only the masters: the eighty or so of them were merely the better-paid end of a wide spectrum. A boy at the school would, in all sorts of ways, continually come up against a wide selection of the others, though not all of them. I personally never had anything to do with the Scouts, nor was I ever good enough at any of the sports to be taught by the professionals.

What I missed most was the daily intake of music to which I had been accustomed, and which I felt I needed. My dominating love of orchestral music and opera was now established, but at school I had no access to either of them, nor to a radio or a record player. Some houses had a radio in the dayroom, but Snugs refused to let us have one in Barnes A. The only music to be heard was that in the chapel, plus chamber-music recitals given by the music teachers. Actually some of these teachers were good players, and their recitals were of a high quality. However, the outstanding instrumentalist in the school was not a teacher but a boy, Colin Davis, who played the clarinet. It was not his technique so much as his musicality that gripped everyone. He played the music as if he were inside it, communicating from somewhere within it. He was so good that when he gave a public performance he was accompanied not by other boys but by music teachers. The first time I heard the Brahms Clarinet Quintet, soon after I arrived, it was played by him, and I carry the sound of that performance in my mind's ear. He was to become an internationally famous conductor. Another boy who was in an altogether higher class than his teachers was David Mason, in my house, who played the trumpet. We all used to say, in our ignorant and parochial way, that he was the best trumpet player in the country, but he very nearly was: when Sir Thomas Beecham created the Royal Philharmonic Orchestra only some four years later he engaged Mason as a permanent member from the start. The first time I heard the tune of Cherubino's aria from Act II of *The Marriage of Figaro* it was played by him, in the house music competitions of my first term. This had the bizarre consequence that that tune is permanently engraved on my mind in the sound of a trumpet. (Among opera-lovers it is referred to as '*Voi che sapete*', but on our programme sheet it was 'Say ye who borrow', and that is how I still think of it.) These music competitions took place once a year, with each house putting on a short concert. Mine won it in my first term, and again the following year, which made me think I had come to the right place.

As far as music in chapel went, there were the hymns and psalms, of course, but not many of those had interesting tunes. Vaughan Williams had composed a service specially for the school, but that was performed only occasionally. Worth listening to on a daily basis were the organ voluntaries, which were played while we all trooped in and out. The one at the beginning would just arbitrarily stop when the service was ready to begin, but the one at the end was played through to the end, so if you wanted to hear it you could slip into an empty pew on the way out and stay until it finished. Most of the organ-playing was shared between the head of music, Dr Lang (nephew of the then Archbishop of Canterbury, about whom there was a well-known piece of doggerel ending: 'Auld Lang Swyne, how full of Cantuar'), and a Mr Cochrane, known to the boys as Corks for his addiction to the bottle. Corks was at that time a blond and handsome young clergyman with a beautiful baritone voice. The first time I heard Brahms's *Four Serious Songs* they were sung by him, very movingly.

In chapel he tended, quite rightly, to play the most popular classics of the organ repertoire, so it was from him that I first heard them, ranging from Bach's Toccata and Fugue in D Minor to such recent moderns as Karg-Elert (who dedicated one of his works to the school). He also played his own arrangements of popular classics from the orchestral repertoire: Borodin's overture to *Prince Igor* was a favourite of his, and became one of mine. If he was drunk he would play one of his much-loved pub songs at the end of a service – say, 'Moonlight and Roses' – in an improvised arrangement that would be suitably enriched and lachrymose. It always delighted the boys, who would look at the headmaster to see his reaction, but he affected not to notice. Music-starved as I was, I certainly got some pleasure out of all this organ music; but the snag for me was that I did not really care for the instrument itself; indeed I never have. The organ in the Christ's Hospital chapel was thought to be of special interest, having five manuals and an unusually wide range of stops, and I suppose I feel a certain gratitude towards it.

There was a school orchestra, and I heard it at the end of my first term. Although I had been hearing live orchestras since I could remember, mostly in theatres, where some of them were truly dire, I was unprepared for anything so awful. It was a revelation that an orchestra could be so bad. Even so, the music somehow managed to convey itself to me in spite of its performance; indeed it was that occasion that gave me my first conscious lesson in the distinction between a performance and the work being played. The work in this case was the first movement of Schubert's 'Unfinished' Symphony, and I thought it was marvellous. When I went home for my first school holiday I was given some money as a Christmas present, and bought a recording of this symphony – which meant I then heard the second movement for the first time. It was the first classical recording I bought for myself.

Although Christ's Hospital could claim to be a musical school, my love of music developed mainly at home, during the holidays, through playing my father's records, listening to the radio, and going increasingly to operas and concerts. The school extended my range to other areas of music – mostly chamber music and the organ repertoire – but these were areas I was less interested in, and on the whole the performances were not up to the same standard.

CHAPTER SEVENTEEN

The overriding experience of being at any boarding school in those days was that the school was your life while you were there – and this was for most of the time. Since then, most of them have become more integrated with their surrounding communities: parents want to go on seeing their children during term, and send them to schools that are not too far away, and the children go home at weekends. In those days there was no going home during term, and half-term did not exist. You visited your family three times a year; and the total amount of time you spent with them added up to about a quarter. For three-quarters of the year, in uninterruptedly long stretches of time, you were at school, and not allowed out of bounds. So it became your world. This made it a more conditioning experience than it is now. And at Christ's Hospital that conditioning went deeper than at other public schools, because it started younger and went on for longer: for the other schools the normal age of intake was thirteen, but at Christ's Hospital it was eleven, in order to co-ordinate the state and private systems. For a lot of individuals it was younger still, because the school had its own preparatory school, at one end of the Avenue, and this fed most of its output into the main school. Boys who left Christ's Hospital at eighteen had been there for between seven years and nine, as against the usual five.

The fact that the school existed for children with a special need for boarding education increased still further the difference it made to them. They were not problem children, but a sizeable majority came from problem homes, mostly well-educated families that had fallen on hard times – this, of course, being before the welfare state. Perhaps father had died, or become chronically ill, or was a failed businessman (of whom there were many during the Depression); or mother was an invalid; or there was a seriously handicapped sibling living permanently at home – there was no end to the variety of circumstances that could bring a boy to Christ's Hospital. In all such cases the boy's being there significantly improved his situation, and this increased the school's importance to him. It was also likely to be his only chance of getting the sort of public-school education that alone in those days opened up all the doors of opportunity.

If you go to a day school, being at school consists mostly of being in a classroom, but if you live at school you are in a classroom for only a small proportion of your time, so it constitutes a much smaller part of the experience. For most of us, I think, it was not all that important – it was never my chief concern. I was brimming over with interest and curiosity, but not for the sorts of things that were taught in class. In fact I was distantly perplexed by the fact that what was of greatest interest in life – things like music, theatre, politics, ideas in general – were not what schools were most concerned to teach you. The things they cared most about bore little relationship to anything else: they were just what you did at school, that's all. My own attitude towards them was that they must be expected to be boring, but would be less so if you paid attention to them than if you did not. Most of the time I did. I performed well enough in my work to keep out of trouble, and those two considerations, rather than interest in the work for its own sake, constituted my main motive for doing it. I could see no point in a lot of it – I could not, for instance, see any point in learning Latin (though I am pleased now that I did). I think these are, or were, normal attitudes among schoolboys, and were the attitudes of most of my fellows. A small number of them had an active interest in work – they positively enjoyed Latin, say, and would put in extra time on it – but I thought they were dull dogs: anyone who preferred doing Latin to being in the hurly-burly of a dayroom talking nineteen to the dozen with his friends, or sitting alone reading some work of imagination, perhaps an adventure story, was a grey creature, I thought. That anyone could prefer classroom work to music was incomprehensible to me.

Since I did enough work to stay out of trouble, my position in the class drifted lazily upwards. Having in my first year been near the bottom in those subjects that the boys around me had been doing before, by the end of my second I was quite near the top, though without actually being top at anything. I found that this was a good position to be in, because it meant that I was mildly approved of by the masters without their paying any special attention to me – I did not want to come under pressure to perform, or make a show of interest. So I stayed very happily there, and allowed myself to float along with the current.

The first subject to ignite my imagination was geometry, in my second year. It was so counterintuitive as to be thrilling. Even the most elementary things in it were amazing. When you considered that the variety of shapes a triangle could have was infinite – and how bizarrely shaped a lot of them were – it was almost incredible that their angles should always and inevitably add up to 180 degrees. I learnt to prove that it was so, but I found it almost impossible to believe. And the fact was that if you made a right-angle between two lines, each of which was one unit long, and then completed the triangle by joining up the ends, it was impossible even in theory to give a precise measurement of this third line: its length, in whatever your units, was the square root of two, and that was an irrational number, inexpressible in either fractions or decimals. Again I knew that this was so, but found it mystifying. There the line was, in front of you, just a line, one of the three making up this simplest of triangles, and yet, unlike the others, you could not measure it exactly. Why not? If you could measure the other two, why not this one? I found it so peculiar that I could not get my mind round it. And yet I could *prove* it.

When, also in the maths periods, we did what we called statics and dynamics, I felt the same combination of fascination and puzzlement. That everything around me should consist of a balance of forces, and that counter to every one of these forces was an equal and opposite force, which was why things were as they were, took my breath away. It meant that this apparently stable world was really an almighty struggle of forces going on all the time, everywhere in everything, and that stability existed not in spite of that but as an outcome of it, created by it. Each new piece of information that the master gave us was equally astonishing. For instance, if you dropped something, it would fall towards the centre of the earth with the same acceleration regardless of what it was – minus, obviously, the effect of whatever forces there might be acting against it; that went without saying. It meant that in a vacuum a feather would fall at the same rate as a ton of lead. This seemed self-evidently impossible: surely if other things were equal, the heavier a thing was, the faster it would fall. But that was not so. In lesson after lesson, mathematics and the mechanical sciences were revealing the world around me to be quite contrary to what any thinking person would assume – and therefore contrary to common sense. There was something hugely exciting about all this – the unexpectedness of it, the experience of perpetual discovery, the sense of revelation. Never before had I felt like this in a classroom.

No other subject was to have this effect on me until I started doing physics. Meanwhile the next most interesting, in my second year, was chemistry; but that was because it was about sex. The school followed a laudable plan of giving every boy an introduction to biology in his first year, to chemistry in his second, and to physics in his third; but for reasons to do with our age (for most of us it was the last year before puberty) the chemistry got diverted into the biochemistry of human reproduction. What is more, we were taught by a woman, and an unmarried one, Miss Harvie. Perhaps this needs to be explained before we get to the sex.

When the war began, the senior school had only ever had male teachers, all of them graduates of Oxford or Cambridge. The younger able-bodied ones, and some of the others too, were quickly called up, and could not be replaced. This created a problem that lasted throughout the war. The school tried to solve it in three successive ways. First, it invited retired masters to come back out of retirement. Several volunteered, but most of these (not all) no longer had enough energy to do the job properly, and to us boys they seemed ancient, a collection of old buffers and duffers. In any case, one or two of them proceeded to get ill or die. So *that* arrangement was unsatisfactory. The school then took what it considered the adventurous step of taking on women, young ladies not long out of Oxford or Cambridge. There had, I believe, been a woman teacher in the prep school, so the decision was not altogether without precedent. Nevertheless, having women in the closed world of a male boarding school led to problems – not chiefly with the boys, I understand, although one woman was thought to have been to bed with several of them before she was dismissed. With that, and in the depths of the war, the school was pushed into thinking the unthinkable, and took on a male graduate from a university that was not Oxford or Cambridge – Leeds, would you believe it – but found him so unassimilable that it reluctantly fell back again on Oxbridge women as a lesser evil. In the final stages of the war, the school's original masters started to get special release from the forces so that they could come back and teach, and the problem began at last to resolve itself.

I lived through all these phases, and had experiences with each of them. The first of the two old buffers who taught me called himself – absurdly, it seemed to me – Captain or Major (I forget which) Blamire-Brown, I assumed because he would wish any invading Germans to know what rank he had held during his previous encounter with them. He was a pig, boorish and fierce; and I still remember some of his more unpleasant remarks, not that any of them were directed at me. He terrorised his classes. But despite his defects of character he did teach me some Latin. He also taught me one of the mnemonics that have stuck in my mind ever since, one that explains which Latin nouns and proper names carry inflected meanings without the use of a preposition:

> With island small, and little town,
> We put no preposition down;
> Also with *humus*, *rus* and *domus*
> We cast the preposition from us.

I do not think there has been a single occasion when this has been of any use to me. I sometimes think I have a bigger store of useless knowledge than anyone I know – but that comes inevitably from having a good memory.

The first of the two women I was taught by was Miss Harvie. She was clear, efficient, likeable and cool. She took it for granted, as she needed to in her situation, that we knew already about the mechanics of sex, and confined herself to explaining the biochemistry of it. Actually, I am not sure that we did know all that much about the mechanics, beyond the basic fact of penetration; but I do not blame her for not trying to tell us. What she explained was the structure and functioning of spermatozoa and ova, telling us what chromosomes were, and genes, and what was known about inherited characteristics, and how they were transmitted; and also a bit about how a baby develops in the womb. So it was not so much about sex as about the consequences of sex. It was fascinating and highly informative; but there was nothing there about emotions or relationships, or the social aspects of any of it. And nobody ever attempted to talk to me about those things. My parents never said anything, in fact never mentioned sex at all: they just started assuming, after I had reached a certain age, that I knew about it.

Sex was a subject of obsessional fascination among us juniors; but when I think of how much time we spent talking about it, I am struck by how little we actually knew. I knew a bit more than the others, being streetwise for my age, and they hung on my every word; but I must have given them at least as much misinformation as information. It shows how little free talk there can have been about such matters between the younger and the older boys – a lot must have been known to the older ones that was unknown to us. I had only the dimmest, most distant ideas about orgasm, and did not know of the existence of masturbation. I was taken aback when I went for the first time to the school swimming baths, where most of the boys swam naked, and saw pubic hair on the older boys. It looked grotesque to me, not at all aesthetically pleasing. I had liked it on girls, but that was different. This was ugly. Given all this ignorance, little of our sex-talk in the house was about the realities that were going to face us in the near future: most of it was speculation and dirty jokes, the casual, flippant and yet obsessive obscenity common among boys. New jokes, riddles, limericks and songs kept arriving from goodness knows where to keep our supply of such things refreshed. I suppose most of it must in fact have trickled down from the older boys, but new items were continually coming in from outside the school. I contributed a few myself, having a capacious background of this sort of thing in my Hoxton street lore. But it was all very infantile.

That wide gulf between the smallest boys and the biggest was due to the exceptionally wide age range of the school, with boys from eleven to eighteen living in the same house. One institution that helped to bridge the gap was fagging. Each of the house monitors was allowed a fag, a small boy who acted as his personal servant – cleaned his shoes, made his bed, ran his errands. This was a voluntary arrangement on both sides: no one had to fag, and the fag could give it up whenever he liked. There were two inducements to do it. One was pay. The going rate was ten shillings a term, the same again as the pocket money a fag would get from his parents. The other was that he was excused from what were known as 'trades'. Every other boy apart from the monitors had two trades, a house trade and a (dining) hall trade. These were domestic chores. One boy would have to sweep the floor round one of the dayroom tables twice a day, two more would share responsibility for putting up and taking down the blackout shutters from two of the windows; and so on. In the dining hall a pair would have the task of setting out the big plates on the house's table, another pair the small ones, another pair the tea bowls – and other sets of boys would clear them away again. It was all well organised and, with forty-something boys available, most of the domestic chores could be briskly dispatched. The trades ranked in order of status, like so many other things in our lives – like us ourselves – and were reallocated each term. The individual boy had no say in choosing his trades, they were given to him by the monitors who supervised them.

After experiencing my share of trades I decided to try fagging. I have always rebelled against compulsion, and I have always especially disliked doing housework. I told myself that if I came to the conclusion that being a fag was worse than trades, I would go back to trades. But I was lucky with my fag-master, a boy called Homfray. He had one of the two studies at the top of the dayroom. A thin but tough young man, some inches more than six feet tall, he was of an ironic, easy-going disposition, inclined to accept whatever I did for him provided it was passable – the right sort of person to work for. My daily duties started with waking him in the morning after the rest of us were up, and then making his bed when I made my own. (The school – on the assumption that the air raids were over, at least for the time being – had gone back to sleeping in the dormitories, which were on the first and second floors of all the houses.) I also cleaned his shoes when I cleaned my own. I tidied his study, and made up the fire; and if he and his friends had had a fry-up the previous evening I did the washing-up. Admittedly this was housework, but the fact that I was doing it of my own volition, and could give it up whenever I liked, made it acceptable to me. It also interested me to see the life of the eighteen-year-olds from close to. One of the things I learnt from Homfray without realising it was how to treat a fag. Years later, when I became a monitor with a study and had fags of my own, I treated them that much better for it.

Another of our many sub-worlds was the life of the dormitory – seniors on the first floor, juniors on the second, two dozen beds in each. Those who had studies had their own cubicles, but apart from that the beds were laid out in a great open space like an old-fashioned hospital ward, a regulation distance apart. The horsehair mattresses were unsprung, and so were the beds themselves, which had removable wooden slats. The school doctor propounded a theory that this was good for us, and perhaps it was: at first the beds felt hard, but we soon became comfortable in them, so much so that boys complained that their beds at home were too soft. Alongside each bed was an iron settle with a flat wooden top, to keep pyjamas and other things in, and to act as our bedside table: these were said to be ancient and to have come from the school in London. Each day when we got up we stripped our beds completely, folded the blankets and sheets, and piled them neatly, army-style, and half-turned the mattress, before going off to breakfast. After breakfast we had regulation bed-making, supervised by a monitor. The beds had to be made in a certain way, with hospital corners. Then they were poled. It was one boy's house trade to take a long wooden pole that existed uniquely for this purpose and roll it up each bed to smooth out its surface. He poled two beds at a time, walking between each pair holding his pole like a tightrope walker. The whole dormitory could be poled in a few minutes and would then look regimentally perfect.

At both ends of each dormitory were what we called lav-ends, each with rows of washbasins and lavatories, and a bath with a shower. During the war the government exhorted the population to save fuel on hot water by not having more than one bath a week, and by not putting more than five inches of water in the bath. A black line was painted on our baths at this level, and we were forbidden to exceed it. It was just like sitting in a puddle. Each boy was allotted his weekly bath night, two boys to a night. On other nights we were expected to wash ourselves all over while standing at a washbasin. There was always a lot of wet and noisy larking around when the boys were washing, but ultimately that would be kept within bounds by the monitor supervising them.

The moment we were all in bed the lights had to go out. By this time we were usually so tired that we fell asleep quickly. For the first hour or two we were supervised by a monitor sitting at a desk in the dormitory, where he did his prep. So that we would not be disturbed by his light, his desk had a tent-like superstructure that almost enclosed him. At weekends, when he was not expected to be doing prep, he read a short story aloud to us. On pitch-dark winter evenings it would be a horror story, and on light summer evenings a funny one, or an episode from a comic novel – perhaps one of the set pieces from P. G. Wodehouse, or *Three Men in a Boat*, or *England Their England*. Over the years I got to know most of the classics in both genres. Among my sharpest memories of school are of lying in bed listening to a disembodied voice in the darkness telling a ghost story, best of all with a wind sighing outside, and perhaps in some distant part of the house a window whose sash cord had broken banging menacingly. We all had our favourites, and when in due course I became a monitor I read mine. These included 'The Beast with Five Fingers', 'The Monkey's Paw' and 'The Room in the Tower'. There are some quotations that cling to one through life, and I still occasionally find myself saying: 'Jack will show you your room: I have given you the room in the tower.'

Another sub-world was the dining hall, a high, handsome place hung about with those immense pictures. We were there for three half-hours a day, and always more than eight hundred people would be sitting down to a meal. Each house had a long table that seated all its fifty or so boys, and on a dais was a high table for masters and visitors. Sometimes these would be joined by the house captains, but otherwise a house captain would sit at the head of his own long table, with his most senior colleagues on either side of him and the rest of us stretching down in order of precedence to the eleven-year-olds at the far-distant bottom. As the years went by we progressed up the table. All the serving, waiting and clearing away was done by boys, with the most junior doing the most menial jobs. The kitchen staff appeared only to bring and remove the Brobdingnagian metal containers in which everything came to us. All the dining-hall equipment had to be big and tough, including the cutlery and crockery. We were given our tea not in cups or mugs but in bowls. When these were full they were heavy, but they had no handles, and we became dexterous at using them with one hand. Once, standing at a table of empty bowls before a meal, I dropped one that landed on another in such a way that it exactly replaced it on the table while sending the other crashing to the floor, exploding in a fountain of glitter. It looked like a trick, the sort of thing a performer might do on a stage. I was so entranced by it that I called Batts over to tell him what had happened, and while I was trying to explain, with two other bowls, I let one slip, and precisely the same thing happened a second time.

Halfway along one of the long sides of the hall was an ancient wooden pulpit of unknown origin, from which grace would be said by a boy. Opposite this, against the other wall, was a raised desk for the hall warden, the master supervising the meal. To start things off, the hall warden would bang his gavel for grace, and then again for us to sit down and begin. At the end of the meal he would do more banging for grace and our dispersal. In between, there was not usually much for him to do, but he was present to cope with emergencies, and to arbitrate problems. In my day the role was played with chilly authority by Noel Sergent, the only French master who was a real Frenchman – had, indeed, played rugby for France – a fact which made it all the more impressive that he completed the *Times* crossword every day during our breakfast. In his absence his place was taken by Fred Haslehust, a classics master who was even quicker with the *Times* crossword, but had to cede points on this because he was a setter of crossword puzzles for the *Daily Telegraph*.

The food . . . Language quails. Words cannot describe it. The fish pie stank. The stew consisted of lumps of grey gristle floating in a fatty brown grease with skin on top. The spaghetti we called 'worms in carbolic'. Whatever leftovers there were from these nightmare dishes were recycled into an all-purpose pie. It defies serious understanding. The official excuse was wartime rationing, but older boys swore that the food had been just as bad before the war; and in no other place during six years of war did I encounter anything like it. But we ate it, because it was what we lived on: we were hungry children, and there was nothing else; and in any case we were not allowed to leave food on our plates. We conditioned ourselves to eat it without thinking about it. Years of doing this had a lifelong effect on some of my attitudes: I enjoy good food with a special and keen-edged enjoyment that has an element of surprise in it, as if it is not what I expect to be given; and I will eat without fuss whatever is set in front of me, no matter how bad it is, and feel an inner impatience with anyone who complains about it. Having said that, I have to admit that I was defeated by the fish pie. As soon as I entered the hall and smelt it my gorge rose. I would go to any lengths to avoid eating it. Usually I managed to get somebody else to take my helping, but if not I would wrap it in my handkerchief and smuggle it out of hall under my clothes, to put it where it belonged, down the lavatory.

Some of my readers may suspect me of exaggerating. After all, in most institutions where food is served, the people who have to eat it complain about it. But I am not exaggerating. In the mind of everyone who was at the school in those years the memory of the food is encrusted with scar tissue. Wherever they meet, more than half a century later, it is one of the first subjects to be mentioned. I have heard one say, not wholly jokingly, that the conditioning it gave him enabled him to survive in a Chinese prisoner-of-war camp during and after the Korean War when his friends were dying all round him. The black joke among us at the time was that we had two complaints about the food: it was impossible to eat, and there was not enough of it. We never felt satisfied, and were always slightly hungry. One curious thing is that although this was so, and although the food was vile, it constituted an adequate and perfectly balanced diet, owing to the dedicated fanaticism in this regard of the school doctor, who enjoyed a national reputation as a child dietician. We were a tough and healthy lot – most of us, anyway – lean and muscular, rarely ill. I doubt if I have ever again been as fit as I was at school. This is especially remarkable given the meagreness of wartime rations – meat once a week, one egg a week, one piece of cheese a week, and all the rest of it – and speaks volumes about our peacetime eating habits.

Yet another sub-world in our daily lives was chapel. The problem with that was boredom. The daily services were bad enough, but matins and evensong on Sundays were like oceans of time that had no shores. I had never at any age believed in God, and I saw these services as mumbo-jumbo that I was compelled to take part in. Once the novelty wore off I found them offensively tedious – I was being trapped in chapel and compulsorily bored. Inside me a huge rebellion swelled up against this, which I had great diffi-culty in controlling. Later, it became a serious problem for me. It was to be in the school chapel that the panic attacks and claus-trophobia began that have plagued me ever since.

The chapel, like the dining hall and Big School, was built to hold a thousand people. These were seated on two sides of a central aisle, six raked-up rows on each side, so that one half of the school confronted the other. Above the heads of those in the top row ran a succession of murals by Frank Brangwyn, eight on each side, big enough to dominate the interior of the chapel. In sixteen crowded tableaux they told the story of the spread of the gospel from the preaching of the Apostles to an Edwardian street mission in the East End of London. The scenes are jostling with highly individualised characters and faces, and are brightly coloured. In a book written about the school before I went there, when the pictures were new – *Christ's Hospital* by G.A.T. Allan – there appears this passage (p.94): 'I cannot but feel that such wonderfully imaginative drawings would look better in some building designed for less sacred use. To my mind they produce no religious atmosphere, rather the reverse; and I think it is a pity to provide boys with grotesque pictures, to be studied during divine service, amongst which may be found apparent caricatures of masters and others waiting to be spotted.' This is, indeed, spot on. It is precisely what I did. In my epic struggles against boredom, and the feeling of being trapped, I studied those pictures with grateful intensity, seeking from them all the different kinds of distraction they could yield. I found likenesses of my friends, the masters, my family, people I had known in Hoxton and Market Harborough. I cannot imagine how I would have survived those services without them. They left me with a sense of personal indebtedness to Frank Brangwyn, who at that time was alive and famous – he was knighted in the year I went to the school. (Later I discovered a Brangwyn Museum in Bruges.) When Teddy Edwards asked us to write a poem about some aspect of our experience of life at the school, I penned a hymn of gratitude to him that finished, after two lines ending with the words 'know' and 'sanguine':

> I'd've died of boredom long ago
> If it hadn't been for Brangwyn.

Teddy reproved me dolefully for this in front of the class, but I had the feeling that the boys were nearer to being on my side than on his.

Every school contains worlds within worlds, and every school has its own distinctive character, but Christ's Hospital is extra-different in that its history, diversity of intake, physical scale and wealth are all unique. In keeping with this it developed over the centuries a language of its own. The terms sixth form and fifth form were not used: instead there were Grecians and Deputy Grecians; and below them the Great Erasmus and Little Erasmus forms. The school itself was Housey, and this was adjective as well as noun – housey food, housey clothes and the rest. These usages are in the Oxford Dictionary, and other dictionaries too, so they can be said to have entered the English language. As for the slang, it was so extensive that two or three separate dictionaries of it have been published. Among the private slangs of other schools, it is said that only Winchester's equals it in extent. It would weary my readers if I were to print a mini-dictionary here, but a few words will give the feel of it. A fag was a swob, a dormitory feast a bonfast; a blow to the head was a fotch; lavatory paper was bodge. Not surprisingly, the largest special vocabulary had to do with food: bread was crug, butter flab, tea kiff (so the bowls out of which we drank were kiff bowls), waste food was skiffage, or skiff for short. A high proportion of the words were curt, bold and crude-sounding, like Anglo-Saxon. In addition to our own slang we used some ordinary English words in eccentric ways: for instance our all-purpose word of commendation, perpetually on our tongues to mean just good or nice, was genial. Because German was the school's main foreign language we took everyday words from that too: beautiful was always *schön*, and we as often said *danke schön* as thank you. If a boy was lacking in vitality he was said to be *tot* (the German word for dead, pronounced 'tote'). About most of our speech there was an unadorned directness that was characteristic of most things to do with the school, not least its buildings; but our sentences were so thick with specially used words that some of what we said would have been unintelligible to outsiders. This encouraged play with language, and there was a lot of that in our conversation.

One way and another, the school constituted an environment that exerted an enormous pressure on its members. A few of them hated it altogether, and a few loved it uncritically, but most of us had divided feelings that were strong in both directions, loving some things and hating others. Never did I wish I were not there – on the contrary, I would always have chosen that rather than any of the alternatives – but there were things about it that I detested. Compulsory chapel came first, but there was an atmosphere of compulsion generally that I resented. Most aspects of our lives were governed by rules and regulations. Compulsory sport and religious services were only two of them, but both put me off for life: I have taken no physical exercise since my earliest undergraduate days, and for years after leaving school I was unable to bring myself to go to a religious service. If I was invited to a friend's wedding I would go to the party afterwards, but not to the service. I can only thank heaven that I had started to see Shakespeare's plays in live performances in the theatre before they were introduced to me in the classroom: I never thought of them as belonging in class, where they had been dragged from another world. On a desk instead of a stage they were like fish out of water, gasping their lives away.

Compulsory activities brought to the surface disabilities which, whether or not I had had them before, I had not been aware of. Late in middle age I was told by doctors that I had almost certainly had undiagnosed asthma as a small child, and that it had left me with inadequate lung capacity. This would explain why my mother was always going on about me having had 'a weak chest' before I could remember. It also explains why, at school, whenever I exercised to the point of getting out of breath, I would get into a distressed condition: I would gasp noisily, and gulp for air, desperate, and have fierce stabbing pains in the chest. At its worst, if I were made to go on, I would become almost distraught. Yet it never occurred to me at the time to think of this as a problem to do with my lungs: I supposed it to be a more general physical weakness, something all over, muscular if anything. I was a little puzzled in that my arms and legs were strong, but beyond that I resigned myself to it in an unthinking way. I just supposed that the other boys were physically hearty, sturdy, in a way I was not, and I felt slightly ashamed of my weakness, and tried to hide it. Any activity that involved sustained running was torture to me. Cross-country runs were among the worst, because we were not allowed ever to stop, so it meant unremittingly driving myself forward into the pain, and they seemed never-ending.

However, there was something more to be feared than cross-country runs, and that was the institution of punishment drills.

These were like something in the eighteenth-century navy. They were the school's alternative to corporal punishment, which was not used at all by most masters, who instead gave out these drills. One of our three retired sergeant majors, Sergeant Usher, who was the school's village policeman, conducted these drills a couple of times a week. The malefactors changed into games clothes but kept their leather shoes on, and reported on the asphalt playground behind the houses. Here Sergeant Usher ran them deliberately to exhaustion over a period of half an hour. His explicit aim was to make them suffer, and this he was skilled at doing. For me the experience bordered on the intolerable. My hatred and fear of these punishment drills was such that, after I had ingested the public-school ethos, there was only one occasion on which I lied when called on to own up, and I did that to avoid a punishment drill. It shamed me profoundly in the eyes of two of my friends, and in my own eyes too.

The other disability that was brought out in me by the school's physical activities was a psychological one. Again, I had never been aware of it, but I now found myself in extreme terror of anything that would take me, even momentarily, out of control of myself. The simplest example occurred during morning PT. We would be asked to do a headstand – that was easy enough – and then roll over backwards on to our feet again. It was simplicity itself, and the other boys, perhaps after an initial awkwardness, did it with a fluent, effortless movement: they merely let their upended bodies crumple into a roll, and their own weight carried them up on to their feet. But I could not do it, because I could not let myself go. I had a complete mental block against it. If anyone had asked me what I was afraid of I would not have been able to answer. There was no danger of pain or injury. Yet I had what can only be described as a phobic terror of letting go control of my own body, and it was a terror that I could not, by any act of will, overcome. I felt it even more on the rugger field. When I saw how, when a boy was tackled, he was swept along off his feet, I felt an unnameable horror of being tackled. It was nothing to do with a fear of being hurt: it was fear of control of myself being taken away from me; and it was panic of an extreme kind. I felt it even when a scrum lifted me off my feet. Being carried along helplessly, not being in control of my body, was intolerable to me: I would willingly have borne any amount of pain in preference to it. So throughout each game, my efforts were focused on never getting possession of the ball, so that I would not be tackled; and also on never being in a scrum; and on disguising as much as I could the fact that I was doing these things. It put me in a very odd relationship to the game.

If I were asked now to explain how I came to have this phobia, my guess would be that I was physically abused by my mother, violently shaken, when I was a baby, and that the experience was an all-engulfing terror from which there was no escape; and that this annihilating sense of powerlessness implanted in me a panic fear of being helpless in someone else's hands. I am fairly certain that such abuse took place, because it happened also during the period of my earliest memories, and I emerged into conscious-ness being frightened of my mother. But when I was a pre-teenager at Christ's Hospital it never occurred to me to make any such connection between these things. I just felt swamped by irrational fear, and then all my thoughts had to go into coping with it on the spur of the moment. I never understood it. And I was concerned to conceal it from others.

All the things I have described in this chapter were elements of daily life. But what I was most conscious of living with was the unique individuality of each of the other boys close to me. Our lives together were full of incident: friendships and rows, feuds and peacemakings, showdowns with authority, misunderstand-ings, two-day dramas, crazes that swept us all up and then ebbed away leaving no trace, passionate arguments, crimes and punishments, victories and defeats, entertainments, diversions, plans, stories from outside, crises offstage at home; it all flowed on like a formless drama, with our relationships among ourselves at the centre. This was what filled my consciousness most of the time. We were learning always from one another, the most important things having to do with living together, coping, managing, getting along, in a variety of different and often stressful circumstances; and this was probably the most valuable part of the education I received at school. In addition to all that, we were learning specific things from one another. One boy, Bailey, had a passion for chess, and through watching him and listening to his stories I learnt the classic openings and defences, and something of the history of the game, and heard the most famous anecdotes about well-known players. Another boy, Garrard, had a gift for caricature: he had a disenchanted eye for the peculiarities of all of us; and to leaf with him through the dayroom's copy of *Punch* was to get a funny and instructive introduction to the art of the cartoon. One boy was hooked on aeroplanes, so from him we learnt about the different planes on both sides of the war. I was forever talking about music, and I seem to have sparked off an interest in it in one or two of the others. It was a rich soil for us all to grow up in.

In later life, the boys in my house went into nearly as wide a range of occupations as Old Blues had done in the sixteenth century. George Neighbour, house captain in my first term, was to become head of the Performing Rights Society and marry a well-known opera singer. His deputy, Peter Glare, became the leading lexicographer of my lifetime in both Latin and Greek, an extraordinary achievement. Another of the leavers in my early days, Whattoff, became a waiter, and another, Glauert, a chemist who spent most of his life as a Fellow of Trinity College, Cambridge. Most of the boys went into industry or public service; and a surprising number of those close to me in age became professional soldiers, including one, Dick Gerrard-Wright, who became a major general. The range was exceptional; and because we all spent our formative years together, we all benefited from it.

CHAPTER EIGHTEEN

When the school holidays came round I would exchange this rich world for Arnos Grove, where I had no world at all except for my family – and I did not see them until the evening of each day. They would get up in the morning and go off to their jobs, leaving me asleep. They preferred it that way: with three of them competing for one bathroom they did not want me using it too, nor did they want to have to get me breakfast when they were in a hurry. So I would wake up each morning in an empty flat. I would get out of bed when I felt like it – which, as so often with children and adolescents, was late – and wash or bath at leisure, and make breakfast for myself. Most days I stayed at home till lunchtime – playing records, listening to the radio, reading the newspaper. Because I got up so late, the mornings were short. I listened to the same records over and over again, playing some of my favourites almost every day. In fact, quite often, when a record finished, I would put the needle back to the beginning and listen to it again. It astonishes me now that I did not get tired of those records. There could not have been more than two hundred of them, and each side lasted only four minutes and a bit, so the total amount of music on them must have been well under thirty hours. Yet for years I played a selection from them almost every day that I was at home.

In those days before refrigerators, it would not have occurred to anyone that I should eat lunch at home, and in any case there was food rationing – and in any case again my mother would not have wanted to spend her time preparing anything. It occurred to neither her nor me that I should prepare lunch myself. So I went out to eat. The family was unprecedentedly well off now. After my sister left school there were three earners in the home – and my father had two pay packets. The vital consequence for me was that I had enough pocket money for my needs. It was always given to me by my father, who I am sure was the one who actually paid it. He felt a certain guilt at my being abandoned all day, and realised that I had to go somewhere and do something. He always gave me enough to go into the West End on the tube and get a meal at a greasy spoon. These cheap cafés for workmen were plentiful everywhere in those days – they are still not uncommon – and I nearly always ate my lunch in one. The main dishes were fried, and would include such things as egg and chips, tomato and chips, fish and chips. At the top or bottom of the menu it would often say: 'Chips with Everything', a phrase that was later made famous as the title of a play. It was the food I enjoyed most at that age anyway, and we never had it at school. The people around me would include not only workers in overalls but also impecunious office workers and shop assistants, especially women and young girls, and there would be a sprinkling of shoppers too, and perhaps a few retired people, so the clientele was sufficiently variegated for no one to take any particular notice of me.

After lunch I would spend my time in ways that changed as I grew older. I always had a great love for the life of the streets, which I had grown up with. I would wander along the pavements of the West End full of curiosity about everything: they were nothing like as crowded as they are now, and still less was there the amount of traffic. I had space and elbow room to look at my leisure – people, shops, buildings – and gravitate towards any group or event. If a salesman was selling items out of an open suitcase on the pavement I would stand in the group around him and watch, and listen – to the group as well as to him. Street musicians, auctioneers, tipsters, men doing the three-card trick, political speakers, religious preachers, loonies announcing the end of the world, all had me in their audiences. I would usually listen for a long time before moving on. If I saw men working I would stop and watch them, as I would any altercation or fight, or accident, or police incident – any incident of any kind. I loved window-shopping, and even more going inside the department stores: I could happily spend a whole afternoon in one without buying anything. I loved their colour and variety, and the endless swirl of people, whom I would watch individually, and I relished the quality of the goods. My favourite would have been Fortnum and Mason if it had been bigger, but as things were I divided my chief affections between Harrods and Selfridges, and spent many an afternoon in each. I would wander into the parks, mostly Green Park but also St James's Park and Hyde Park, where there was a bandstand that occasionally offered music. Everything I have mentioned was free, except for my lunch and the tube fares. Until I got older I had no money to buy anything, but I took that for granted, and did not feel deprived. I was having an exciting time.

Because I had this dominating curiosity I was always exploring, always finding new places to go, new things to do. At first they had to be things that were free. First of all there were the touristy things, like the changing of the guard. Then I realised that there were free museums all over the place, most of which were boring but some of which were interesting – I found the British Museum fascinating, and went there many times. Then, as I grew older, I was given more pocket money, and this transformed the situation. I could do touristy things that charged admission fees – go up the Monument, visit Kew Gardens, the Tower of London, the Zoo, Madame Tussaud's. I discovered the Charing Cross Road bookshops, and for years haunted that street like an addicted ghost.

The sort of shops I patronised sold many of their second-hand books for a penny or tuppence, and would leave their customers free to browse; so I could spend a whole afternoon in one and emerge with two penn'orth of books, or indeed no books. My finances eventually rose to the dizzy height of affording sometimes to go to a matinee at the theatre, either at the back of the gods or in standing room, or on a returned ticket – I found all the ways there were of getting in for little money – but it was a further while before this happened, and I was then a lot bigger physically (though I still sometimes had to pretend I was buying a ticket for someone else).

Although I went to the West End on most days when my family were not at home I did not go every day: sometimes they would want me to carry out errands locally, since I was the only one of us with free time. On those days I would go to Palmers Green or Southgate, and have lunch there, and perhaps go to a cinema, or visit my grandmother or my aunt Peggy. Whatever I did, I was always home in time for our evening meal, and would then see my family for the first time that day – unless they or one of them were coming to the West End to meet me for a theatre. Because our evenings were the only time we saw one another, we spent them mostly talking. Sometimes one or two would read while the others talked, and sometimes we would listen together to a radio programme.

Since for three-quarters of the year my life was at Christ's Hospital, I had a great urge to talk about it to my family. In fact I felt a need for them to share it with me. My father did that unprompted. In his usual warm and intelligent way his interest in the school had been ignited by my going there, and he had already bought and read a book about it, with the result that for a long time he knew more about its history than I did. He interrogated me with keen realism about the life there, and about my friends, and what we did, and about the masters, and what we were learning. As a lover of language and a connoisseur of cockney slang, he was especially interested in the school's slang, so different from that of the London that surrounded it when it came into existence. (Some of it goes back a long way: Charles Lamb mentions it.) We had uproarious conversations in which he would laugh delightedly, comment, criticise, mimic, mock, ask. He saw most of the limitations of a boarding school for what they were, but he was an enthusiastic and encouraging ally, a supporter of mine in what had become my new life. He wanted me to be happy, and I think he may have identified with me too: it was a life he had come very close to having himself, and perhaps would have loved to have. For me, what mattered more than anything was that he cared, was interested. My mother was coldly indifferent. My sister Joan was actively hostile, and reacted disparagingly to any talk of Christ's Hospital. She thought it was unfair that I went to such a good school when she had not done so. The eighteen pounds a year my parents were contributing became a basis for her to tell herself that they were spending money on my education when they had not been willing to spend money on hers, and that the whole family's standard of living, including hers, was being sacrificed to help me. She voiced these sentiments frequently, and although both my father and I pointed out that they were completely untrue, it made no difference. This made *me* resentful, inevitably. I felt that her attitude was appallingly unfair, and what is more there was nothing I could do about it: I could scarcely be expected to leave the school to satisfy her jealousy; and nothing else would have done so.

This trait of hers was directed not only at me. I remember her complaining to my father that a girl at her office ought to be stopped from taking an extra holiday because Joan had not been offered it too. He responded with weary exasperation: 'I've talked to you about this before. If somebody else has got something that you haven't got, your attitude shouldn't be that they ought not to have it, it should be that you *should* have it. Taking it away from her would make you no better off, and would make her worse off. If *you* had it, you'd both be better off.'

This remark of his made a great impression on me, because it expressed a general attitude to life that I had always had but been incapable of expressing myself. I never minded others having things that I wanted and lacked, and this was nothing to do with unselfishness on my part. It was because their not having them would not make me better off. My father never felt that sort of envy either, nor did my grandfather.

Joan had left school at sixteen. Most people at grammar and public schools left at about that age – the general school-leaving age being fourteen – and only a tiny number went on to universities. She had now left Huntingdon and come to live with our parents. In London she took a secretarial course, and got a job at one of the leading advertising agencies, Pritchard Wood and Partners. This was in Fetter Lane, just off Fleet Street. That was the centre of the area where most of the national press was, so it was an exciting part of London to be in every day. She was starting a new life which included her own pursuits in the West End. Like the rest of the family, she loved the theatre, and went as often as she could. It was around this time that she began to develop a particular interest in ballet, which was to become something special to her within the family, though my father had always liked it too.

All of us now went to the theatre more often than before. Except for my mother, we thought it by far the most enjoyable of all the ready-to-hand things to do, the one most worth spending time and money on. My mother strung along with the rest of us most of the time, sometimes dragging. When I now look up the listings for the West End theatre in the early 1940s, I am amazed at the sheer number of things I saw, dozens of them, all during school holidays. They include some of the best things I have ever seen, such as Frederick Valk in *Othello* – twice, in fact, once with Bernard Miles as Iago and once with Donald Wolfit – and Wolfit in *King Lear*. There were powerfully cast classics besides Shakespeare – I saw Wolfit and Valk twice each in Ibsen's *The Master Builder*. But we were far from living on a diet of classics: the theatre was our chief source of light entertainment, which was why we went so often. Usually we could agree what to go and see, but I remember one early-closing day when we were unable to decide between two plays; so my father suggested we go to both, a matinee and an evening performance. My mother said: 'It's too much,' and I did not understand what she could mean. Too much what? My sister and I were laughing with excitement at the idea; and off we all went. Evening performances began so early, because of the blackout, that we had to run from the first theatre to the second. I have a clear memory of the four of us running panting along Coventry Street, three of us laughing, and my mother protesting through her gasps: 'I said it was too much!'

Revues were in vogue, and we saw all the main ones; their names indicate what sort of shows they were – *Up and Doing, Rise Above It, Fine and Dandy, Strike a New Note, Sweet and Low*. If Terence Rattigan was bringing out a new play (*Flare Path* and *While the Sun Shines*) or Ivor Novello a new musical (*Arc de Triomphe*) or Agatha Christie a new thriller (*Ten Little Niggers*), we went to see it as a matter of course. Some of the new plays we saw have established themselves as modern classics, such as *Blithe Spirit, The Man Who Came to Dinner*, and *Arsenic and Old Lace*. In 1943 I saw Noël Coward act in a new play of his own, *Present Laughter*. Most of the plays I saw then are now forgotten, by me as well as everyone else. Even so, the best actors of the day appeared in them, and I continued to see the same actors – many good, some bad, a few great – for the rest of their careers. At the time of writing, some are still around, after more than sixty years. I saw George Cole on the stage for the first time in 1941 in *Cottage to Let*; in 1943 I

saw Paul Scofield, in *The Moon is Down* – not to mention Deborah
Kerr in the same year in *Heartbreak House.* (Bernard Shaw was still
alive then.) I find it impossible to convey what all this meant to
me. Apart from music, I thought theatre the most wonderful thing
in the whole of life. Everything about it was associated with excitement. The thrill of anticipation each time we settled into our seats
and waited for a play to begin never dimmed with repetition; and
the magic of that instant when the lights began to fade as the
curtain was about to rise brought it to an almost uncontainable
pitch. At one such moment, when I was about to see Valk as
Othello for the second time, the impossible thought flashed into
my mind: 'This is as good as music.'

Because theatre had such a powerful effect on me, it was capable
of causing me serious emotional disturbance. This happened with
John Gielgud's *Macbeth* in 1942. A fact unappreciated by me
at the time was that the production was an unequalled combination of talents: William Walton composed music specially for it, a
nineteen-year-old Michael Ayrton painted the scenery, and the
cast was a list of distinguished names right down to the three
witches, one of whom was played by Ernest Thesiger. The judgement of the critics was that, given all this, it was not especially
good. In spite of them, though, it ran for most of a year – during
which time no fewer than four people working in it died, thus
confirming the play's reputation for being unlucky (merely to
utter its name is unlucky: many actors refer to it as 'the Scottish
play'). Oblivious to all this as a twelve-year-old, what I was aware
of seeing was Gielgud giving an anguished performance of ever-
increasing intensity that made my scalp prickle and itch. The
witches' scenes appalled me, and so did the scene with Banquo's
ghost. When I got home to bed and was alone in the dark I was
plunged into uncontainable terror, with the most lurid scenes of
the play re-enacting themselves in the blackness around me. I had
to get up and go into my sister's room, and ask if I could spend

the rest of the night on her floor, wrapped in my bedding; and that is what I did. I was still frightened of going to my own bed the next night, though I did in the end.

Incidents like this made my family begin to wonder whether it was a good thing for me to be alone for most of every day. My father had the thought that I might re-establish contact with Norman Tillson, the closest friend of my pre-war years. His family owned two sweetshops in Hoxton Street, and had lived above the one further away from us. Norman had gone to a different school from me, and had been evacuated to Bedfordshire. Boys of our age did not write to one another, and we had no telephones, so we lost contact. Now bomb blast had made the rooms over his family's shop uninhabitable, while leaving the shop itself intact, so they had moved out to the northern suburbs and were commuting daily to their shop. All this was exactly parallel to my family's history. They moved further out than we did, to Potters Bar. Norman was still an evacuee in Bedfordshire, but like me he was revisiting his parents during the school holidays, which meant that whenever I was in Arnos Grove he was in Potters Bar. We began meeting again, a couple of times a week, and this set a pattern that continued until he left school and started work after the war.

Out there in Potters Bar it was a different world: a new redbrick suburbia with a life of its own. The people were mostly the first generation of their families to have decent living conditions – indoor lavatories, running hot water, bathrooms, small gardens. Because they had moved into modern homes from what were often dilapidated ones, 'new' and 'modern' were fundamental values for them: they wanted everything new and modern. And they were proud of their homes. Being better off than they had ever been – the war having created jobs not only for all the men but for most of the women too – they were all the time planning and saving to buy things for their homes. In the conditions of wartime their problem was not so much the availability of money as of goods. Even so, what was happening was the beginning of a way of life that was to become the predominant lifestyle of the British people. It was essentially future-oriented and optimistic. People took it for granted that they were going to be better off next year than last. But in those early days they were still self-consciously getting away from the past, a past that had been poor, drab and lacking in opportunity, and had held them down.

The social shake-up provided by the war freed them in other ways. Millions were being sent away from home, to live and work in other parts of the country – even us children, of whom more than a million had been sent away unaccompanied – and huge numbers were travelling abroad for the first time. It was changing their attitudes and outlook, their traditional ways of thinking. It was also changing their expectations. Mr Tillson's brother Johnnie became an officer in the army, something that would not have been thinkable only four years previously: a combination of his personality and the barriers of social class would have made that impossible. But now the barriers were coming down, and everyone was aware of it. A future was opening up where there had been none before. And people wanted this to continue; in fact they demanded that it should: if the authorities expected them to fight a war, it was certainly not going to be so that they could go back to life as it had been before. The one thing they were determined on, above all else, was that there was to be no going back. It was this attitude that was to bring about the Labour landslide of 1945, in which Winston Churchill was swept out of power before the war was even over.

To this day, when I read about people's suburban childhoods, it conjures up the world I came to know in Potters Bar: teenagers on bikes, little front gardens, local cinema, open-air swimming pool, the shopping centre and the railway station, a sense of being in a lesser community outside a greater world. Norman's mother,

Beattie, stayed at home with him when he was there, instead of going to Hoxton to help in the shop. She mothered the two of us unobtrusively, caring for us happily without getting in the way. She was a person I liked enormously – affectionate, easy-going, generous-hearted, non-judgemental: the direct opposite of my own mother – and I came to feel almost like a member of the Tillson family. At first Norman and I would do the things we had always done together, chiefly roaming the streets and playing games. Sometimes we went to the cinema. Sometimes I borrowed a bike and we went off cycling together. In summer we went to an open-air swimming pool called the Watersplash, which I especially liked. When the weather was bad we had to content ourselves with indoor pursuits, and these would usually be card games. Both of our families were keen on cards – our parents had been playing together since before we were born – so we had grown up with card games. Norman taught me cribbage, the best of all games for two. I taught him chess, but neither of us enjoyed that as much as crib.

His two grandmothers were on the scene a lot, Nan Tillson and Nan Luff, and both were demon card-players who welcomed having us there to play with. They were wicked old women, both of them, in their different ways, and highly diverting. Nan Tillson had kept a pub in Southend, and possessed the right sort of personality to go with that – ready to get on with anyone but not standing for any nonsense: bawdy and outspoken, extrovert, hard-drinking, capable, funny and likeable. This made her ideal company for boys. She was never without a cigarette in her mouth, and somehow managed to cough round it perpetually without moving it. She was a tough old party altogether, not someone to get on the wrong side of. Nan Luff presented a complete contrast to this: diminutive, quiet, devious, manipulative. Nan Tillson was hilariously rude to her, but in fact the two of them were so evenly matched that watching how they behaved was an entertainment in itself, like successive rounds between a cunning little boxer and a tearaway. Without realising it at the time, I was learning from both of them. From Nan Tillson I picked up quite a lot of worldly wisdom, while Nan Luff alerted me to some of the invisible patterns of deceit: I found her deviousness so intriguing that it was sometimes I who suggested to Norman that we visit her.

Occasionally Norman would come to me in Arnos Grove. But since I was the only person there during the day, and there was nothing for us to do in the surrounding streets, we would then have to go either to Southgate or into the West End; so he came only rarely. I tried to have sessions at home with him playing records, but this was of no interest to him. Our interests were beginning to diverge. We had always been a contrasting pair. We looked different: he was stocky, barrel-chested, with a round freckled face and thin, flat ginger hair, whereas I was tall and stringy, with a long white face and piles of wiry, wavy hair of so dark a brown as to be almost black. Our personalities contrasted too: he was serene, sure-footed, practical, ready to talk but not running off at the mouth, while I was high-strung and gabby; and although I talked too much, I lived more inside myself, and was less good at practical things. In most of the indoor games we played we were an even match. But now, for the first time, each of us was beginning to develop along a path that the other did not want to pursue. Norman was acquiring a passion for sport, many sports, and was good at them all, whereas I, who had compulsory sport at school, was no good at any of it and disliked it intensely – and certainly did not want to have anything to do with it during school holidays.

However, I do remember one fête that we went to together, in which we both entered for all the events we were eligible for. Norman won nearly all of them, and I came nowhere. By the end he was cradling both arms full of prizes. I offered to help him carry them, but naturally he wanted to go on holding them. As we made to leave, people gathered round him to congratulate him and ask who he was. The little crowd became so thick that as we walked away I had to fall behind to make space for them to talk to him. I walked along a few paces in the rear, looking at him surrounded by these admiring people all trying to talk to him at once, and felt that I was being separated from him not only physically but in a more important sense – it was as if he was being airlifted away from me by those people. The conscious realisation entered my mind for the first time that from now on, as we grew up into our lives, we were going to move in different directions, and grow further apart. But there were still some years to go – we shall come to it later – before he and I became obsessional billiard players, and the dozens of afternoons we spent together at the billiard table were the happiest of our friendship.

Norman went to Hoxton every Saturday with his mother to help out in their main shop (the other had been put out of action by the bombing). But there was no point in my going with him; he would be too busy to spend time with me. On a Saturday he and his parents would be on the go all day without respite. Being a sweetshop, they sold their goods over the counter in ha'p'orths and penn'orths, weighing out each purchase on the scales; and this meant that at the end of their longest, busiest day they would have grossed something like fifty pounds – of which, of course, their profit would be only a portion. My family's clothes shop would be at its busiest on Saturdays too, and they would not want me there either, because I was too young to help with the services required; and in any case they would need to make only a fraction of the sales to earn the same amount of money.

There was one day, unforgettable, when I did go back to Hoxton. It came about in the following way. I had been a couple of years younger than most of my pre-war classmates, and this meant that when they left school in Market Harborough at fourteen or fifteen, and came back to London to live with their families again, I was thirteen or fourteen, and had been at Christ's Hospital for two or three years. Suddenly, after the years of Hoxton's emptiness, I once more had a lot of former school-mates who were living there. One Saturday in the West End I bumped into one of them, and we arranged that I should come to Hoxton the following Saturday afternoon, when most of them did not have to work, and meet some of the others. He would fix it up, he said. I arrived at the meeting place full of excite-ment, and there they were, a wonderful collection of the old faces. We all started talking at once. As I was greeting them, there were new ones still arriving behind me, chattering as they came in, so I was conscious of people and voices behind me as well as in front. So when those in front burst into a laughing, jovial chorus of 'Blimey, 'ark at 'im!' and 'Don' 'e talk posh!' and 'Cor, listen to 'im, talkin' all la-di-da!' I looked round to see who the new arrival was that they were greeting with this friendly derision, my ears pricking up for the voice they were describing. There was nobody there, the new arrivals having melted in. I turned back, and saw that they were laughing at me. My first reaction was disorientation: for a moment I stood bewildered. It was a long time now since anyone had talked about how I spoke, and I had long ceased to think about it myself. The chorus went on, and people were nudging one another, winking, laughing incredulously as if they could scarcely believe their ears. Then one of them said: 'It's no good you talking like that to *us*, you know. We know where you come from.' The idea that I would put on an accent to differentiate myself from them was so alien to me, and so hurtful, that I brushed their reactions impatiently aside and went on greeting people. But the damage had been done. They saw me as different. I was put out by it. For a long time they interrogated me about my school – none of them was at school now – and my life there, and how it had made me different. To them almost everything I said sounded like something out of a comic, and they said so: housemasters, rugger, Latin, chapel, the incredible uniform that they had all seen on the streets, none of this had any counterpart in their experience of life, and the whole caboodle seemed to them like a Never-Never Land that existed in comics alone – Lord Snooty and his Pals, said one (a strip cartoon in the *Beano*). They were cheerful about it, and warmed towards me in a friendly way, but they regarded what I was talking about as simply not real life, some sort of enacted entertainment, as it might be a street pageant or play. And it was the actuality of my life, the reality of it now, that they were dismissing. It was a while before I could get them away from all this and on to the subject of their own lives – their jobs, what Hoxton was like now after the bombing, and so on. I was deeply interested in that; but when I left, I would not have wanted to repeat the experience.

Just as when you encounter a new word, you immediately start coming across it in other places, so I soon encountered other comments on the way I spoke. Norman and I were playing cards with Nan Luff, and he made some cockney crack at her that reminded her of the way Nan Tillson insulted her, and she said: 'Why joo aff ter talk like that, Norm? Why doncher talk nice, like Bryan do?' And again I felt mortified. The way I talked was being used as a stick to beat Norman with. From time to time others commented, usually approvingly. (*'Don' 'e talk nice?'*) Since I talked spontaneously, however it came out, I felt helpless about it. But – exactly as had happened at Christ's Hospital a couple of years before, only the other way round now – people got used to it, and stopped remarking on it, and it became one more aspect of the way they were used to seeing me.

CHAPTER NINETEEN

My father had kept his promise, and let me start learning the piano in my second year. The lessons were with the handsome young clergyman 'Corks' Cochrane, in his study at the other end of the Avenue. As a musician he was a talented all-rounder. More at home on the organ than the piano, he could not only sight-read anything but transpose it into any key, or put a full orchestral score on the music rest and play it. He was an outstanding choral conductor, and a good singer. He had perfect pitch, which means (contrary to what many people seem to imagine) that if, without sounding a note of any kind, you asked him to sing, shall we say, a B flat, he would do so. Perfect pitch is a form of memory, the ability to remember pitches, and most professional musicians, including singers and composers (indeed most great composers), do not have it – it develops in early infancy if it develops at all. Corks, so gifted and so attractive, was fated to deteriorate catastrophically in his later years, when he became bloated with drink and almost disgustingly gross. I am pretty sure repressed homosexuality played a role in that development.

He decided to teach me differently from the way he had taught his pupils hitherto. Usually, after learning to read the notes, they went on to learn the different keys, and used these in the most elementary way possible at first, by playing scales, and then learnt how to move from one to another. After that they graduated to short and simple pieces, and developed steadily upwards from there. Notoriously, though, beginners found playing scales boring. Scales are not music. The pupil might be learning the relationships between the keys, and their written signatures, and developing the requisite suppleness in his hands, and being introduced to the basics of fingering – and all this was essential – but he was not getting any music. This made the endless repetition of scales mind-numbing, and many people were so put off at this early stage that they dropped out altogether. This now led Corks to decide, without having thought it through, that scales could be dispensed with. He saw no reason why a pupil should not begin straight away on simple pieces, and learn to read music – and familiarise himself with the different keys – through playing those. Such a pupil would proceed slowly, of course, and it would take time, but the process as a whole would be much more interesting, because he would be playing music, real music, from the beginning.

In my first lesson Corks explained to me that this was what he was going to do. He took up the score of Schumann's *Album for the Young* and played the first few pieces. Then he played the first again, two or three times, with a running commentary. Then he told me to take it away and practise it for the following week's lesson. Daily I went to the Music School, which contained a dozen or more practice rooms with pianos, and struggled through the piece. At first I had to locate each printed note on the keyboard. Then I had to make my two hands play together. It was an agonisingly slow process. But because it was so slow, and because the piece was so short, by the time I had struggled through to the end of it I knew it by heart. After that I played it over and over, trying to reduce the number of mistakes, and to achieve an even tempo, and then to get this tempo up to a proper speed; but never again after that first time was I reading the printed music. This was to set the pattern for all my subsequent work with Corks. The pieces got harder and longer, but my capacity to remember them developed with practice, and in every case the process of working my way through a piece for the first time lodged it in my head, and after that I was playing it from memory. The playing itself became quite good, and when I had been learning for three or four years I won a school prize for piano-playing; yet I never became even a minimally good sight-reader; I had no technique, and at that stage I had scarcely any understanding of the relationship between the keys. All I was learning to do was to play from memory the individual pieces: I acquired no other skill. It was something I could have taught myself with no tuition at all. Corks, full of weak good intentions, behaved irresponsibly with me: he had given no systematic consideration either to what he was doing or what the consequences of it would be. In later years, after I left school, I launched into the study of composition, and that was made unnecessarily difficult for me by the fact that I had never learnt properly to sight-read at the keyboard.

Corks and I spent a lot of our time simply talking about music. His interests were wide, but his love of Elgar knew no bounds. Elgar, he asserted, was as great a composer as Beethoven. When I said the polite equivalent of 'Aw, come off it,' his reply was that we should judge a composer by his greatest work, and Beethoven never wrote anything better than *The Dream of Gerontius*. Elgar, said Corks, composed only a handful of things on that level, and Beethoven many, but the level was just as high. This view, coming on top of my father's love of Elgar (and particularly *The Dream of Gerontius*), made me familiar with the idea of Elgar as a great composer. I never took the patronising attitude towards his music that was common at that time; in fact from my teens onwards he became a special love of mine.

Corks played piano pieces to me by widely differing composers, pointing out things about them that I would not have noticed for myself. I have remembered some of his performances: the last movement of Beethoven's 'Moonlight' Sonata, for instance; and

Chopin's 'Revolutionary' Study; in both cases it was the first time
I heard them. He gave a hilarious rendition of the overture to
Wagner's *Tannhäuser* in which, while his left hand intoned the
Pilgrim's Chorus with po-faced solemnity, his right suddenly
darted out and seized a hearth brush lying within reach and started
crazily whacking the upper part of the keyboard in simulation of
the violin accompaniment. Because of my passion for Wagner he
invited me one evening to his study to listen to a broadcast by
Kirsten Flagstad. He lent me the first of the innumerable biog-
raphies of Wagner that I have read – and also, naturally, a biog-
raphy of Elgar.

Another music master, Philip Dore, arrived at my house as the
junior housemaster, and I saw him constantly. During the holidays he earned large sums of money by playing one of the seafront
organs at Blackpool, from which he also broadcast on BBC radio
– his signature tune was 'Oh I Do Like to Be Beside the Seaside!'
– and this gave him kudos with the boys. He was a good musician, and was the first to record the complete organ sonatas of
Mendelssohn. Short, very fat, very jolly, he was just the right sort
of person to have around boys. At that time there was a popular
song whose words went (they had to be sung in an old-style black
American accent; and I quote them from memory):

> Mr Five-by-five
> He's as tall as he's wide
> He don't measure no more
> From his head to the floor
> Than he do from side to side

and this led to Dore being nicknamed Mr Five-by-five. This was
then shortened to Five – and then, because of our propensity to
say things in German, Fünf. (One of our jokes was: 'What comes
between fear and sex?' and the answer was 'Fünf.')

In Big School there was a beautiful early-nineteenth-century organ that had been brought to Sussex from the school in London, and whenever Five wanted to get into practice for one of his Blackpool appearances he would take a group of us up to its loft and give us a recital of popular songs. He always began with his signature tune, which he would launch into with terrific brio, instant swing that made my skin jump into goose pimples; and while playing it he would turn his face back over his shoulder and beam at us with his great big bespectacled features, just as he was going to do with his audience in Blackpool: he was rehearsing his beaming as well as his playing. I was so transported by these sessions that I was seduced into playing that organ myself when no one else was around. It was a mad thing to do, because it was strictly against the rules for any boy to touch the organ without permission, and sooner or later I was bound to be heard. I got away with it for a surprisingly long time. Unluckily for me, the person who heard me was the one who cared most about the organ, the head of the music department, Dr Lang. He summoned me to his study and gave me six of the best – the only time I was given the full six in all my years at Christ's Hospital – and it hurt more than I would have believed possible. He was one of the two or three masters who were notorious for perceptibly getting an erection when they beat a boy, and he laid it on with a kind of mad ferociousness.

My addiction to music led me to take up the bass trombone, though it happened partly by accident. I wanted to learn the clarinet, so I went along to the bandmaster, Mr Stagge, and asked if I could do so. He said the clarinet was the most popular instrument in the band, and he had people queuing up to learn it, so his answer had to be no. On the other hand, he was going to be short of a bass trombone in a year's time, and would I be interested in learning that? One of my father's closest friends, Chopper, was a trombonist in a Salvation Army band, and I had often

watched him play: I think this may have been one of the factors
in my saying yes. I made a start, and learnt the rudiments of the
instrument. But whereas Chopper was a tenor trombonist, and
had splendid tunes to play, the bass trombone scarcely ever did
anything but provide bass notes for the harmony. It was not even
oompah, oompah, but only half that. This caused me to lose interest.
I gave the instrument up before getting as far as playing in
the band.

The authorities at Christ's Hospital were not unanimously keen
on music. Quite a lot of the masters resented it for taking boys
away from games, or from their prep; and the headmaster himself
once famously complained that there was 'too much music going
on'. Fortunately there was enough of it to have a momentum of
its own that enabled it to survive this opposition. Corks had discovered that a particular note on a particular stop of the chapel
organ set up sympathetic vibrations in the wooden panel against
which the headmaster, Mr Flecker, leant his head during the services, so whenever Flecker made difficulties for the music staff
Corks extemporised *fortissimo* voluntaries centring on this note.

It was at Christ's Hospital that I first heard – and saw – Gilbert
and Sullivan. *Trial By Jury* was staged at the end of my first year.
From some source – I think it must have been my father – I had
acquired a snooty attitude towards Gilbert and Sullivan, but I
thought *Trial By Jury* was great fun. Its attitude of derision towards
authorities and accepted hypocrisies was to my taste, and the match
between words and music seemed right. The role of the Plaintiff
was sung pleadingly by the attractive young wife of the most notoriously sadistic of the masters, thus insinuating sexual implications
from an intriguing quarter. A boy, Bob Pitman, sang the Usher,
and made himself the star of the show. For some time afterwards
the rest of us went around singing 'From bias free of every kind
this trial must be tried'; and the first three or six of those words
became our standard comment on any kind of stitch-up. The

following year *HMS Pinafore* was done. It was brimming with tunes, and both words and music contributed permanently to the school's stock of standard references. Again Pitman performed, this time the role of Sir Joseph Porter. I was astonished that a boy could be so good. With his stage presence, good baritone and satanic looks, which included black eyebrows meeting in the middle, he came close to stealing the show. I think he could have had a future as that kind of singer, but he was destined to become a star of a different sort, the star columnist on *Express* newspapers.

Stage productions of any kind came on at the end of term, when discipline was lax and the audience about to go home. But the whole term would be filled with preparations, so even boys not involved in a production would be constantly aware of it. Actors with roles to learn would be asking their friends to hold the book for them and prompt them, or would walk about declaiming their lines. Particularly good lines or jokes would go around and become quotations. If the production was a musical one the songs would become well known. Disasters at rehearsal were always plentiful, and stories about these would go the rounds too. Every house put on a play or plays in the winter term. The first such programme in my time included that unforgettable fable *The Monkey's Paw,* by W. W. Jacobs (who was then still living). A level up from house plays were school plays. The first of these was Shakespeare's *Twelfth Night.* The role of Maria was played by a boy called Ivan Yates, who from then on made a speciality of playing female comedy roles, in which he was uncommonly sophisticated without being camp. He gave us Lady Teazle a year later, and Lady Bracknell two years after that. He was to become a friend of mine at Oxford, and remain so for the rest of his life, though at school I never met him.

Whereas the school plays were chosen from the classics, the most popular kind of house play would be a recent success in the commercial theatre. A famous production by another house was *Arsenic and Old Lace*, in which the two old ladies were Ivan Yates and Bernard Levin. Those in my own house included Noël Coward's *Hay Fever* and Terence Rattigan's *French Without Tears*. I appeared in a couple of one-acters; but to this day the only full-length play I have ever acted in was R.C. Sherriff's *Journey's End*, a tragedy set in the trenches of the First World War. With us, casting was always type-casting: every role would be given to the boy who seemed closest to it. So I played Trotter, the cockney officer who had risen from the ranks. He is a sympathetic character, and the one with most of the funny lines, so I got most of the laughs. It was, I found, satisfying to play. But the experience taught me that I was no better at acting than any of the other boys, in spite of my special love for the theatre and the fact that I was soaking it in during the school holidays.

I reached puberty at what was then, I believe, the normal age for a boy, thirteen. What apprised me of the fact was that I had an explicit sexual dream that climaxed in orgasm, and I woke up having the orgasm, never having had one before. Still half-asleep, I had no idea what was going on – except that, whatever it was, it was alarmingly violent. As I came to in the darkness of the dormitory my whole consciousness was being electrified as if it had been plugged in to the mains, and a massive charge pumped through it, convulsing my brain. My first thought was that I was having an epileptic fit, or going mad. But then the convulsions died away and I became aware of something entirely different, a warm sticky mess in the bed. I felt for it with my hands, and found that my pyjamas and sheets were soaked with some thick, smooth liquid. I sniffed at it on my hands, and it smelt like mushrooms. It was some seconds before I realised that it had come from my penis. And then, of course, when I was properly awake, I put two and two together, and the realisation swept over me: 'My God, so this is . . .'

Central to the whole experience was that it was outside my framework of understanding. The container of the only reality I knew had split, and something of a radically different order had come flooding in from outside, from some totally other elsewhere. There was already something else that I experienced in this way, and that was music. Just as people in love often think that no one else in history can possibly have felt the way they feel, so I did not believe that anyone else could have the same experiences as I had when I listened to music. It was not possible. Music came to me not *as if* from a different world but actually from a different world, from some order of being and reality unconnected with anything in the space I occupied. And from now on it was the same with orgasm, only more so, because orgasm was intense and climactic, more emotionally violent. The power behind it was at a higher voltage.

Fundamental to the difference in experience between men and women is that from puberty onwards boys have orgasms frequently whether they want to or not. Their bodies are unceasingly producing sperm that has to be got rid of, and if they do not induce orgasms in themselves, Nature does it for them in so-called wet dreams. So orgasms are inescapable. Boys grow up in the grip of this situation, and for most of them there is something overwhelming about it. They cannot ignore their own sexuality; and their sex drives and desires are as strong now as at any time in their lives. Yet the situation is new to them, and they have no experience in dealing with it. In fact, the truth is they are still children. And because of their age it is impossible for them to find the sexual outlets they feel a ravenous need for, and dream about. At the age of fourteen or fifteen I made some absurd attempts to have sex with one of the housemaids, a sixteen-year-old girl, but it all petered out into nothing. We were both terrified, first of all of the sex itself, and also because we knew we would be sacked on the spot if we were caught. We were more ignorant of how to do what we wanted to do than either of us realised, and both of us were pitifully lacking in self-confidence. Our fumblings and gropings were almost paralysed by ignorance and inhibition, with the result that nothing of consequence took place, except for a lot of red-faced and inarticulate embarrassment. It is so painful a memory that even now I shy away from thinking about it. But behind all that, as the cause of it, was a drive of tremendous power, something which on my side came close to desperation. I was obsessed by sex, and tempestuously in need of it. I thought about it more than anything else during the years between puberty and my first relationship, which occurred when I was seventeen and still at school – but that is a story we shall come to later.

Meanwhile the only outlets we boys had for our animal sex drives were with one another. But the inner as well as the social inhibitions against this were very powerful, and exposure was usually met with immediate expulsion, so by no means everybody took part in that sort of activity, though many did. It went on patchily and in semi-secret – the activity itself was always hush-hush, and yet it was the subject of endless rumours and excited whisperings. It was on everybody's mind. I never heard of anything happening that went beyond mutual masturbation. In later life I was surprised to be told by people who had been to Eton that buggery had been commonplace there. I never heard of it at Christ's Hospital, nor do I think it occurred: I was as active sexually as any of the other boys, and so voraciously interested in sex that I tapped in to all the grapevines, and it would have been almost impossible for something like that to be going on without reaching my ears. What we did do was fairly mild, and always *faute de mieux*, or so it seemed to me. When I was involved I used to fantasise about the boy being a girl, and afterwards I would always feel guilty and ashamed, and swear to myself that I would never do it again.

In case what I have written has activated the curiosity of readers, perhaps I ought to pre-empt mistaken guesses by saying that I never got involved in sex with anyone in my own year or older. My preference was for boys younger than myself, who I was able to fantasise about being girls. And none of them is named in this book.

In adult life I have found that a great deal of misunderstanding exists regarding the nature of sexual activity in boys' boarding schools. Wherever heterosexual males are segregated from females and forced together for long periods there will be sexual activity among them. It happens in the armed services, in camps and on ships, and in prisons, prisoner-of-war camps, and so on. These men are not homosexuals, nor are they being turned into homosexuals: they are normal heterosexual males. Their sex drive is so urgent, especially when they are young, that it compels an outlet, and if they are denied the outlet that they want they will seize on whatever is available until the real thing comes along. The vast majority of males who take part in homosexual acts in these circumstances have no desire to do so in other conditions, and do not do so during the remainder of their lives. The minority who do are those who are homosexual anyway, or at least bisexual. It is not, I believe, possible for a normal boy to be turned into a homosexual by being sent to a boarding school.

At about the same time as all this started to happen, I was made to specialise as regards my academic work. I was really too young to be doing this, but it was normal in all of Britain's best schools at that time – they were notorious for it in other countries. The advantage was that by the time a boy went to university he was well advanced in his special subject, and the university could begin with him at a high level. The disadvantage was that his general education was not as broad-based as it should be: for instance, at the age of fourteen I gave up the sciences altogether, after only one year each of biology, chemistry and physics.

Near the end of our second year we were asked what we wanted to specialise in, but were warned that we might not get our choice – there had to be a limit to class sizes, so we might need to be spread. I said I wanted to specialise in modern languages, which for me would have meant taking up German in addition to my French. But when, on the first day of my third year, I looked at the noticeboard, I saw my name down for classics – and that meant taking up Greek as well as the Latin I was already doing.

I was appalled. For the second time I was being denied German, when I so passionately wanted to learn it. Apart from that I was dismayed at the prospect of having to study Greek, by which I was, if I can so express it, bored in advance. The natural step was for me to talk to my housemaster, which I did. He said that this was something that only the headmaster could alter, so he made an appointment for me to see God.

H.L.O. (Henry Lael Oswald) Flecker was a fearsome figure even to the masters. Looking down from a height of several inches over six feet, he was domineering in manner, and given to volcanic eruptions in which his speech would turn into a scream, and he would rant on and on, and stamp not only his foot but the whole of a giant leg. Everyone found him alarming. His nickname was Oily, or The Oil. At first I assumed this was because of his appearance – his skin was quite a dark brown, and shone – but in fact the name came from something he had said when he was new to the school, introducing himself via a sermon in chapel. He was describing how he saw his role, and having characterised the school as an already well-running machine he added: 'I am the oil.' From that moment he was known as The Oil, and then, by a natural extension, Oily. Although he was now at the top of his profession, the first thing anyone said about him was that he was the brother of James Elroy Flecker, who was then a famous poet

– he had died in 1915 – and who possessed what was already, in my eyes, the distinction of having written a play for which Delius had composed the incidental music: *Hassan, or The Golden Journey to Samarkand*. It enraged The Oil that he should go through life being known to everybody as his brother's brother, even all these years after his brother's death; but there was nothing he could do about it.

As I crept into his study it seemed to me shadowed and congested, and full of dark wood; and he standing in the middle of it taller than any human being I had ever seen. He told me to speak up, and I said how much I wanted to learn German. He said I could not, because there was a unique problem with it: most of the German speakers among the staff had been called up for war work, so the school had a special shortage of teachers in that subject. In which case, I said, could I specialise in something other than Greek? He gave an exaggerated look of surprise. Classics was absolutely the right thing for me, he said. I was a bright boy, and the brightest boys in the school always specialised in classics, as a matter of course. Latin was already one of my best subjects. It was obvious I ought to do classics, anyway, which was really why they had put me down for it. I resisted. I started to say that I was better at maths than at Latin, so could I please specialise in maths; but before I was halfway through my second sentence a scream rent the air, bouncing back off the walls and drowning everything in the room. It was so loud, so violent, so sudden, and so totally unexpected that it had happened before I realised that anything at all had happened. By the time I took in that he was yelling an unbroken stream of imprecations down into my upturned face, it had been going on for several seconds. I stood there bewildered, utterly overwhelmed. His words poured over me like molten lava. There were no pauses between them, and I was too dazed to take most of them in – all I heard was that I was a something little something who something somethinged and needed to something something. One of his legs, which by itself seemed taller than I was, stamped again and again as he screamed. The only complete sentence I registered, because it was shouted louder than the rest, and in tones of cosmic incredulity, was: 'Do you think you know better than I do?' At last the screaming rose to its highest peak on the words 'Get out! Get out! Get out!' and I found myself physically bundled into the corridor. His study door slammed behind me with an almighty *thunk.*

I reeled back to my house, a cauldron of inner upheaval. The only recourse I had beyond the headmaster was my parents, so as soon as I got back to the dayroom I sat down and wrote them a letter, asking them to write to him. It was several days before a reply came, and then, to my surprise, it was from my mother. Neither she nor my father had written to the headmaster. Her letter admonished me to accept my fate, and gave inane reasons for doing so – for instance, that Greek was worth doing 'if only to be able to say that you have learnt it'. My disgust went beyond words.

There was nothing more I could do, yet something inside me would not accept the situation. I had no choice but to attend Greek classes, but I did not take anything in. It was not that I made a conscious decision to go on strike – the blockage was there of its own accord, insuperable. By the end of the school year I knew almost as little Greek as I had known at the beginning; and whereas in every other subject I was near the top of the class, in Greek I was bottom.

The headmaster sent for me again. I went to his study in terror, expecting another explosion. When I arrived he was sitting at his desk, and he turned towards me with a disconcerting smile.

'All right,' he said. 'You win. You can do German if you're still determined to. But I warn you: if you do, you'll have to take it in School Certificate next year. And if you get a bad result it'll be on your own head.'

That was that. My year of Greek left me with nothing more than an ability to read the Greek alphabet. I suppose I could, just, add to that the fact that my Greek teacher – A.H. Buck, known to us all as Buckie – was to become a friend when I was in my early forties. He had been a boy at the school, which meant that his whole life had been Christ's Hospital. I was sitting in his class one day, in the depths of a depression brought on by a bad cold, when he appeared at my elbow.

'Got a cold?'

'Yes, sir.'

'Feeling lousy?' (I can still hear his articulation of 'lousy'.)

I was astounded by the question. It went against the whole way we lived. You never talked about how you felt, or asked anyone how they felt. If you had troubles, you dealt with them by your-self without discussing them with anyone else; and no one else would refer to them either, however well they knew you had them. A surge of astonished gratitude welled up inside me.

'Yes, sir.'

'Well, you'd better go back to your house, then. You can make yourself a bit more comfortable there. No point in staying here if you feel like that.'

This tiny bit of sympathetic concern, not only expressed but acted upon, was unique in my experience of the school – until my last couple of years, when I began to deal with masters on more equal terms.

Decades later, Buckie made sexual overtures to a boy, who told his parents, who told the headmaster, and Buckie was out, his whole world in ruins about his ears. He was looked on as disgraced beyond redemption, and felt himself to be so. In obscurity he got a low-paid (and also, I think, part-time) job with Oxford University Press as a proofreader of Ancient Greek, and went to live in a bedsit in the poorest part of Oxford. When I found myself in Oxford too, as a Visiting Fellow at All Souls College, we met several times. I was touched to find that Christ's Hospital was still central to his inner life. Among other things, he marinaded in the books of writers who had been there, and seemed to know the essays of Charles Lamb almost by heart.

When my voice broke I joined the choir, and found a similar problem to the one I had had at Worth. Although my speaking voice was high, my singing voice lay awkwardly between tenor and bass, so that I was not able to sing either part properly – neither the higher notes of the tenors, which is where the best bits usually were, nor the lower ones of the basses, their juiciest bits to sing. I joined the tenors to get the tunes, and simply left out the notes I could not reach.

Rehearsals with Corks were among my most enjoyable experiences. He had a fine ear for the balance of voices within a choir, and his love of romantic harmony led him to put a slight touch of emphasis on whichever note within a chord was the least expected, so there was a trademark warmth and richness to the sound he produced. He shaped phrases beautifully. Repeated rehearsals of a work under him would make that work a special possession for me, and this happened with Handel's *Messiah* and *Acis and Galatea*, Brahms's *Requiem*, and Christmas carols by surprising composers such as Tchaikovsky. From this choral singing I learnt more about music, and about how to read music, than I did from my piano lessons with him.

For a couple of years in my early teens my best friend was Jennings, who had been my nursemaid when I was new. Perhaps partly for that reason he usually had the edge on me when it came to taking a lead. I first heard about a great many things through him, and learnt a lot from him. His nickname was Spint, our slang word for anyone of slight build. He showed me a photograph of his father, who looked Asian, but Spint said he was Eurasian and his mother English. Spint had spent his pre-school life in Malaya, where he had been born. His father, he told me, had edited a newspaper in Singapore before the war, and had published a book under the nom de plume Southern Cross. It was Spint more than I who had the sort of personality that was supposed to go with being cockney: cheeky and chirpy, amusing in repartee, independent-minded, pleasure-loving, irreverent of authority. His approach to life was like that of a man tucking in to a gourmet meal, all smile and elbows. One of the things that pleased him most was language. He would latch on to particular words and phrases and repeat them as if they were music, his eyes lighting up as he said them. For a term he found himself rehearsing the role of Laertes in a school production of *Hamlet*, and during those rehearsals he absorbed not only his own part but most of the play. In the same way as a boy might suddenly start whistling, he would, apropos of nothing at all, come out with one of the ordinary, un-famous lines, like 'It is a nipping and an eager air,' with a look of wonderment on his face, as if this was something truly marvel-lous, which of course it was. I helped him learn his lines, and absorbed a lot of *Hamlet* myself. My father had taken me to see John Gielgud in it, so the whole play was already alive for me, and I came to think of it as the best play I knew.

Jennings and I were schoolboy socialists. For him, I think, this was part of a general bolshiness whose chief target was the school, but my attitude was quite independent of the school. The chief influence on me in this, as in so many things, was my father. I had grown up absorbing a lot of his ideas, and now that I was old enough to understand some of them I was getting enthusiastic about them. The prevailing ethos of the school was conservative, among boys as well as masters. There were the odd few socialists here and there, especially among the older boys, but they were either smiled at indulgently or disapproved of. In a distant house there was a communist who was none other than Bernard Levin.

Since we were all known by our surnames, I gave him the nickname 'Lenin' at our end of the Avenue. He and I got to know
each other quite well in later life, and he told me he had never
realised that this soubriquet was coined by me.

Jennings and I read some of the notorious Yellow Books of that
time, hard-covered pamphlets written by Labour politicians and
published by Victor Gollancz in lurid yellow jackets. They
expressed not so much support for socialism as hatred of the
Conservatives. Because there was a wartime truce between the
political parties their authors hid behind Latin pseudonyms, but
the publishers made no secret of who they were. The most famous
and influential of the pamphlets, *Guilty Men*, was by Michael Foot.
Another, ineptly titled *Why Not Trust the Tories*, was by Aneurin
Bevan. Basically, they blamed the Conservatives for the war, and
argued that the Conservative Party ought never again to govern
Britain. These books broke the party truce, of course, but that
did not bother me, and I was a great enthusiast for them. From
them I imbibed what was the standard left-wing view of inter-war
history, and it informed my outlook until I found myself studying
something closer to the real thing at Oxford. The left-wing view
glossed over the fact that the Labour Party had persistently voted
against any attempt to prepare for a fight against Hitler, and the
fact that the only significant voice calling for such preparation
had been that of a Conservative, Winston Churchill. It also over-
looked the more general connivance of the left – communists
more than socialists – with fascist power. It demonised Ramsay
MacDonald, the Labour Party leader who left the party and led
a national coalition government after the debacle of the Labour-
led government of 1929–31. Partly on that basis, it encouraged
the myth that in any large left-wing organisation the leaders usually
betrayed the rank-and-file when they reached the top.

The wartime truce between the parties was broken not only by
Victor Gollancz's pamphlets but by a new left-wing party that was

formed expressly for that purpose, the Common Wealth Party. It was founded by J.B. Priestley and Sir Richard Acland. When a Conservative MP died, Labour was precluded by the truce from putting up a candidate in the ensuing by-election, so Common Wealth did, with more or less the same policy. I supported them joyfully, and wrote off to them for their literature.

One day Jennings showed me some literature he had obtained from the Young Communist League: junior newspapers, pamphlets, brochures, leaflets – a whole parcel of the stuff, including two membership forms for us to fill in. Neither of us had seen anything like it before, and we fell on it avidly. Most of it was crude, and therefore right up our street. Then I realised that there was one aspect of it that was deeply alien to me. This was the romanticisation of factory life. It cut right across one of the most disturbing experiences I had had, an experience that was still recent.

My mother's brother Len, who before the war had worked for a tea company in Ceylon, was now in London as personnel manager in a factory. During one of my school holidays he had shown me round his factory, and it was the first time I had ever been in one. I was aghast. It seemed to me the negation of life itself: soul-destroying. Individuals would sit or stand in one place for the whole of each day, at a machine or a conveyor belt, making one single repetitive movement which might be of just an arm or a hand; and they did this every day for literally years. They did it under lighting that was a dim yellow and made their grim surroundings look even more depressing than they were. There was no hint of daylight or bright colour anywhere, and not a breath of fresh air. Yet the people did not seem depressed. When I mentioned this to Len he said they were well paid, and thought of their jobs as good ones that they were pleased to have. One of the groups I had seen had been particularly jolly, and this had depressed me more than anything. They were women sitting round a table on which were two heaps, one of little screw tops to go on toothpaste tubes, the other of tiny white caps to go in the screw tops – and this was their job, putting the white caps in the screw tops. They did it by hand with a small instrument at a speed that eluded the eye, and while they were doing it there was a continual babble of conversation among them, a lot of mutual interaction and quite frequent outbursts of laughter. At any moment one or two might be distracted from the group, looking silently down at their work, absorbed in it; but after a while they would look up again and join in. That these women should spend all day every day for years and years putting caps into screw tops overwhelmed me with its appallingness, and yet the most appalling thing of all was that they were happy doing it. It induced in me a feeling of despair. My whole visit to that factory got under my skin in a way that disturbed me. It seemed to me a terrible world in which these people were living, a terrible life they were leading; and I knew that millions of people all over the world were living in the same way. I was actively depressed by it for weeks – and again, after that, whenever I thought about it. I even had one or two nightmares about it. As a young socialist I thought that one of the chief motives of political activity had to be to get human beings out of conditions like that. Yet here in a newspaper that Jennings had got from the Young Communist League was an article holding factory life up as some sort of ideal. Far from representing it as the nightmare it was, it was showing factory life in Russia as an idyll; and the photographs of sunlit factories and handsome workers were like the chorus scenes of happy peasants in some of the operas I was seeing. It was grotesquely false, and it turned my stomach over. I was perplexed. How could any sort of socialist not be against such a spirit-crushing life? How could anyone at all, socialist or not, be in favour of it, except for the factory-owners? I came to the conclusion that this political bumf must be produced by journalists sitting in an office somewhere who had never set foot in a factory.

Jennings wanted the two of us to join the Young Communist League. I was not keen, but did not know how to put into words the way I felt. 'But you agree, don't you,' he said, 'with what they are saying against x, and against y, and against z?' 'Yes,' I replied. 'Well,' he said, 'why don't we join and see what it's like? If we don't like it we can leave. Or you can leave if I still want to stay in.'

We were having this discussion on an open-air bench outside the dayroom, overlooking the front lawn, surrounded by pamphlets at our sides, on our laps, on the ground at our feet. I could feel the argument slipping away from me when our house-master, Snugs Burleigh, came riding along the path on his bike. Seeing the pamphlets, he stopped and asked what they were. When we told him he looked concerned, picked up one or two, and started looking at them. He saw the letter inviting us to join the Young Communist League, and quizzed us about that. It was not clear to me why he was taking so much interest. In the end he told us he would keep all this to read through carefully, and meanwhile we were not to get in touch with the organisation until he had spoken to us again.

After a few days he summoned us to his study. He had come to the conclusion, he said, that this was something for our parents to decide. If they had no objection to our joining the Young Communist League we were free to do so. But we must get their permission first, and show it to him.

The moment we were outside the study door Jennings turned to me and said there was no chance of his getting his mother's permission. I did not think there was much chance of my getting my father's, either. Now that the Russians were our allies against Hitler, and it was on the Russian front that the war against Nazism was being decided, he had moved away from the blanket disapproval of the Russians into which the Nazi–Soviet Pact had plunged him, and returned to being ambivalent about them. We had even started taking the *Daily Worker* at home as a second newspaper, to get the Russian point of view. (Everyone knew that the British Communist Party and its newspaper were financed by the Russians, and in fact it turned out years later that it had been the Russians who kept the newspaper in existence.) But my father still disapproved of Stalin and his methods. His overriding attitude to communists had become that they said the right things but did the wrong ones, and were not to be trusted. He would have been alarmed at the thought of my getting involved with them at any age, but especially as a child, and he would certainly have talked me out of it. In any case, I was not keen to join. And I would be left with no desire to at all if Jennings were not a member. So we pursued the matter no further. But I had come within a hair's breadth of joining the Communist Party as a junior member. If Snugs Burleigh had not come along at just that moment I would have done so.

The incident affected Burleigh's attitude towards me. He took to addressing me as Trotsky; and once when he handed me a letter he said: 'I knew it must be for you when I saw it had a red stamp on it.' The masters in general seemed unable to take my left-wingery in their stride, as they ought to have done. Teddy Edwards, whom I loved, once told us to write an essay about our attitude to the British Empire, so naturally I fired off an anti-imperialist salvo in which I said all the standard left-wing things about exploitation. When the essays were handed back, marked out of a hundred, mine had a giant nought underlined several times. Sitting in my desk at the back of the class I was gazing at this with astonishment when Teddy shouted from his dais at the front, over the heads of all the other boys: 'Yes, Magee, you may well look askance . . .' and launched into a tirade that went on for several minutes. Like me, only on the other side, he said all the standard things – that the British Empire was the greatest force for good in the modern world because it brought peace and the rule of law to barbarous societies all round the globe, developing their economies and raising their standards to a point where they would be able to cope with democratic self-government, so that we could then leave them to govern themselves; and that no other empire in the history of the world had done this. Over many centuries, he shouted, thousands of boys from this school, including many he had taught personally, had devoted their lives to that cause, going out to live and work in distant parts of the world and giving their all in primitive, unrewarding circumstances. One of the most important things we were being trained in here was a conception of leadership that saw it as a form of service, so that we too could play such a role, in whatever society we chose to live. People who ran all this down, he yelled, were Enemies of the Good, and were not to be listened to. They usually had an agenda of their own that was anti-democratic.

At the end of all this I felt as if I had been chewed up and spat out, but it did not change my views. Fortunately I was not called on to reply: I would not have been able to stand up to Teddy. I began to get used to it, though, for I became the object of a number of such public dressings-down. Lionel Carey, who taught us divinity that year, asked us to write an essay about whichever of the twelve apostles we found the most sympathetic, so naturally I chose Judas Iscariot. It was an act of provocation, of course, but I had a few good debating points to make, and they were fun to write. I managed quite an amusing piece, and was unprepared for the explosion that greeted it in class. Carey too shouted at me in front of everyone, louder than Teddy but not for so long, and he went redder in the face. He said he had not given my essay any mark because he did not know how such an essay *could* be marked, it being beneath consideration. He ended, his voice going almost to a falsetto when it got to the name: 'This is *Bernard Shaw* sort of stuff!' For me there could have been no higher praise: my current idol as a prose writer was the Bernard Shaw of the *Prefaces* – in fact I may well have been imitating him unconsciously.

It says something to the school's discredit that nonconformist opinions were publicly lashed and thrashed in this way. The school was supposed to be teaching us to think for ourselves, but in fact the degree of latitude that was accepted by most of the masters was pitifully narrow. A few years later, at university, I came to know people who congratulated themselves on their bravery in outraging convention by wearing burgundy-coloured waistcoats, and Christ's Hospital's attitude to diversity of opinion was something like that. Genuine liberalism was looked on as a dangerous form of radicalism that stretched tolerance to its limits. Anything more radical than that was beyond the pale. The school itself embodied classical conservative values: all power flowed downwards, and all structures were hierarchical. Each individual had his place and knew what it was, and was punished if he stepped out of it. The whole system was in thrall to its own past: the reason why most things were done in the way they were was that this was how they had always been done. Each member of it was expected to devote himself to it, and to display attitudes that sustained it. Questioning, criticism and dissent were tolerated in only the most anodyne of forms, and were otherwise taboo. Religion played an important role in all this, and was consciously used to manipulate our beliefs and behaviour in the required ways. The whole institution was essentially tribal. The school's ancient device expressed its ethos: 'Fear God, Honour the King, Love the Brotherhood.' Its traditional toast took the same points in the same order: 'The Religious, Royal and Ancient Foundation of Christ's Hospital. May those prosper that love it, and may God increase their number.'

A couple of years after the scenes I have described I came near to being expelled for my beliefs. In chapel, one half of the school faced the other across a centre aisle, but when it came to saying the creed, all nine hundred of us (that figure included the masters) turned towards the altar. I decided that I was not going to say the creed, a profession of a belief that I did not hold, so I would not pretend I was doing so by turning towards the altar. When everyone else turned, I stayed facing the front. Immediately, my face stood out, being the only one everybody, indeed anybody, could see. I did this every Sunday for about a year. Later I learned that it had caused consternation among the masters, who were afraid that other boys would follow my example. Several of them said I must be presented with an ultimatum: either turn to the altar or leave the school. None of this reached my ears at the time. Without knowing it, I had been fought for and saved by the master in charge of my special subject, which by then was history. He said that this was mere adolescent rebelliousness on my part and that I would grow out of it; that the staff ought just to let it pass; that I was a certainty to get a scholarship to Oxbridge, and would be penalised for life if I were made to leave the school before that happened. Of course he was right. I came to feel of my own accord that my gesture was a bit of meaningless self-indulgence that was making no difference to anything, so I started turning towards the altar again. No one commented. This was typical of the school: everyone saw what was happening, and everyone carried on as if nothing was happening – a form of behaviour that is looked on all over the world as typically English.

Among the people most outraged by my behaviour, apparently, was the headmaster, who had already got me marked down in capital letters as a member of the awkward squad. He said nothing to me privately, but issued a prolonged and public denunciation of me in his Latin class. In something I had written I made a mistake about one of the plural forms of *quis*, so in class he asked me to decline it aloud. Again I got it wrong. His now-familiar scream rent the air, bouncing back into the classroom off the walls and making all the boys sit up astonished. I was astonished too, but this time I managed to take in most of what he was saying, even though it went on for several minutes. As before, the white-hot words came streaming out like molten metal, with no breaks, and one whole leg banging its foot loudly and repeatedly against the floor. One passage went: 'You're of no use now, you never were of any use, and you're never going to be of any use. What will become of you I don't know. If they nationalise the banks *they* might take you, but otherwise you're going to end up sleeping on the Embankment . . .' The nationalisation of the banks was an obvious reference to my left-wing views.

When I told this story, many years later, to Colin Davis, he capped it with a better one of his own. It was again set in the Latin class of the headmaster, who was dobbing his finger round the room asking each boy in turn what he wanted to be in later life. When he reached the young Davis, Colin said: 'A musician, sir.'

The headmaster laughed with fat joviality: 'Do you know, Davis, for a moment there I thought you said you wanted to be a musician.'

'I did, sir.'

'What, you mean you *seriously* want to be a musician? You want to earn your living at music?'

'Yes, sir.'

The headmaster laughed again, derisively this time, and said: 'Will you let me hold the hat for you?'

Colin said to me: 'Ever since, there's been a tiny voice at the back of my head saying: "I'm going to show that bastard."'

CHAPTER TWENTY

One difficulty about encapsulating day-to-day life in any big, complex institution is the many-sidedness of it: there are so many different things going on at one time and being taken for granted simultaneously. As well as those I have mentioned there were many others. For instance, I was a member of the Officers' Training Corps, known as the Corps. Once a week we dressed up in First World War uniforms – puttees and peaked caps – and carried out military training. It came as a great surprise to me to discover that I was a good shot – it did not seem to fit in with the rest of my character.

The school possessed a sizeable armoury of military weapons. This was kept under tight security, but there were one or two thefts from it while I was there. One of these occasioned a scene of unforgettable drama. The headmaster summoned the entire school to a special meeting in Big School and told us, in tones of majestic gravity, that a gang of older boys had carried out a theft of explosives and detonators from the armoury. We naturally thought this was tremendous news, and were agog for more. Who were these boys, and what were they planning to do with the explosives? Blow up the school? With what may have been an inborn sense of theatre, the headmaster brought his narrative to a climax, and then thundered: 'Douglas, stand forth!' The hero-villain of the school at that time was a sinisterly handsome boy whom we called Black Douglas because of his hair. He now emerged from his seat as if on cue, and stood alone in the centre aisle. The headmaster denounced him in front of everybody as the ringleader of this criminal escapade, dwelling on the terrible consequences it could have had if the explosives had fallen into the hands of young children. Douglas stood calm and self-possessed, neither defiant nor intimidated, just looking the head-master coolly in the eye while every other eye was on him. I happened to be in front of him and quite near, so I got a full-frontal view. What impressed me was that he looked so like his normal self, neither cocky nor abashed. How can he do it, I wondered: how can he be so at home inside his own skin in circumstances like these? The headmaster brought his denuncia-tion to another climax, made another dramatic pause, and then, with Jehovah-like magnificence, proclaimed: 'Douglas, you are expelled!' Gasp. The intake of breath was audible from hundreds of throats. I thought it was impossible now for Douglas to know what to do. I expected him to slink back to his seat. But with the simple self-possession that had distinguished him throughout, he turned and walked up the long aisle between the rest of us and out of the building. He had been expelled so he was going. His demeanour said quietly: 'There is a world elsewhere.'

There was another boy in my house who had more the char-acter of a small-time criminal. Being a monitor he was allowed to beat boys, and he delighted in punishing. He made himself a rubber truncheon, filled with lead, and used to whack it into his palm in a kind of foreplay of threatening. Not long after leaving the school he held up the post office in one of the local villages at gunpoint. Although he was wearing a mask at the time he was identified and caught. It turned out that he had stolen the gun from the Christ's Hospital armoury, which was why he had carried out the crime so close to the school.

We were all trained in using the military small arms of the day – I was particularly good with a Sten gun. Militarism was not only in the air, it was encouraged – we were, after all, in the middle of a war in which the older boys were going to have to fight, and the younger ones too if it went on long enough. So the more we prepared for it now, the better. On what were called Field Days we used to take a whole day off class and carry out far-ranging military manoeuvres across the Sussex countryside. These were cunningly plotted to challenge the map-reading skills in which we had been trained. The skill they actually developed was that of finding out-of-the-way pubs that would let us in because of our army uniforms, and where we could remain unlocated for a couple of hours, saying afterwards that we had got lost. This was certainly a realistic training for warfare. And it was on these days that we came to know the extended countryside round Christ's Hospital. Not until we were sixteen were we allowed to have bicycles, or even go out of bounds unaccompanied.

Until that age, apart from Field Days, most of us went beyond the ring fence only when we had visitors from outside, usually from home. Boys who were good enough at any game to play it for the school would visit other schools – our standard fixture list was Brighton, Charterhouse, Cranleigh, Dulwich, Epsom, Lancing, St Paul's, Tonbridge, Whitgift and St John's, Leatherhead – but I never had that experience. I was no good at games, and lucky if I played for the house. Even then, I was lucky at, say, cricket if I was brought in as fourth bowler; and my highest innings ever was 34. My performances were bold but insecure – I might hit runs off half a dozen balls and then be clean bowled. And that was the way I was in most sports. On a good day I might appear to be a reasonable player for a couple of minutes, but the luck always ran out very quickly. The most I can say is that I was not as hopeless at any other games as I was at rugger. There were some at which I was not far below average, even able to fill in unnoticeably. It contributed to my education that I got the inside feel of so many games by playing them for several years: rugger, cricket, fives, squash, hockey, soccer. But my lack of prowess confined me to the school.

It was only when I had visitors that I even went as far as Horsham, two and a half miles away. Horsham was the shopping centre for the staff, an essential part of their ordinary lives, but for us boys it was remote: it was out of bounds. Our uniforms were too conspicuous for us to go there unobserved, and we did not have the money for shopping anyway. We went when we were taken; and what we knew chiefly were the eating places and the cinemas.

My father visited me every term. Usually I met him at the station, and we would go for a gentle stroll round the school, then take a train into Horsham. If we were having lunch there we would go to the King's Head, which we preferred to the Black Horse. These were Horsham's only two hotels, and in the England of that day there were rarely restaurants in small towns, so one ate in hotels. More usually we just had tea, and for that our favourite place was Wakefield's. This had a clock sticking sideways out of its front on the first floor, and we always asked for a table beside the window next to it so that we would not forget the time, as we had once done somewhere else. There was a day when we ordered the set tea at Wakefield's and it turned out to include an especially delicious apricot melba. At the end of it my father said with a note of surprise and inspiration: 'Shall we have it again?' We had it again. Heaven, I thought, could only be like this.

Other members of the family came occasionally to visit me. At that time women wore hats, and they felt under a compulsion to wear something different from the norm if the occasion was seen by them as being special, say a wedding – or, unfortunately, a visit to a boys' school. Then they felt it necessary to make a splash by dressing up. Even if normally they looked very nice, they still felt they had to look different, so they spoilt their appearance for special occasions. No amount of remonstration with them availed;

they would explain that this was something they had to do. Boys dreaded being visited by their female relations: they hated seeing their mothers or sisters making themselves look ridiculous in front of everyone. Mine were no different, and after early experiences of their visits I told them they could come again only if they wore the hats they normally wore. They disregarded this, so I felt compelled to say I would receive them only if they wore no hats at all. This stopped them coming. Although it had not been part of my intention I found I welcomed it, because it meant I had my father to myself.

By this stage he and I were talking about everything under the sun, but most of all the chief of our shared enthusiasms, which were music and politics. As a socialist I was so much of an idealist that my attitude to socialism came near to being religious: I saw it as the only form of society that was morally right, and therefore I thought one must crusade for it regardless of circumstances. My father, who was a humane pragmatist, shocked me by saying that if all private employers were good employers there would be no need for socialism. He made other sorts of remark that were outside the range of my understanding. He once observed that the imposing, elaborate set of brick buildings that constituted Christ's Hospital station were a typical example of the nineteenth century's overcapitalisation of the railways, and I simply had no idea what that meant. But most of the time we talked on equal terms – which I was not able to do with my schoolmates when it came to those particular passions.

Apart from such one-day visits, the only escape most of us had from the colossal weight of organisation that governed our lives was when we were ill. However, after I ceased to live with my mother I was scarcely ever ill. I had a short spell in the infirmary with mumps, and a longer one with a chest infection, but that was all. The doctor did not know what the chest infection was, or how to cure it. This was before the general use of antibiotics. If you got any kind of infection you waited for it to run its course, and either you got better or you lost the infected part, which might be all of you. My illness was bad enough to keep me in bed for three or four weeks, during which time I lost an alarming amount of weight. The school doctor was on the point of having me transferred to the hospital in Horsham when I started to get better. I remained skeletally thin, and when I went home for the school holidays I was given a medical prescription for more than my ration of milk and eggs. However, my mother appropriated these for family use, declaring with a gritty laugh that I obviously did not need them now that I was getting better.

The weeks in which I was bedridden became a memorable experience. There had always been a contemplative side to my nature, and I was now able to lie in bed all day and just think. I did a lot of this, and somehow it was clarifying, and made me feel better generally. Something was happening to me that had to do with my age, connected I think with puberty. I was reaching what people used to call the age of reason, and beginning to relate to life more in terms of concepts and less in terms of emotional re- action. Concepts were new things to me, or at least many of them were, and they filled my head. They lit up so much that I found them wonderful and fascinating. Above all, they liberated me from the here and now, the hereness and nowness of feeling. I began to find myself living in a wide-open landscape of the mind, in which thoughts moved forward, backward and sideways almost simultaneously: if such-and-such was happening now then so-and- so must have occurred at some point in the past without my noticing it, and if that was already the case then I ought to expect such-and-so to happen in the future. I had thought like this before in some individual situations, but not all the time about everything, and it made the world in which I found myself a clearer and more meaningful place. But there was a downside to it. Concepts, so useful and illuminating, got in the way of my spontaneous reactions. All my life up to now I had been immediately up against everything I experienced, unthinkingly identified with it, as if I *was* it, and nothing else existed. The sensory immediacy of it filled me. There was a naked presence and engulfingness about living that for most of the time I enjoyed, though sometimes I found it overbearing. It was this that was now coming to an end. Sensory experience now found itself at one remove. Between me and it came thoughts, ideas and concepts of every kind, forming chains of connection. Along with them there arrived a new kind of self-consciousness, so that I was aware not only of the experience I was having but also of myself as having it. Sometimes I felt that this devalued the experience itself. There was no longer that unthinking, self-forgetful spontaneity of before. It was a felt loss. I was ceasing to be the natural animal that small boys are, and becoming a creature living in the light of the mind. It was not a process I would un-wish, but I was far from thinking that it was all gain.

In the school infirmary there was a radio speaker in each ward, and among the few things on it that were thought suitable for us was classical music, so I listened to a concert every day. Among the most thrilling moments was hearing, for the first time in my life, that wide-open-spaces horn motif that leaps up out of the orchestra near the beginning of Dvorak's 'New World' Symphony. It seemed to take the top of my head with it, and my brain was suddenly out there in the open spaces with the wind blowing round it. To this day that moment can give me the same exhilaration, while also bringing back the memory of myself lying in a hospital bed feeling it for the first time. Another revelatory work was Borodin's Second String Quartet. As an orchestra chauvinist I thought I did not like string quartets: I found their sound too gaunt, too undernourished. But here was sensuously beautiful sound as a vehicle for superbly lyrical music. It opened the gates of chamber music for me.

In that bed I read a book whose influence on me I find even now impossible to evaluate. It was a novel by Howard Spring called *Fame is the Spur*, and recounted the life of a boy, Hamer Shawcross, as he emerged from the slums of Manchester to become one of the country's leading socialist politicians. For some time I had believed that I was destined to lead Britain and the world into a Golden Age of Socialism. And I had always been unaware that these daydreams were fantasies: I thought of them as facts about the future. These were things that were going to happen. I could not foresee exactly how they were going to come about, because that was not the sort of thing anyone could know in advance. No one could foretell the future in detail: the detail was bound to depend on ever-changing circumstances. But now I found myself reading the life story of just such a person. My identification with him was complete, and abnormally intense – until quite late in the book, when it became clear that he was going to succeed in career terms only, while failing in terms of achievement. Then I began to think: Well, there's the difference. He failed. I'm going to succeed. But before I reached that point, a specific life path had been laid before my eyes. When Hamer Shawcross emerged from the education system he travelled abroad, and lived and worked in foreign countries, and became a man of the world. Then, while still young, he returned to England and plunged into political activity, attending party conferences and making speeches. He was, in particular, a good public speaker. Then he became a parliamentary candidate, though he failed to get in to the House of Commons at his first attempt. Eventually he became a Labour MP. And while all this was going on he acquired, along the way, a wife and child, and published several books.

Now I did in fact go on to do all these things. And the disconcerting truth is that from the time I read *Fame is the Spur* I saw this as the life path I was going to follow. I do not mean by this that the book became a point of reference for decisions or actions:

I never thought of it in connection with any decision I made – in fact, after my teens I scarcely thought of it at all. But it caused me when I read it to form a much more specific conception than I had had before of the path I was going to follow in life. I am entirely certain that I did not do anything significant – did not marry my wife, or write my books – because I had read *Fame is the Spur*: that would be an absurd proposition in the light of the way things actually turned out. Also, before I became an MP, I did a great many things that Hamer Shawcross did not do – I served in the army, went to Oxford and Yale, trained in industry, worked as a music and theatre critic, earned my living in broadcasting. So the similarities are selective. Even so, the fact remains that I did see myself, in the very broadest of terms, as following a course in life that had been crystallised in my mind by the reading of *Fame is the Spur*. It must have corresponded to something deep inside me; and, that being so, I might well have followed such a course in any case. It could be that the only difference made by reading the book is that it put into my hands a partial sketch map of my future journey when without it I would have made the same journey without maps. Yet even that is something for a book to have done.

Because Jennings was my special friend I let him in on the secret that I was going to save the world. At first he believed me, and was awestricken. For a brief time he prepared himself to act as my St Peter, the leader of my apostles, my first pope. But then suddenly – he must have talked about it to someone else – he began to jeer at me. He addressed me in terms of derision as the greatest man who had ever lived. I felt betrayed. Here was the only person to whom I had fully divulged my secret, and this was how he reacted. He even made jokes about it in front of other people, and this cut me to the quick, because I knew that no one else would understand. In fact it was this, not anything he said to me directly, that brought to an end the friendship between us.

It was only about a year after this that Jennings left the school altogether, at the age of sixteen. All the boys at Christ's Hospital sat the General School Certificate at fifteen or sixteen, usually in eight subjects; and on the basis of their performance, plus whatever judgement the school had formed of their abilities up to that point, an assessment was made whether they had a chance of getting in to Oxford or Cambridge. If the answer was no, they were asked to leave, to make room for a new boy. If the answer was yes, they stayed on till they were eighteen and took one of the college entrance examinations. In practice there were several things wrong with the way this system worked. One is that few, if any, of us took Higher Certificate. Another, related, is that it was rare for any university other than Oxford or Cambridge to be considered, which meant that large numbers of boys who could have got in to good universities left school at sixteen and received no higher education at all. More drastic still is that the school was a defective judge of ability: some of the ablest boys in my time were asked to leave before they were eighteen, including the two who were to become the most famous, Colin Davis and Bernard Levin. I was later to get to know Ian Trethowan: he had been at the school before me, and in due course became Director-General of the BBC, but he too had been made to leave early. Many such people bore lasting resentment against the school, which they saw as having misjudged them and handicapped them seriously in life. Perhaps Jennings did too; I do not know. I was never in the same class as him, so I have no idea what his academic work was like. It may have been poor. But he was intelligent, and quick, and had a marvellous feeling for language. The school let him down, I fear, as it did many. Because he and I had drifted apart before he left I never heard from him again. But he had provided me with almost daily stimulus and delight during a couple of the most formative years of my life.

Despite the unrealism of the fantasies I had shared with

245

Jennings, the facts that I had passed puberty and was beginning to think meant that I was taking the earliest steps into becoming an adult. That whole period of my life constituted a turning point: I was beginning to find my feet and become an autonomous person. Perhaps not surprisingly, a contribution was made by the fact that the war had also passed its turning point. Everyone began to realise that the outcome had been decided in Russia, where the two biggest armies that the world had ever seen had been locked in combat on a one-thousand-mile front, the whole thing on such a scale as to make our battles in the West look like skirmishes. After the Battle of Stalingrad it was borne in on us that the tide of the war had now irrevocably turned, and that from now on the Germans were going to be on the defensive. There were bound to be years more of fighting, and millions more of dead, but the outcome could no longer be doubted. The difference this made to the psychology of the people of Britain was incalculable. Until then they had been defiant, defensive, grim, closed in, determined to endure whatever fate might have in store for them. Now they began to relax and open up, to become more sure of themselves, to look outward, then optimistically forward, and to think in terms of the future, a future in which everything would be getting better. They began to enjoy life – being on the winning side in a just war was exalting. Inevitably, I was caught up in this. I began to feel more confident about the world I was growing up into, and to look outwards into it more, and to start thinking excitedly about the future.

What we were all looking forward to immediately was the creation of a Second Front, so that the Russians would be carrying a less disproportionate share of the burden, and the Germans would have to fight a war on two fronts. A gigantic build-up was taking place in Britain for the invasion of western Europe, chiefly by the Americans but with England as their indispensable launching pad. Well over a million US servicemen were stationed

in Britain – a fact which by itself made an all-pervading difference to the social life of the country. Some of this difference can
be inferred from what were said to be the three main complaints
against American soldiers: 'They're overpaid, oversexed, and over
here.'

Being less than twenty miles from the south coast, Christ's
Hospital had Americans encamped all round it. Some visited the
school – Jennings and I once guided one round. A heavy American
military vehicle, having lost its way, once came clanking loudly up
the Avenue, the officer in charge of it standing up and looking
wonderingly around at this environment from outer space; but
the headmaster, hearing the noise, came running out of his house
screaming and waving his arms like a windmill, until the bewildered man and his vehicle went scuttling back to wherever they
had come from. Some boys formed out-of-bounds friendships in
the military camps, from which they would return at dead of night
with armfuls of contraband, usually alcohol and cigarettes. One
was given a loaded gun by some drunken Canadian soldiers (or
so he said – he may have stolen it from them). There were British
troops too, and their supremo, Field Marshal Montgomery,
decided once to visit the school without notice. Since he was the
biggest national hero after Churchill, a hasty welcome was scrab-
bled together for him, and the boys were summoned out of their
classrooms to Big School so that he could talk to us. And there
he was, up there on the dais, Monty, wearing his famous battle
dress and his equally famous beret, telling us that it was our job
above all to become good leaders. Leadership, he said, was the
most important contribution that any individual could make to
society, especially in time of war. Do you know, he asked us, to
what our troops in North Africa owed all their wonderful victories? Brilliant leadership. That was the secret. They had had brilliant leadership. I could not quite believe that I was hearing this,
because he had been the leader of our troops in North Africa.

He was talking in a way that affronted everything his audience believed in, so much so that I thought at first I must be misunderstanding him. But everyone in Big School was feeling the same way, masters as well as boys. Having thought of him as a supreme hero we sat there looking at him with stony faced disapproval. The report of his visit that appeared later in the school magazine, written by a master, consisted of four lines.

Then at last came the day we had all been waiting for – D-Day, as we had been calling it. I was emerging from the chapel by myself (perhaps I had been at a singing practice) when I saw Corks scampering excitedly towards me across the empty lawns, his clothes flapping outwards, his tie flying over one shoulder, his face shining like a sun.

'It's happened!' he shouted as he approached me. 'It's happened!'

'What's happened?'

'D-Day. We've invaded France. Normandy.'

He was beside himself.

Should we be so pleased? I wondered. It was going to be a bloodbath.

I said something to this effect.

He bridled with surprise, and then with dismissive impatience. 'Well, yes, it will be a bloodbath. Of course. But it's got to happen if we're going to win the war. And we've certainly got to win the war. So we can only be pleased.' Off he scampered to tell everybody, still in a state of radiant excitement, leaving me standing there thinking, yes, of course, he must be right.

From then on everybody followed the news greedily, and talked about it every day. The aeroplane activity over our heads was like nothing there had been before: sometimes the whole sky was dark with gigantic bombers flying in close formation. In addition to this our home-front war continued on its way – later that same month, June 1944, the school itself was bombed. The Germans were using unmanned flying bombs, correctly called V-1s but referred to by everyone as doodlebugs. They made a distinctive chugging noise until the engine cut out, and then they began their long descent in silence until the explosion. When you heard one coming, the sound naturally got louder and louder until it was right over your head, and if it cut out then you were safe, because it took a long time to come down, still moving forward; but if it cut out while it was on its way towards you, you froze. The silence then was terrible. When you heard the explosion, however near and ear-splitting, you would be flooded with a sense of relief. I was so frightened of the V-1s that this relief was overwhelming. I would then feel guilty towards whoever the bombs had fallen on.

I do not think any of us heard the approach of the doodlebug that fell on the school, because it arrived at five o'clock in the morning. We were woken by an almighty explosion that brought glass from the dormitory windows shattering on to the floor all round our beds. The bomb had landed a couple of hundred yards from my house, beside the garages. Of course, if it had landed on our block it would have killed up to a hundred of us, but in fact it killed no one. It did, however, destroy all the masters' cars, and when that became known it released a suffusion of *Schadenfreude* throughout the school. However, it also put the masters in a filthy temper for the rest of term.

By late 1944 the war had entered its endgame. Victory could not be far off – bound to come in 1945. Everyone's thoughts started turning towards the new life that was about to open up in front of us. I could not imagine what it would be like to live in a country that was not at war, did not have bombing, blackout, rationing and the rest. I tried unsuccessfully to picture it. In an American magazine I read that it was not healthy for me to eat meat every day, so I should do my best to have at least one day a week on which I did not eat meat. The magazine fell to my lap, my gaze drifting out of the window. I was lost in wonderment. For five years there had been only one day a week on which I *did* eat meat, and then not much of it. Could there be people in the world who ate meat every day, and as much as they wanted? I found it unimaginable.

In fact the long process of returning to normality began before the war ended, and lasted for some years after it. For instance, the authorities were anxious to spread demobilisation over as much time as possible to forestall the mass unemployment that had followed the First World War, so they started releasing various categories of people from the armed forces while the fighting was still on, people who they could be fairly sure were not going to be needed to fight again. They started with the older men who had skilled jobs waiting for them to go back to. Masters who had fought in the war, and whom I had never met – I may have sighted one or two when they were visiting the school on leave – came back to us, still living in their uniforms until they could get enough civilian clothes together (clothes were tightly rationed). The first one I was taught by was Arthur Rider, who took us for French. He dealt with us quite differently from other masters. Though maintaining his authority with ease, he talked to us as if we were his equals. He was a colonel, and I assumed this must be how he was used to talking to his men. I suppose the point was that he treated us as if we were grown-ups, not children. No teacher had talked to me like this before. I was coming up to fifteen at the time, and I found it thrilling to be addressed as an adult.

Just before the war ended, something occurred that was traumatic not only at the time but for ever afterwards. Advancing American troops, now sweeping through Germany itself, liberated a concentration camp at Buchenwald, near Weimar. It was the first of the extermination camps to be opened, and the revelation of what was inside simply flabbergasted the world: the prisoners like walking skeletons; the mountains of corpses; a whole organisation for applying the techniques of mass production to mass murder. People could not take it in: nothing like it had been known before (or, if it had, in the Soviet Union, the reality of it was to remain concealed from most people for a few more years yet). For me, as for the majority of people, the first I saw of it was on newsreels in the cinemas. Never to this day have I been so traumatised by anything I have seen. I could not look at the screen for most of the time. I felt faint, and sick. We had heard rumours of this whispered in our wartime propaganda, but reading scraps in newspapers was one thing, seeing larger-than-life moving pictures of it another.

The revelations of Buchenwald were followed almost immediately by those of Belsen, which was run by sadists who whipped and tortured their victims before killing them (and then made a lampshade out of the skin of one of them). The horror of it was overwhelming, and lay not just in the revelation of the facts but in the uncovering of an abyss. Here were human beings below anything one would have imagined possible, whether in the degradations they could suffer or in those they could inflict. Here was wickedness beyond believing, evil beyond understanding. At the time the experience was like being scalded, scorched, burnt inside oneself beyond endurance; and deep down something was being injured, permanently damaged, permanently altered. For many years I could not bear to talk about it, or read about it, or look again at any of those pictures – I was terrified of anything to do with it touching my mind. It had gone beyond what I could bear. Because I avoided it as much as I could, it was some decades before I realised that my personal experience of all this was widely shared.

The liberation of the concentration camps affected everyone's attitude to the war. People forget this now, but the truth about those camps was not known until the war's last few weeks. It brought home to us, in a way nothing else could possibly have

done, the fact that we had been fighting a regime of unimaginable evil. A tidal wave of moral justification swept over us and
lifted us up. Everything we had done – everything we had suffered
all these years, and everything we had inflicted on others – was
now justified. And the end, when it came only a couple of weeks
later, brought an apocalyptic sense of triumph, the triumph of
Good over Evil, an attitude all the more exhilarating because it
was new.

When the news of victory came, everyone within the widest
school community made automatically for the centre, so that we
could be together. Then we all trooped in to our daily evening
chapel – to find that the hymn, scheduled weeks or months beforehand, began:

> The strife is o'er, the battle done,
> Now is the victor's triumph won.

I have never heard such singing. It was not so much singing as
roaring from a thousand throats. It was animal-like, primitive, and
it made us all delirious. Whether we then did it straight away or
the following evening I do not remember, but all the boys swarmed
up on to Sharpenhurst Hill, the highest point in our surroundings, and set fire to a condemned hayrick, producing an instant
bonfire the size of a house. We made improvised guys of the Nazi
leaders and burnt them as spectacularly as we could, and then
completed hand-to-hand circles round the mighty blaze and sang
our hearts out.

The feeling we had of a new age dawning was carried forward,
for me at least, by the general election that followed immediately.
In spite of the fact that we were still at war with Japan, once
Germany had been defeated Britain's wartime coalition government dissolved itself. The truth is that, as far as we were concerned,
our war was pretty well over: we left it to the Americans to deal

with Japan. So now came my first proper general election, the first one I was old enough to understand and care about.

Although I wanted the Labour Party to win, I was too ignorant to have clearly formulated expectations. People in general seemed to think it self-evident that the Conservatives would win because their leader, Winston Churchill, was idolised by most of the population. I shared in the general adulation, but did not want a Conservative government. And this turned out to be the view of the people as a whole. Not only did the Labour Party win an overall majority for the first time in history, it won by a landslide. The voters themselves were astounded. I was cock-a-hoop. Bernard Levin endangered his life by climbing to the top of Big School and attaching a red flag to its clock tower, thus inducing a life-threatening rage in the headmaster, who was only just restrained by his colleagues from expelling Levin on the spot. I was taken aback by the reaction of most of the adults round me. It was not so much that they did not want a Labour victory as that they were terrified by it. They thought it was going to bring a full-blooded socialist revolution in Britain. I, who actually wanted full-blooded socialism, knew perfectly well that it would mean no such thing; indeed that there would be no real socialism but only a few steps in that direction. Even so, when I expressed my pleasure at this modest prospect people got furious with me. Erskine-Tulloch said to other boys in our year that my attitude was insupportable, and that if I went on any longer about Labour's victory he was going to beat me up. Rarely have I been so shocked. The thought that in my beloved England someone I knew, an actual friend, would beat me up because of his political opinions was beyond my comprehension. Given the nature of the war we had just been fighting it should not have been, and it was a much-needed revelation.

In fact, that whole general election campaign was an education for me. It shocked me beyond words when Churchill said, or implied, that a Labour victory would lead Britain towards being a totalitarian state, and used the word 'Gestapo' in this connection. Although I was only fifteen, the nonsense of it was transparent to me, and I did not see why it was not transparent to everyone else – although actually, as things turned out, it was. In this way, and in others, Churchill insulted the intelligence of the electorate, not to mention the personal, barbarous insult to his colleagues in the wartime government. A left-wing newspaper explained that he was talking this vile rubbish because his thinking had come under the influence of a writer called Hayek, in a book called *The Road to Serfdom*, and the paper displayed a photograph of the book's dust jacket. This was how I first heard of Hayek. For some years afterwards I assumed, without reading him, that he was a demonic writer of black-hearted, reactionary malevolence.

The whole business of choosing a government, and thus choosing the direction in which the country was going to develop from now on, excited me. The time span over which the campaign was stretched was an unusually long one, because we needed to wait for the votes of the servicemen overseas to be collected and brought back to England for counting. During this time I was introduced to electioneering, the cut-and-thrust of party politics, so different from anything that had gone on during the war. The Conservatives based their campaign on an appeal to Churchill's popularity: he was a historic figure now, hailed all over the world for his great leadership; and it must be obvious, said the Tories, that he was the right man to lead us into the peace. Labour dwelt on the horrors of Conservative rule before the war, when the country had been blighted by mass poverty and mass unemployment. They called for a new and different social order based on public ownership and a welfare state. It was this that captured the public mind. The general feeling, put crudely, was that the people had not fought their way successfully through six years of world war in order to go back to the Bad Old Days. They wanted a Brave

New World. So not only did the workers in the factories vote Labour: the servicemen did too, and also, decisively, the lower middle class in the modest suburbs.

I was partisan in all this, but my partisanship was chiefly negative. I detested the Conservatives. I was in favour of Labour but cool about them. My coolness was not because I had doubts about their declared beliefs but because I had doubts about the commitment with which they would put them into practice. I had got it firmly into my head that when people came to power in the Labour Party they sold out on the party's principles, and that leaders of the big trade unions did the same. Now that the Labour movement had itself come to power nationally, my fear was that it would betray the people it was most supposed to help. This fear was reinforced by my father. When I next went to London for the school holidays, and he met me at Victoria station, my first words to him were an expression of delight at the general election result, but his immediate reply was: 'Yes, provided they stay on the right lines. It's up to people like Aneurin Bevan and Emmanuel Shinwell to keep them to it. Otherwise they won't.'

CHAPTER TWENTY-ONE

At the beginning and end of each term the school used to hire a private train to take us to and from Victoria: we called it 'the Housey Special'. As was the general custom in those days, each of us had a trunk which made the journey separately from door to door, collected the day before we travelled and delivered the day after we arrived. This meant that on the journey we were empty-handed – and that was an invitation to misbehave, given that we had a whole train to ourselves. On the last morning of term we made an early start, because many of us would face long connecting journeys from London. House by house we marched down to the station, singing. I always knew there would be a member of my family waiting for me on the platform at Victoria, and hoped it would be my father. From there, in a state of excitement, I would be swept into a different life.

I loved London with an immoderate love. I was happy enough at school, but I took for granted that London was the hub of the universe. To me the most exciting part of it was the West End, with its crowded streets and department stores, theatres and concerts, parks, greasy-spoon restaurants and second-hand book-shops. And to these there had to be added one or two more local pleasures, such as the cinemas in Palmers Green and the billiard hall at Southgate. All this was lived against a background of my parents and sister in Arnos Grove, plus the rest of my family in Southgate, and the Tillsons at Potters Bar. The whole of it was bound together by London's buses and tubes, the tube above all. And it was mine. (During or not long after this period a novel came out called *London Belongs to Me*, and that was how I felt.) Not a single one of these things had any counterpart at Christ's Hospital. When the school had been in London it had famously been part of the warp and woof of London's life; but now that it was in the Sussex countryside it might just as well have been on Mars.

One of the keenest of my pleasures, now that I was so full-bloodedly political, was to go to Hyde Park on a Sunday afternoon, to Speakers' Corner. One often reads mistaken references to the speakers as being at Hyde Park Corner, but Speakers' Corner is at the other end of Park Lane, by Marble Arch. It is a child's picture-book illustration of free speech. Spread across a large asphalted open space there would in those days be anything between six and a dozen speakers addressing different audiences simultaneously, each far enough away from the others to be heard by his listeners, and each raised above his crowd by a makeshift podium that he and his organisation had brought with them, a collapsible platform constructed on the same principle as a stepladder. The audiences could be of widely differing sizes, ranging from almost none to several hundred. There were all the time people arriving and leaving, or wandering from one crowd to another to sample the different speakers, so there was perpetual coming and going. The speakers were on two main subjects: politics and religion. I never took much notice of the religious ones, so I never knew much about them – they seemed to be mostly of an evangelical cast. The political groups were mainly fringe parties of the Left, and that suited me to the ground. One or two of the speakers represented no one but themselves, but these were nearly always cranky and uninteresting, and seldom lasted for long – though there was one who was outstandingly entertaining, a little man who invariably wore a black suit and a wide-brimmed black hat, and sold a regularly produced, privately printed sheet of articles written by himself called *The Black Hat*, price one penny. He was Bonar Thompson, a Swiftian of the left, a socialist cynic convinced that all political parties, not least those represented by the speakers round him, were corrupted by inescapable, universal, gross and ridiculous human failings, such that nothing could ever be expected of them or anybody else. Of course, he implied, we all knew how society ought to be run, but it could never be like that because of the hopeless folly and absurdity of human beings, which would never change. I spent hours listening to him. I was too much of an idealist to believe him, but I found him endlessly amusing, and learnt more from him than I realised at the time.

As far as the fringe parties were concerned, each one thought all the others were wrong. But among them there was one speaker who, by common consent, was supreme as an orator, a man called Tony Turner. He spoke for the Socialist Party of Great Britain, an organisation of immaculate socialist purity that had existed since the early twentieth century without ever acquiring more than a thousand members. It was fortunate in having a rich patron, and it brought out a well-produced paper, the *Socialist Standard*; but Tony Turner remained the only member of the party of whom anyone outside it had heard. To this day I think of him not just as the best open-air speaker I have heard but as in a class by himself. This is not a judgement peculiar to me. Many have expressed it. Bernard Levin, one of them, told me that when he was a student at the London School of Economics he used to listen regularly to Tony Turner, who on weekdays would address the lunchtime office workers in Lincoln's Inn Fields, and Bernard was spellbound by him as by no speaker before or after. Turner was in his late twenties then; small, and with an unusual face, having been born in New Zealand as the illegitimate child of a Maori and a housemaid from England. He had a normal European skin colour with half-Maori features. His mother had returned to

England with him and brought him up in poverty in the Old Kent Road, where eventually she married a Mr Turner. Tony joined the navy for seven years at the age of fourteen, and it was the navy that gave him his education, a good one, ranging from Far Eastern travel to the mathematics required for navigation. He grew into an intelligent, disciplined, forceful personality. He was not ill-looking, and women found him unusually attractive. More than three decades later, when I was a Labour MP, he and I became friends – I stayed with him at his home in Nairobi, where he spent the second half of his life, and travelled all over Kenya with him; and we used to meet whenever he came to London. When he died he left me his library – and there I found the intellectual substructure of all those speeches I had stood listening to as a schoolboy. At that time, though, I would not have dreamt that he and I would ever know one another, and I looked up to him as something of a hero.

His special gift as a speaker was to be dramatic without being phoney. He pictorialised: whatever he was talking about, he gave you a picture of it, painted in clear, bold colours, though not unsubtle. His wording was economical, so his thoughts must have moved fast. And the logic was good – it was rare for him to say something that was not reasonably arguable. But as with all truly great speakers, the key to his success lay in a highly distinctive personality which conveyed itself to his audience in everything he said, but is not itself conveyable in words. He was charismatic. Instinctively, he had all the gifts of timing and phrasing, pausing and pacing, contrast. He would play his speeches off his audience, perceptive of their reactions, responding to them instant by instant. What he said had plenty of substance always: his comments on current affairs, about which he was well informed, rested on an additional foundation of reflection and reading, solidly acquired. The whole was pervaded by sharp humour, so that although serious in argument it was entertaining, and one stood listening in a state of chuckling delight. It was normal for him to have an audience of some hundreds, always the biggest in the park.

As I came more fully to understand years later, when I acquired his library and read through the comments he had written in the margins of his books over many years, he had slowly formed a classical socialist outlook, pondered with unusual intelligence, thus equipping himself with an ideology that could explain everything. This meant he could apply it to anything that happened; and he did this with great brilliance, making clever and illuminating comments about whatever occurred – comments which always, however spontaneous, fitted in with his larger world view. These practical applications of an underlying outlook were the speeches I was hearing on Sunday after Sunday. Their staple consisted of criticisms of existing society and its current affairs. But of special interest to me were his attacks on other left-wing viewpoints that put themselves forward as alternatives to his own. He saw the Labour Party and the trade unions as too complicitly involved in the society they were claiming to be critics of, always running with the hare while hunting with the hounds, compromised at every turn. On the communists he was both withering and devastating: the gulf between the Marxist theory which they espoused and the nightmare social reality of Soviet Russia, which they invariably and abjectly defended, was unbridgeable, and all the evidence of their behaviour ought to warn us that if communists were to come to power in any other country they would implement not Marx's theory but Stalin's practice. Their conduct in non-communist countries was marked by a breath taking lack of principle: for instance the Communist Party of Great Britain here at Speakers' Corner had passionately opposed the war against Hitler – in reality, of course, because Hitler was an ally of Stalin, but ostensibly because the war was between capitalist states, and therefore one in which the workers had no interest – until the Germans invaded Russia, whereupon they somersaulted overnight and became passionate supporters of the war, saying it was a people's crusade against fascism. The consistent cynicism with which they conducted all their affairs provided him with endless material for his savage but wonderful humour. And he had equally little difficulty picking off the remaining left-wing parties – the Trotskyists, the anarchists and the rest. His words had a cutting edge all the sharper for the fact that speakers for those parties, and crowds of their supporters, were only a few yards away.

His positive message was milk-of-the-word socialism, such as the other left-wing parties claimed to believe in but showed by their actions that they did not. The underlying theory was a fusion of Marxism and democracy, arrived at from the writings of Marx himself as a starting point but then as criticised by the philosophical anarchists, and after that reconstructed by the so-called revisionists. There is a body of literature there that constitutes a rich tradition of political thought, one that has had a much greater influence on the continent of Europe than in the English-speaking world. For me at that age it was the perfect brew. I did not, needless to say, read any of the books on which it was based, but through Tony Turner their influence fed into a political outlook that was forming itself from different sources – of which the most important was my father. And to hear it articulated week after week with such charismatic brilliance came close to being an orgastic experience for me. I continued to believe something like it until disenchantment set in at university. Until then I too found, as I thought, that it enabled me to understand everything, and gave me clever answers to all the criticisms I encountered. Being outside the Labour Party and to its left I could easily be mistaken unthinkingly for a communist, but in fact I was fiercely anti-communist. At that time there were a number of anti-communist socialists who were more famous than Tony Turner, but I did not as yet have the same acquaintance with them – people like Bertrand Russell, George Orwell, and Arthur Koestler.

Tony lost his faith in socialism during the post-war years, and by the end of the 1950s had ceased to believe in it altogether. The whole belief system, he then told me, came to seem to him like a gigantic work of art, or like a religion: glitteringly attractive to contemplate, inspirational, huge in scale, seriously thought through, full of good ideas and penetrating insights which all connected up with one another, marvellous in its ability to meet our emotional needs, brimming with life – and the whole thing an illusion. Although he had thought of himself as anti-religious when he believed in socialism, it now seemed to him a religion substitute, and he sometimes referred to that period of his life as his religious period.

My father would often come to Speakers' Corner with me. He and I were close companions now. He delighted in introducing me to new things of every kind – new venues of art and entertainment, new sports and games, new cafés, restaurants, shops. 'Don't you know this one? Oh, you must have a look at this one. Let's go in, shall we?' He would wander into men's clothing shops and examine their wares with professional interest, explaining their points to me as he did so. Even if he came out without buying anything he had usually charmed one of the staff in the process. We watched billiards and snooker at Thurston's Hall in Leicester Square, and cricket at Lord's. Those were years of legendary English cricket players, against equally legendary visitors from Australia, and it gave me warm, huggy pleasure to watch them. All sorts of things that are boring to me now, from cricket to ballet, excited me in my teens, when they were part of a new world opening up around me. One way in which my father's policy of introducing me to as many different things as possible paid off was that not only did I discover and pursue those interests that were to become lifelong passions, I also found out about a lot of other things too, with a curiosity which, although it turned out to be more short-lived, was genuine as far as it went, and extended my horizons.

He taught me things about the life of the streets that I would not have known at that age – how to deal with traders of all kinds without being taken in, and what the commonest deceptions were. He explained to me how pickpockets operated – Hoxton had always been the best-known base of the whizz mob, as they were called, and he must have known some of them personally. He explained not only these low-level scams, but also the stings used by confidence men, and these fascinated me. At the races we stood watching the three-card trick, and he pointed out in whispers how it was being worked not only by the man with the cards but by associates of his in the crowd – he would identify them and explain what they were doing. His normal phrase for a truly silly fellow, a ninny, a gull, was: 'He'd fall for the three-card trick.' One of his lessons to me was: 'Never, ever assume you can get the better of any of these people just because you know what they're up to. Those who think like that are the biggest mugs of all. ['Mug' here meant victim or target, not fool.] If you imagine the whizz mob can't whizz you because you know their tricks, you're a sitting duck. Mugs are set up by their own complacency.'

One of the most useful things he taught me was how to get in to public events that were full up, or at any rate sold out. 'If you're turned away at the door, find another door – there has to be one, like a stage door or a players' entrance, that people use who work there. There'll probably be a bloke on duty there. Talk to him nicely, and tell him you've tried to buy a ticket, and give him a couple of bob. Usually he'll let you in, and show you where you can stand. Often he'll show you to an empty seat. If there's no one at that door, walk through it as if it's normal for you to be there – as if you're somebody's son who works there, say, and you're used to coming. You won't be challenged, normally. If you are, just pretend you've made a mistake. But be nice about it, as if you really have made a mistake. Don't bluster. Half the time they'll say: "Oh, all right then, go on through." And you're in.' I did these things many times, for a long while only with him, but later, when I had gained confidence, by myself. He never encouraged me to try to get in to things for nothing. It was a point of honour with him to try first to buy tickets. But if he could not get them, it became equally a point of honour to get in regardless of that fact. He would always tip whoever helped him, and was prepared to pay as much as he would have paid for tickets. I never knew him fail. This goes a long way to explain how it is that so many of the outstanding events of those years in London, by way of championships and star performances, were part of my experience of growing up.

The first Promenade concerts he took me to were still being conducted by Sir Henry Wood, their founder – and incidentally the conductor on my recording of Schubert's 'Unfinished' Symphony. Nearly all the works I heard at any concert then, I was hearing for the first time. This is an aspect of my life during those years whose magic is unrecapturable, the fact that I was doing so many of the most enjoyable things in life for the first time – hearing the symphonies of Beethoven, Brahms, Sibelius, and other great symphonists; seeing the plays of Shakespeare, Ibsen and the rest. If I could live one period again it would be that, the discovery of all those incredible things within such a short space of time. The world was astounding, the discovery of it thrilling. The first time I heard the Brahms Violin Concerto, played at a Prom by Ida Haendel, I was enraptured beyond the power of speech to describe. I had been hearing the violin all my life, but I had never known it could sound like that. When I first heard Brahms's Third Symphony I was chilled with gooseflesh from the first bars, my hair prickling up all over my scalp. Performance after performance was a seismic shift in my being. And then, always to come, was the excitement of hearing these works for a second time. As for the third, that was in some ways the best of all, because you knew the work well enough by now to get more out of it, yet it was not familiar. Often it was during that third performance that a work *became* familiar, was ingested. With many of them – the *Eroica* is an example – it was the third performance that was the blockbusting experience, and remains the memory.

One of the great things about the Proms was the breadth of repertoire, ideal for a newcomer like me. It seemed I could hear everything. Outside the Proms, concert life was narrow. What had been London's only concert hall, the Queen's Hall, had been destroyed in the Blitz, so symphony concerts had to take place in ad hoc venues, the chief being the Albert Hall and two of the West End's theatres, the Cambridge and the Phoenix. Because rehearsal time was expensive, and in order to bring in audiences, the same popular classics were played over and over again – by the same artists, too. No foreign artists were able to come to Britain during the war, so we heard the same handful of conductors and instrumentalists. Since both Beecham and Barbirolli were in the USA, the only 'great' conductor on the London scene was Adrian Boult. Luckily, he was a good all-rounder, trained to be so by working as the BBC's all-purpose conductor – though as good at Brahms as anyone; and Brahms was my favourite symphonic composer. The outstanding pianists were Solomon and Moiseiwitsch: I first heard most of the popular piano concertos played by one or the other. I became a particular fan of Moiseiwitsch. He excelled not only in the classical repertoire but also, indeed especially, in the big romantic concertos. Rachmaninov himself had said that Moiseiwitsch played his piano music better than anyone else. He had a sourpuss demeanour at the keyboard, but his playing was huge in romantic expression. This was true of Rachmaninov himself, incidentally, who I used to see on cinema newsreels.

A surprising number of individual concerts remain in my memory. At one, the programme consisted of Tchaikovsky's *Romeo and Juliet* overture, Liszt's First Piano Concerto and Sibelius's First Symphony. I had never heard any of these before, and the first and last made indelible impressions, though in different ways. The Tchaikovsky contained one of the most sumptuously beautiful tunes I had ever heard; yet it was the Sibelius which, as it were, changed my life. It started quietly, as if groping for a tune, but then suddenly pulled the cord tight and started to pour out intense, compelling musical utterance, as if addressing me personally. It was as if I had suddenly discovered my own musical voice. If I had been a great composer, I thought, this was how I would compose. From that day I became an addicted lover of Sibelius's music. He seems to me among the greatest of composers, and his music has talked to me in this way ever since.

It was at the Proms that I heard most of the core repertoire for the first time – and then again for the second, and the third. There were rarities at the Proms too, and a great many first performances. I saw several of the leading British composers conduct their own music, for instance Vaughan Williams, William Walton and E.J. Moeran (whose neglected G minor Symphony is a beautiful work). Monday night, by tradition, was Wagner night, when bleeding chunks were torn from the carcasses of Wagner's operas (which were not themselves staged in Britain during the war) and served up as concert items, sometimes for a whole programme, though more often for half of it. I knew by heart those excerpts that my father had recordings of, but the others I had never heard at all. One such concert ended with Eva Turner singing the closing scene of *Götterdämmerung*. I stood enraptured, and afterwards remembered every moment of the performance, hyper-vividly, yet I never knew what happened between the end of the music and finding myself, more than half an hour later, in Piccadilly Circus, nearly two miles away. I must have walked out of that concert in a complete daze: gone, sent, zonked: and instead of getting on the tube at Knightsbridge gone on walking – past, unnoticing, additional tube stations at Hyde Park Corner and Green Park. When my awareness of myself returned I was in Piccadilly Circus, gaping round like a man torn from a dream, with no idea why I was there or how I had got there.

Once the Proms had come into my life they never left it. One year my father gave me a season ticket for the second half of the Proms, and a season ticket for the tube, so that I could go every night. Later, during the forty years when I lived within walking distance of the Albert Hall, not a summer went by without my going to some of the Proms. By the late 1990s I was taking a teenage granddaughter to them.

London's concert life was transfigured by the ending of the war. It meant that foreign artists could again visit Britain. Beecham returned from the USA and founded the Royal Philharmonic Orchestra. I saw conductors such as Furtwängler and de Sabata (whom I still think of as the most exciting to watch of all conductors), and legendary pianists and violinists. Claudio Arrau's playing of Brahms's Second Piano Concerto came as a revelation to me, not only of the work itself but of what piano-playing could be. Life in Britain crawled out of the imposed provincialism of wartime on to an international scene. I had been more than happy with concert-going as it had been before, but now I was introduced to standards I had never experienced, and a new kind of excitement came into my life. For years past the supreme thrill had been to hear the greatest works for the first time, but now that I had heard most of the central repertoire I was experiencing the quite different thrill of hearing those works played better than before, sometimes better than I would have imagined possible. In some ways it was like hearing them again for the first time.

As the years went by, London established the richest, most extensive concert life of any of the world's great cities. This went on for most of my adult life, and I lived through the development as one of its most avid beneficiaries: the whole experience, from the beginning, was part of the inner framework of my life. London was also, during the same period, the city of the world that was most richly endowed with theatre. For someone whose greatest passions were music and theatre it was an incomparable place to live in during the second half of the twentieth century. I became a Londoner in a special sense, in that the life I lived there could not have been lived anywhere else, not even in New York, which was the city that came closest to it. When I emerged from the education system, I would not have considered living anywhere else. Whatever the career advantages, I would never have taken a job that involved living out of central London. Nothing mattered more to me than music and theatre. The deep foundations of all this were laid in the 1940s.

If I were asked to single out one especially formative set of theatre experiences it would be the run of seasons by the Old Vic Company between 1944 and 1947. Laurence Olivier had just returned from the United States,* and ran the company in harness with Ralph Richardson. Its own theatre had been bombed, so the seasons were played at the New Theatre (now the Noël Coward). They launched themselves in the late summer of 1944 with three plays in repertoire: Ibsen's *Peer Gynt*, Shaw's *Arms and the Man*, and Shakespeare's *Richard III*. The supporting company consisted of people who were major actors in their own right. Richardson's

---

* It was sourly remarked on at the time how many people who were at the apex of Britain's artistic and intellectual life spent all or part of the war in the United States: in addition to Laurence Olivier and his wife, Vivien Leigh, there were Bertrand Russell, W.H. Auden, Aldous Huxley, Somerset Maugham, Benjamin Britten, Sir Thomas Beecham and John Barbirolli, to name only a few of those who were of interest to me as a teenager. It gave rise to bitter comment from 'ordinary' people, who tended to see them as 'dodging the war', and gave less credit than they should have done to those who came back while the war was still on.

Peer and Olivier's Richard were among the supreme theatrical experiences of anyone who saw them. Audiences reacted with something akin to shock. There had never, not even before the war, been theatre like this. We had seen stellar performances – Valk's Othello, Wolfit's Lear, Gielgud's Hamlet – but not two performers of that standard in one play with the entire production at a comparable level – and then two or more such productions running together in repertoire. It was as if every aspect of them was of the highest quality. For instance, Tyrone Guthrie as director brought a kind of genius to *Peer Gynt*, and even the tiny part of the Button Moulder in its last act was played by Laurence Olivier.

The following year the same company achieved the same levels in both parts of Shakespeare's *Henry IV*, Sophocles' *Oedipus Rex*, Sheridan's *The Critic*, and Chekhov's *Uncle Vanya*. If anything, Richardson's Falstaff and Olivier's Oedipus out-topped their Peer and Richard. And again there were twenty-four-carat performances in supporting roles – Justice Shallow in *Henry IV, Part 2* was played by Olivier. For years afterwards I thought of this *Oedipus Rex* as the best production of any play I had seen. It was with this run of performances that Olivier became, in most people's estimation, the supreme actor of the age – a position that had been occupied hitherto by John Gielgud – and he continued to be thought so for the rest of his life. The following year, 1946, he played King Lear, with Alec Guinness as the Fool, while Ralph Richardson starred in *Cyrano de Bergerac*; and only a couple of months after that, in January 1947, Richardson and Guinness gave us Ben Jonson's *The Alchemist*. It was pure magic, all of it. Richardson's performances were to my mind as good as Olivier's, though he was less charismatic. He was great, but in a different way, full of inwardness, while with Olivier everything was externalised. Each was a perfect foil for the other. For me the experience ran parallel to the one I was having at concerts: here were supremely great works being performed better than they could have been even in my imagination, unpossessed as that was of the combined genius of, shall we say, Ralph Richardson and Tyrone Guthrie.

There has been nothing like it since. I have seen single productions which are as good, but not year after year of whole seasons of them in repertory. And there have not been better actors since. It caught me at just the right age. It is all sixty years ago now, but it provided me with a touchstone of theatrical excellence throughout my life. I have found that others who lived through those seasons are at one with me on this – Kenneth Tynan once said that whenever two such people meet they start reminiscing like First World War veterans who shared a trench on the Somme.

The same theatre was used by the Sadler's Wells opera and ballet companies for their London seasons (they spent most of their time touring), so going to the New became the high point of my life in most respects. We as a family always bought the cheapest seats, those in the gallery, price one shilling and sixpence, unreserved. To save enthusiasts from having to queue all day, this theatre and some others operated a system of marking places in the queue with little camp-stools. At the New Theatre this was run by a wily old dear called Winnie. On the morning of the performance you found Winnie somewhere near the theatre (possibly in a pub), showed her your tickets, and she sold you numbered slips for your places in the queue, sixpence a time, first come, first served. A couple of hours before the performance she set out as many camp-stools as there were seats in the gallery, each with a slip number attached, several abreast in a long queue up against the theatre wall. If you did not claim yours by a certain time you forfeited it, and with it your place in the queue, which would be allowed to go into the theatre half an hour before the performance. For an hour or more, then, there would be this queue of hundreds of people squatting on little camp-stools in the open air alongside the theatre – chattering to one another, reading newspapers and books, eating food out of paper bags – while the normal occupants of the street walked past them. If it rained they sat on their diminutive stools holding up umbrellas, a sight that was touchingly English. They were a captive audience for buskers, who performed there one after another. These could be musicians, dancers, jugglers, acrobats. One young man declaimed speeches from whatever play we were about to see. He did it rather well, I thought, and I assumed he was an aspiring actor, but I never heard of him in any other connection.

That queue was a world in itself, with a life of its own. Many of the people in it were the same all the year round. Friendships formed, love affairs began, marriages ensued. News would pass up and down the queue. 'Have you heard? The So-and-so's are going to have a baby.' It was where one picked up theatrical gossip, too, and news about forthcoming events in the performing arts generally. In the way she manipulated us all, Winnie combined fairness with corruptibility in proportions that were just right for the regulars who knew her and understood how she operated.

My sister Joan was more a part of all this than I was – she was in London all the year round, and during the ballet seasons she would go almost every night – but when I was at home during school holidays I was the only member of the family whose time was free, so it was my job to go up to the New Theatre in the morning and find Winnie, so that with luck we might be in the front row of the gallery. After that I would be on the loose in the West End for the rest of the day, until the performance in the evening.

These were the circumstances in which I started on a way of life that was to be mine, in essence, for most of my adulthood. In subsequent decades I would book my tickets in advance and sit in better seats in the theatre, eat in better restaurants, travel there perhaps by taxi instead of tube; but all those things are mere outer wrapping. The point of it all, the essential experience, remained the same: the same performances at the same times in the same venues as I would have gone to in any case, however little money I might have had.

Since that was how a whole way of life began, I think of myself as having received the most worthwhile part of my introduction to it in wartime. When I now see photographs of London as it was then, I am taken aback by the greyness and drabness of it, the run-downness, the in-your-face poverty. That is not how I saw it at the time. My life in wartime London was the most exciting and enjoyable I could imagine for myself, and this made it a glamorous place to be. I was responding to the inwardness of it, and it is the inner experience I remember. Although, for example, I made hundreds of journeys late at night on crowded tube trains in the blackout, I can find within myself only the most generalised memory of them. I must, I suppose, have been lost in thought about what I had just been seeing and listening to.

I carried on spending most of my mornings at home, usually playing records. Only four months after I had acquired the 'Unfinished' Symphony, my father made me a birthday present of Grieg's Piano Concerto. This gave me the idea of asking for records as presents. From then on, whenever anyone asked me what I wanted for my birthday or Christmas, I would ask them to give me money so that I could put it together with money from other people to buy a whole symphony or concerto. That way, I could expect to acquire two such works a year. One after another, I bought Beethoven's Fifth Piano Concerto and Eighth Symphony, Mozart's Fortieth Symphony, Brahms's Third, Tchaikovsky's Sixth, Sibelius's Second and Seventh, together with a host of shorter works. Because Sibelius's Seventh occupied only three discs, I was able to buy that and the so-called 'love duet' from *Tristan and Isolde* with money I got for my fourteenth birthday. Deep into Wagner, I acquired several excerpts from his operas, and became specially hooked on Isolde's Narration and the closing scene from *Götterdämmerung*, both sung by Kirsten Flagstad. Goodness knows how many times I played these. Once, sitting alone listening to the historic Lauritz Melchior–Frida Leider duet from *Tristan* for the goodness-knows-how-manyeth time, I burst into tears, overwhelmed by the marvellousness of it and of being conscious and able to hear it, of being in such a world at all. Any description of this will sound squ013gy and sentimental, but the experience itself was unselfconscious and profound. Even so, the recording that I played most often — the only one I actually wore out – was not of Wagner, it was Sibelius's Seventh Symphony. There was a period of about two years when I played it at least once every day I was at home.

My fourteenth birthday was a landmark for me in many ways. Because fourteen was the age at which most people left school and started work, that birthday was treated by most of the population as a staging post on the way to adult life, a sort of miniature twenty-first; and in keeping with that it was accompanied by especially good presents. For me, the day itself fell during a weekend spent in the market town of Shaftesbury, in Dorset. My father had taken me there to visit his old friend Fred Griffin, his regular companion for opera and ballet at Covent Garden before the war. Fred was a highly skilled craftsman who made, by hand under a microscope, minute springs that were used in aircraft controls. To ensure that he should not himself be bombed, the authorities had ordered him to leave London, so he was now living in Shaftesbury's Grosvenor Hotel, with an office and workshop a few yards away in the main street. By our standards he was well-off financially, and he had built up over the years the biggest collection of records I had ever come across. It was his custom to play these all day on a state-of-the-art record player while he was working. He loved Wagner above all, and had almost every Wagner recording that had ever been issued. That weekend I was given free run of the collection, and felt I was in paradise – until, that is, my father made an announcement.

He said there was something special he wanted to talk to me about, and that he and I should go for a country walk (a unique occurrence). On this walk he told me, speaking with difficulty, that he and my mother were going to get divorced. He looked straight in front of him while he was talking. I tried to ease things for him by saying: 'I know.'

His manner turned suddenly to sharpness. 'How do you know?' I can still see the expression on his face as he snapped it towards me.

This was unfair. Here was I trying to help him, and his response was to make it impossibly difficult for me.

'Mum told me,' I said. I was acutely embarrassed.

'What did she say?'

This was terrible, but I had to reply.

'She said you had someone else.'

He swelled up and went bright red with anger, and I thought he was going to burst. But he subsided again, and said in an unnaturally quiet voice, again looking straight in front: 'Absurd.'

Then he started in an oddly scrambled way to assure me that Joan and I would be properly looked after. What I wanted to know (but did not ask) was why the two of them were getting divorced, what had happened, *was* anyone else involved, where and how was each of them going to live. But to my frustration he talked about none of these things, merely about how Joan and I would not need to worry about anything – a concern that was not in my mind.

He died three years later. He was a chain-smoker, and died of cancer of the lung at the age of forty-five. I lived through the whole of those three years expecting him and my mother to break up at any moment in the next few days or weeks. But they never did, and nothing more was said on the subject. In that age, children did not put personal questions to their parents: they waited to be told. I never dared to ask what was happening, or indeed if anything was happening. I was consumed by the questions, but never knew the answers. Had the whole situation changed again? Were they going to stay together after all? In recent years I have asked my aunt Peggy, and she says that the marriage was unquestionably coming to pieces, and would have done so had my father not died. Why there was this delay, neither she nor I knew.

My relations with my mother had never been good, and I was now of an age when she thought I should be earning my living. It riled her that she and my father were keeping me even for those short periods when I was at home from school, and she missed no opportunity of referring to me as a kept person, a parasite. Further education, in her view, was a waste of time, a load of nonsense: real life was what counted: everything else was airy-fairy. But at the same time she did not accept that I was growing up. She was exceedingly upset when I bought books about politics with book tokens that I had been given for my fourteenth birthday. Not only was she disapproving, she was emotionally disturbed – as she had been by my taking harmless adult novels out of the library in Market Harborough. She looked distraught, as if something terrible had happened, and said things like 'Oh dear!' in a frightened voice. I have always been seriously unable, then and now, to understand what the trouble was. When I asked her, she said: 'At your age you ought to be reading story-books.' She tried to make me take the books back, but I refused very firmly, saying that the shops would not dream of accepting them.

My sister, too, seemed alarmed at my growing up. She was a more emotional person than I was, more aware of the feelings of others, and more caring about them. But the downside of these strong feelings was that her judgements were distorted by them to the point where her view of everything was almost completely subjective, a generalisation from the single instances of her own experience. If she met a Dane for the first time, and he struck her as a handsome man, she would say ever afterwards that Danes were a good-looking people. What she supposed to be her factual view of the world was built up almost entirely in this way. She did not at all have a logical mind. And although she was emotionally better developed than I was, I was overtaking her intellectually. This frightened her. She was three and a half years older than me, and had been used all her life to being ahead of me in every respect, so she viewed the new situation as a threat. She became hostile and competitive, and started trying to put me down.

One way and another, then, I was having a troubled time at home. Family conflicts with adolescents are commonplace, and this was the form they took in my life. But they made me all the more determined to go my own way and do my own thing – which again is typical for an adolescent. Even so, and in spite of it all, Joan and I still did a number of things together, as can easily happen within a family. I went to the ballet with her so often that I became familiar with the whole Sadler's Wells Company and repertoire. Margot Fonteyn was in her prime, with Robert Helpmann as her leading man. He was a versatile artist: not a great dancer but a good one, with a special gift for comedy; a successful choreographer; and a talented actor. In 1944 I went twice to see him play the lead in a six-week run of Shakespeare's *Hamlet* (not his ballet of the same name, to Tchaikovsky's music) with the Old Vic Company.

During the forties I was quite a ballet-lover. There was one week in 1946, not long after the Covent Garden theatre reopened from its wartime closure, when I went to the ballet there every night, sitting on those narrow, backless, armless benches at the very top of the gods. The intensity with which I reacted to it is revealed by the clarity and detail of the memories I still have of individual performances. But as I emerged into adult life I felt as if I outgrew it. I can never say this to a ballet-lover, but in all honesty that is what it felt like to me. In any case, ballet is primarily a visual art, and I am primarily an aural person. But in those years there were times, which alas have never recurred, when the beauty of a movement, seen usually as a line alive, would give me the full aesthetic physical response: my whole body would freeze, my skin would stand up into goose pimples all over, and my scalp would prickle.

I enjoyed being an observer of the groupie world that my sister was part of, and rather looked up to it. They were nearly all teenage girls who spent every penny they had on ballet, devouring magazines and books about it, collecting photographs, and so on. They would crowd round the stage door after each performance, surging forward to get their programmes autographed by each of the dancers in turn as they came out. The stars always came out last. The girls would giggle and scream, and bunch round in a tight knot. I never bought a separate programme, but at school during bookbinding lessons I had been given the task of making an autograph album, so I now used this to collect autographs. Having started with ballet dancers, I went on to pick up autographs of other performers at other theatres, and soon had most of the leading figures, from Laurence Olivier and Noël Coward downwards. I was struck by the fact that although they were always nice to me, and exchanged friendly words as they signed, they did not actually register my existence. I had still not met them, nor they me. I did not mind this, but the nullity of it made the activity pointless, and I stopped doing it. (I have never had the collector's instinct anyway.) The only one of them I took against was David Niven, who emerged from the New Theatre one evening in army uniform, not having performed, but as a friend of one of the performers. He made show-off remarks to the groupies, who of course had not been waiting for him at all, about being in battledress and being about to catch a night train to France. He played the hero to them with a narcissism and vulgarity that I found nauseating. And he had not even been in the play.

Engrossed as I was in the performing arts during my time in London, I lost nearly all of my interest in sport. School was turning me off it anyway. I would go to sporting events with my father, or with Norman Tillson, if they suggested it, but I was no longer interested enough to suggest it myself, still less to go alone – except to Thurston's, the Mecca of billiards and snooker. I loved those games more than I have loved any others. We had a local billiard hall in the main shopping street of Southgate, and Norman and I started spending more and more of our time and money there. We called it Burton's because it was over a men's clothing shop with that name, and in fact I do believe it belonged to the shop: Burton's was probably the biggest chain store in the country that sold men's clothes, and above many if not most of their high-street shops there were billiard halls. The amount of time Norman and I spent in this particular one was limited only by how much money we had. We were addicts. There was one Christmas Eve when – being flush with money because it was Christmas – we played for six hours and forty minutes, and were still reluctant to leave. Billiards was our great passion: we would start all our sessions by playing billiards until we felt it was time for a change, and then we would turn to snooker. This made snooker feel like the dessert at the end of a meal, a light-hearted, colourful contrast; and sometimes we did not get that far. Not surprisingly, we became quite good while remaining fairly ordin-ary – the highest break I ever got at billiards was 38, and at snooker 34 (the same as my highest innings at cricket). Occasionally my father would join us. He was in a different class from us, elegant and pleasing to watch, a consistently high scorer. It was he who taught us most of what we knew. When I remarked to him that I was lost to the world while playing, he said: 'You could have all the troubles in the world on your shoulders, and while playing billiards you wouldn't be aware of them.' There was something extraordinarily deep and special about this feeling: inexplicably, it was not unlike how I felt when I listened to music. When, many years later, I discovered that Mozart was addicted to billiards, and would hum new musical ideas while playing it, I felt I understood.

Another game at which my father excelled was poker. He was a regular player in a weekly school where the stakes were high; and although, inevitably, he sometimes lost, on average he won more than his week's wages; so during those years the family's standard of living was dependent on Father's poker I never became anything like as good as he was, in fact I was never much of a poker player at all, but I loved it, and have always regarded it as the king of card games, and one of the greatest games of any kind.

CHAPTER TWENTY-TWO

In my teens I became increasingly fascinated by questions about the nature of reality – and by the word 'reality' I mean, simply, what there is. These were philosophical questions, but at that time no such thought entered my mind: they presented themselves to me as basic questions about what directly confronted me. I would find myself looking at an object immediately in front of my face – it could be anything: an apple, a book – and thinking: 'What *is* it? I can see its size, its shape, its colour, its texture, and all the rest, but what is *it* – what is the something that has those characteristics?' And I was baffled. Despite long periods of concentrated attention I failed to crack the mystery.

If I closed my eyes the object would 'disappear'. When I opened them it came back again. Of course I knew that it was there all the time, that only my image of it disappeared; but what this seemed to tell me was that I was directly in contact with the image and not with the object. It meant that when I could see the object I was reading off details of its colour, texture and all the rest of it from the image; and when I closed my eyes and there was no image I could apprehend nothing, and was not in contact with anything, even though the object itself was in the same place. In other words I was not in contact with the object. Following on from this, I realised that my apprehension of everything was inside my head (where else could it be?). Increasingly there were occasions when I was panicked by this. The first important one happened at school, in chapel, and I had to go out in the middle of the service. The second, not unlike it, occurred in London during the school holidays. I was coming out of a cinema when the realisation hit me that everything I could ever be aware of throughout my whole life was inside my head, while reality itself was outside my head and I could never have direct contact with it. The feeling was of being permanently cut off. In that instant I actually thought I was going mad. I stood in the foyer gasping, drowning, fighting for life. After the hugest struggle, I calmed down. But I had come within a hair's breadth of some kind of breakdown.

Until this time my childish metaphysical reflections had been, on the whole, enjoyable. It is true that they had been baffling and frustrating as well, but at the same time they were intriguing, and I had normally got at least a troubled satisfaction from pursuing them. But from my middle teens I began to find them unpleasant in a way that was somehow sick. They frightened me. Those to do with perception were often nauseating, as if these images in my brain might be hallucinations, and as such symptoms of illness. I could have a new insight, be convinced of its truth, indeed it might *be* true, and yet the perception was accompanied by mental disturbance. My terrors took partly the form of an intellectual conviction of the truth of certain propositions. It was a bizarre combination, indeed identification, and made fighting off the disturbance difficult – I did not want to fight off the truth. The whole problem was that it was not delusions I was grappling with but truths, or possible truths, and my struggles took me to the limits of my endurance. Why I was so churned up and terrified at the thought that certain things were true or might be true, I cannot explain, but I was. It is surprising that I never broke down. I came close to it several times.

Insight and terror proceeded not only hand in hand but as the same thing. The more deeply my gaze penetrated into these problems the more panic-stricken I became. The worst moment came one night in bed, in the dark, in my little room in Arnos Grove. A lot of the Marxisant writings I was reading reiterated that theirs was a materialist philosophy, and that all that existed was matter, so I was lying there wondering if materialism could be true, and what reality must be like if it were. Suddenly I achieved an insight into precisely that: reality conceived as material only. Inexplicably, the thought was all-pervadingly evil, and of the most rampant, all-gobbling hideousness. It was the only thought I have ever had that was accompanied by, literally, a stink as a part of itself. It was an abyss, and I was in it. I was gripped by horror rather than terror, a compound of disbelief, shock, dread and bottomless despair. In the instant of experiencing it I knew that it would not be supportable even for a short time, and I summoned all the forces I possessed to divert my thoughts. As they receded, an ocean of nausea flooded through me and washed them away from me. The whole experience was the ultimate in pure evil, the intolerable. For years I lived in dread of its return, knowing I could not survive it. Never again did I seek to recover that fully achieved insight into the nature of materialism, but I bear to this day the psychological scars. There are no words to articulate it – though I knew that it was what was being referred to when, many years later, I came across these sentences in a book by a philosopher: 'That the world has only a physical and not a moral significance is a fundamental error, one that is the greatest and most pernicious, the real perversity of the mind. At bottom, it is also that which faith has personified as Antichrist.' The philosopher was Schopenhauer, who, like me, was not a Christian, and did not believe in God, still less in hell.

Today it seems obvious that I was an already insecure person whose insecurity was being screwed up to pathological levels by my own persistently radical questioning of my nature, and of the world around me. I was imposing on myself insecurities that I could not bear. My personality was not strong enough to cope with the positions I kept putting myself in. But at the time, all I was aware of were the questions themselves, and the terror they plunged me into. In any case, my questioning was involuntary: I tried to stop myself from doing it, but was only patchily successful. It was a curse of which I could not rid myself, and which visited me every day – in fact my internal nickname for it became 'the curse'.

Luckily for me, although most of my wonderings had this terrifying character, not all of them did. Some were compellingly interesting, and I tried to take refuge in those. One day I was sitting in our living room gazing idly at the standard lamp when the thought wandered into my mind that if it were sentient it could not possibly appear as an object to itself, and therefore could not be an object in its own world. It would be able to see everything else in the room, just as I saw it, but would not be able to see itself. In what terms, then, could it conceive its own existence? There it stood before me, with its wooden base, tall stem and big shade, and I could form no notion of that particular standard lamp in any terms other than these – what they looked like, would feel like, and so on. Allowing for the laws of perspective, it would look the same for any other observer in the room, in any position – any position, that is, except one, the position the standard lamp itself occupied. To the standard lamp, thought of as being itself the observer, no standard lamp was to be seen anywhere in the room, and therefore no wooden base, no tall stem, and no big shade. Only if there had been, which there was not, a mirror in which the standard lamp could see itself would it have had any way of knowing what it looked like. Having no arms, it could not feel its own shape. So if it had spent its entire existence in this room it would never have experienced, and would have no way of conceiving, what were in fact the only elements out of which I could form any conception of it. If it was aware of its own existence this awareness would have to be in terms that were unrecognisably different from those of the only apprehension *I* could form of its existence. What could such terms be? Could it know even that it was a standard lamp? I did not see how. Perhaps all it could do was *be*, inside itself, without any understanding of what or why it was.

I was transfixed by this realisation of the disjunction between being and knowing. Every object in the room would be equally incapable of knowing its own nature if it were sentient. And this must be true of everything everywhere. Then, of course, the penny dropped. It must be true of me. I was a material object, and if I had been born without eyes and arms I would be just as incapable of knowing what I looked like, or what my own shape was, as the standard lamp. Even with eyes, it was only because of mirrors, reflections and photographs – images external to myself, images *outside* me – that I knew what my face looked like. What all this meant was that no sentient being, purely from inside itself, could possibly know, still less understand, its own nature.

For some reason I did not find this frightening – if anything, it gave me a kind of hope. There was something welcome in the fact that there must be more to me than any idea I could form of myself. For a long time, something like a couple of years, I thought about it obsessively, but nearly always with regard to other objects. I would look, for instance, at a building. There it was, a huge great thing: it unquestionably existed. No one could deny that the building *was*. But what was it to be the building? I could see its details, and its overall position and size and shape; but the building itself could not be aware of any of these things; yet nevertheless it existed, it was doing *something*. What was it doing? Being, evidently. But what was that? Whatever it was, I could not get my mind round it – and nor would the building itself have been able to either. I never made an inch of headway out of this impasse. But that fact kept me aware that I was in it.

I have difficulty even now in expressing any of these thoughts in words, and at that time I was quite incapable of doing so. The insights themselves were not in words: they went much deeper than that. So I did not try to talk about them to anybody. But this meant that in some respects a disconnection developed between my outer life and my inner (rather as with the other things I was so obsessionally thinking about). My inner life was partly a cauldron of what I can see now as neuroses and pathological terrors – even what were not terrors were still obsessions. But little or none of this showed on the surface. I was reasonably good at coping with life and getting on with other people. No doubt I often seemed self-absorbed, but that is common, even normal, among adolescents. Perhaps one or two others caught hints of the highly charged goings-on inside me, but I do not think many did, and even they can have had no idea of their nature, extent, depth, power or intensity. I continued much of the time to be with companions at theatres and cinemas, sporting events and social occasions. I was hyper-communicative about everything else, always talking nineteen to the dozen, and being teased about it. An observer's eye would have seen me as a social creature, actively bound up with several other people in many different activities. This disparity between inner and outer became normal to me, and has continued ever since. To this day I have an intense inner life that goes on all the time, and sometimes has a neurotic dimension to it; and yet I reveal very little of it to anyone else. I cannot talk about it to anyone because the words in which it would be possible to do so do not exist. But I continue to function well enough in working and social relationships – for instance, I have never taken a day off work because of it, and my work has always been done as it should be. However, it does make intimacy difficult for me. This fearsome inner world dominates much of my life, and I cannot help that, but there is no way in which any other human being could enter it.

Because I was already so full of terrors, as a young teenager, when the bombing of London started up again in 1944 I found it almost unmanageably frightening. This was in complete contrast to my insouciant enjoyment of air raids only four years earlier. I was offered a way out of this situation, but did not take it. Christ's Hospital made arrangements for boys whose families lived in areas that were being bombed not to go home during the school holidays but to spend that time with other boys' families in safer parts of the country. My mother wanted me join in the scheme, but I refused. The life I lived in London had become indispensable to me, and I could not, even at this price, bring myself to forgo it. I returned to London for every school holiday, bombing or no bombing. Nevertheless, I was frightened out of my wits by the V-1s. If I heard one coming and was alone in the flat I would get under the living-room table and crouch there in mortal terror, listening to the ever-approaching bomb and convinced that I was about to die. Most of the bombs exploded south of us, in central London, but you could never be sure they were going to – quite a few got as far as us and beyond; and I could always hear them coming. One seemed to cut out its engine immediately outside the window, and I thought it was about to plunge into our block of flats and blow me to bits, but it passed over.

The V-2s were even more frightening. Because rockets travelled faster than sound, you heard them coming after you heard them explode. That was ghostly as well as ghastly. There would be an almighty explosion, completely unexpected and out of the blue, and then you would hear the *swoosh* of the rocket as it approached through the sky. It chilled my blood each time I heard it – though the fact is, of course, that if you heard it you were all right. During the V-2 bombings I moved around central London half expecting to be snuffed out instantaneously. Once, just as I was stepping out into daylight from Oxford Circus underground station, there was one of these huge explosions frighteningly close, and for a

moment I felt like turning round and going straight back underground and returning to Arnos Grove – but I did not, I stayed in
the West End. And that is how I managed to carry on, combining
extreme terror with an obstinate attachment to my pursuits.

But it meant I was in a fairly fraught state for most of the time
when I was at home, and that must have aggravated the normal
difficulties of adolescence. I was rubbing up against my parents
in all the usual ways. In the rows that erupted they hurled at me
the fact that I was incredibly lucky, free to come and go as I liked,
generously provided by them with pocket money out of their three
or four pay packets whenever I was at home. All this was true. But
I was painfully conscious that the whole set-up was theirs, not
mine, created by them, belonging to them, run by them; and that
I had no alternative but to fit in; so I did not feel anything like
as free as they said. I was powerless. And I hated Arnos Grove:
the truth is I did not want to be *there* at all. As is usual for adolescents, I wanted to throw off my family's influence on my attitudes
and outlook, and establish my independence of thought and
behaviour; so I opposed them and contradicted them unnecessarily. Inevitably, it was my father, whom I loved most of all, and
whose influence on me had been so much greater than anyone
else's (and also, I could have added, so much more beneficial),
that I felt most need to free myself from. So I started behaving
badly towards him.

My relationships with the other close members of the family
were not good. My mother disapproved of the fact that I had
passed the school-leaving age without leaving school, and she saw
me from now on as a layabout who should be earning his own
living. I was constantly reminded by her of the fact that she and
my father were standing on their own feet when they were my
age, and this grated with me especially, because of the sense I
already had of my lack of independence. Even so, I took the neces-
sity for a good education for granted, and thought my mother

was wrong about that. But then there was also my sister, bitterly resentful for opposite reasons. She was deeply jealous of the fact that I was getting a better education than she had had. One way and another, I was disapproved of by all of them.

By now I rarely had occasion to go to Hoxton any more. I was keeping up with the remaining members of my family during the school holidays by visiting them on Sundays at their homes in Southgate. Often I would spend the first couple of hours of the afternoon with my grandparents and their daughter Hilda – she being my maiden aunt and godmother – and then call in on the Petts, my aunt Peggy and her husband Bill. The two households received me very differently. At the first my grandparents and Hilda would ply me with questions about my life at school, and be interested in the answers. Then they would ask what I was doing now, during the holidays, and be interested in that too. The Petts, on the other hand, took the view – which I heard Bill formulate openly – that to tell somebody something is to exert a kind of dominance over him, while to be told something is to be subjected to the other person's dominance. So they tried to avoid being told anything. The example Bill cited when he urged this course of action on me was: 'You don't want to just sit there saying nothing while he tells you all about the wonderful holiday he's just had: *you* tell *him* about *your* holiday.' They applied this principle to me. As soon as I started telling them anything about what I was doing, Bill would interrupt and insist on telling me what *they* were doing. He was even given to telling me what people unknown to me were doing. 'Oh, I know,' he would interrupt. 'Our friends the So-and-so's have a son at Highgate, which is just like Christ's Hospital, and he . . .' So instead of sharing my life with them, which is what I was longing to do, I would find myself sitting there while they told me about the doings of some total stranger. Peggy's practice was even odder. She would tell me what I myself was doing. 'Oh, I know,' she would interrupt. 'I can just imagine you sitting there and . . .' Given that she knew nothing about what I was telling her, her resourcefulness in keeping up a flow of uninterrogative talk was a phenomenon. 'You must be thinking . . . What you're bound to want is . . . Anyone in your circumstances would naturally . . . Believe me, I fully understand how . . .' and so it would go on. And on. And on. There was something mad about it. I spent hour after hour, year in and year out, listening to a lot of rubbish about my own life from people who knew almost nothing about it and were refusing to let me tell them.

Peggy continued this practice for almost, but not quite, the rest of her life, which was another half-century or more. When I joined the army, she told me what life was like in the army; and when I went to Oxford, she told me about life at Oxford; and so on, with every succeeding stage, until she was in her eighties and I in my sixties. Only in the last few years of her life, before she died at the age of ninety-two, did she ask me questions and listen to the answers. Until then, however determinedly I tried to share anything with her, she interrupted with undiminished determination and stopped me. It was pathetic, of course, and exasperating, but also tragic in its way, because it meant that she and Bill remained almost entirely ignorant of my life. Because they would never allow themselves to be told anything, they never knew anything. After a few years of this I had become a stranger to them. The only consolation was that it was what they wanted, and indeed were insisting on. They behaved like it to other people too. Decades later, when they found themselves in New York on a visit to my sister, the person who tried showing them round found that while he was pointing out the spectacular sights of Manhattan they were not looking or listening at all, but were deep in conversation with one another about their life in Southgate.

Because my family was so disunited the only people we knew in common were one another. Apart from that we each had our own friends, and our own lives, and went our own ways. There were no other families that we visited together, or who visited us. However, my bit of the family would go out quite often together, as indeed we always had, to places of public entertainment – sometimes without my mother, though only at her insistence. Joan got a job in Frith Street, Soho, and from then on the rest of us would meet her in one of the Soho restaurants called Fava, and have dinner before going on to a performance. I was still not allowed to choose freely from the menu in any public eating place – my father always read out to me a choice from the cheapest dishes – and at Fava's my choice was between two, each of which cost four shillings and sixpence. One of these was Vitello Milanese, a veal escalope with spaghetti, and I loved that. We never had veal at home, or spaghetti, so I ordered it every time we went to Fava's, and never got tired of it. Occasionally, at another table, we would see Tony Turner, the Hyde Park orator, with his friends, but we never spoke to him. Years later, when I got to know him, he told me that Fava's had remained his favourite restaurant even after he read in a newspaper that it had been prosecuted for selling horse meat. For years, well into my twenties, it was the Soho restaurant I preferred to all others; and in my memories of those years it figures almost as a character in its own right.

Joan's new job was a turning point in her life, and brought new interests into mine. It was with a printing firm, the Shenval Press, which acted as a publisher in the way printers in the eighteenth century had also been publishers. She was secretary to its boss and owner, James Shand, known to everyone as Hamish. He was intensely interested in everything to do with design, starting with the typefaces of his own printing; and among other things he published a quarterly journal concerned with the relationship between technical design and the arts, whether in industry, architecture, interior decoration, furniture, or popular art such as posters and advertising. The journal was called *Art and Technics* (for which the in-house nickname was *Tarts and Technics*). He also published a journal about printing. Joan brought these home, and talked about her work. And it came to me as a new kind of education.

I had taken the physical objects in my environment for granted, just as they were: the furniture, the books, everything from the vacuum cleaner to the telephone; also public objects such as tube stations and trains. Now I realised that for each and every one of them a host of conscious decisions had been taken by individuals before they were able to come into existence, not just the decision that they should be produced but what their design was to be, what material they were to be made of, how big they were to be, and so on down to the smallest detail. It could never have started out with the decision to produce *this* vacuum cleaner or *this* telephone, because each was itself the outcome of multiple choices. Each time I picked up a book, there was someone who had consciously decided not just to publish it but what format it was to have, what typeface, what quality and thickness of paper, what materials in the binding, what colours in the jacket. Everything had been decided and designed. And in every case someone was responsible, if only by default. I looked at things in a new way, down to each box of matches, and the matches in the box. It was a revelation.

I had a honeymoon period with this, and enjoyed it with all the excitement of discovery. I am not primarily a visual person, and I do not respond to visual experiences with anything like the same depth as I do to music and words. There was to come a time when I had become used to seeing things in terms of their design, and the bloom and freshness of the experience faded. But I never went back to taking the look of everything for granted. The way I saw things had been permanently changed.

While Joan was with the Shenval Press it published a magazine called *Ballet*, and with this she was in her element. She was, so to speak, secretary to the magazine, so the editor and contributors were continually in and out of her office. She found herself moving deeper into a world she already knew and loved. The venture was successful, so the firm launched a sister publication called *Opera*. This has since become the international house magazine of the opera world, and is thriving today. I have a friend, Richard Law, who contributed to the first issue and is still writing for it more than half a century later; and I have written for it myself, many times.

My sister, though living permanently with our parents – not just for a few weeks at a time, like me – was developing a distinctive life of her own. But my parents also had their separate lives. Whether there was more to my mother's than met the eye I doubt, but my father may have been having an affair during those years – I almost find myself hoping so, for his sake. If he was, it may well have been with someone of whose existence I was ignorant. But there is a woman I think it might have been. She had been a colleague of his in Civil Defence, and I had met her when I visited him at his depot – she was always around when I was there, and I found her unusually likeable. She was sexy and warm, and seemed to have a certain softness for my father, and also to show more than a normal interest in me. I must have known her name at that time, but all I can remember now is her nickname, Speedy.

A big change that occurred in my life during this period was that I started getting vacation jobs. Although it was my father who gave me my pocket money it was my mother who insisted that I get a job during the school holidays. How I found the job I no longer remember, but I became a temporary junior clerk in the income tax office in Tottenham. The people there wanted me to start work on a Saturday morning – all offices worked on Saturday mornings in those days, but it was the time people most wanted to take off, which is why they wanted me there then. On my first day I was instructed to man the enquiries counter and deal with the public – who, they said, arrived in maximum numbers on Saturdays. When I protested that I would not know the answers to any of their questions I was told that this did not matter. 'The important thing is to send them away happy. You talk nicely, and you've got good manners, so you can do it. Just tell them that we know all about their problem, and are dealing with it, and that they'll hear from us very soon. Take a note of their name, and let us have it, and we'll then deal with it. There's nothing anyone can do across the counter anyway. If there's anyone who won't take this from you, fetch Mr So-and-so, and he'll deal with them. But you'll find you'll be all right.' And I was. I had no knowledge of tax matters whatsoever, none at all, and to begin with no knowledge of the workings of the office either, but none of this made any difference. And the fact that I was only a teenager, which I expected in itself to annoy the people who came with their problems, appeared not to matter. I was tall, and seemed well educated; and in those days these things in themselves were enough to evoke respect. The whole experience was an eye-opener, if a saddening one. I soon learnt how the office worked, and absorbed some of the basic lessons about how bureaucracy operated at its interface with the public. Most of the individuals who passed their lives in that office were decent, well-intentioned people with a normal sense of fairness; but at the same time they were little people: unimaginative, blinkered, governed by the rule-book, and inclined to laziness. Above all they were fearful for their jobs, and therefore terrified of putting a foot wrong. What governed their behaviour more than any other consideration was fear of doing something that would open them to serious criticism from their colleagues or superiors.

Working on the counter was the most interesting job I was given. Most of the others were mechanical and mindless, like altering with a pen a single digit on each of a pile of out-of-date printed forms, so that they could go on being used – there was no office machinery except for typewriters and telephones. This was an introduction to the realities of life for the lowliest of the people who worked in offices. There were still millions of people doing jobs like that. When I came across Bernard Shaw's remark that, of all the damnable wastages of human life, clerking was the worst, I knew what he was talking about. (So did he. It was an abyss into which many writers, trapped in a way that I was not, had stared.)

What made it bearable was the presence in the office of another temp of my own age, and a congenial one, Ken Connor. He was a local grammar-school boy on the way to becoming an art student. We were often set to the same task in an otherwise empty room, so we spent whole days in animated talk. He loved music, and went to concerts, so we sometimes went off together in the evenings. I also visited his family. His mother was intelligent but authoritarian, formidably harsh-tongued, and his father a bus-driver. Father was haunted by the fact that someone had committed suicide by throwing himself under his bus. His inability to get this out of his mind communicated itself to me, and in his presence I felt the touch of a finger of inconsolable yet resentful melancholy. Ken and I remained friends for a number of years. When my first book was published – a volume of embarrassing poems written in my teens – it was he who designed the jacket. His cover is better than my poems, and is now what makes the book worth having.

It was in my mid-teens that I started to write poetry. My conscious mind had little to do with the process. The poems came to me spontaneously, under some sort of pressure from within, and the only self-aware thing I did was write them down and punctuate them, and occasionally polish one of them up a bit by altering a word here or there to remove an obvious fault. I would always know when a poem was on the way: I would be overcome by a broody, heavy, full, drowsy feeling that I experienced at no other time. This would cause me to withdraw into myself, and then the poem would push its way into my mind. In that sense it was authentic poetry, even if, at the same time, not very good. It is extraordinary that all this versification, with its rhyming, scansion, division into stanzas and the rest of it, can happen unconsciously, but it does. And the fact that the poems are not very good makes it more rather than less surprising. The nearest thing to it I can think of is the tightly plotted structure of some of my dreams, with their intricate organisation and vivid detail, which are also creating themselves spontaneously and involuntarily in an unconscious mind.

It was nearly always in London that I wrote my poems, not at school, because only at home could I find the necessary solitude for uninterrupted parturition – a paradoxical benefit to get from being in London. Altogether, the richness of my London life was extraordinary. In some ways I think of it as the nodal point of my whole development as a human being.

However, and of course, although being in London was so special for me, it was not special to the other members of my family, who lived there all the time. They had a perfectly normal need to get away from it for holidays, sometimes when I was with them. By this time they had taken to going away separately, my mother usually to Bristol. My sister would take charge of the flat while Mother was away, and go off with her friends at another time (perhaps to Stratford-upon-Avon to see some plays). There was one summer – I think it was immediately after the end of the war in Europe – when my mother, sister and I went for a holiday in Bournemouth. I enjoyed it. I have always liked resorts, for the same reason as I have always liked circuses and pantomimes: they are showbiz at its most basic, and are fun. The one special memory I retain is hearing a young Australian pianist called Noel Mewton-Wood play Beethoven's Fourth Piano Concerto with the Bournemouth Municipal Orchestra. He was altogether exceptional, and became internationally recognised as such. But he committed suicide while still very young, over a homosexual love affair.

I was still in London with my parents at the end of that summer when the war against Japan came to an end, and with it the Second World War. It happened precipitately, because of the dropping of the two atom bombs on Hiroshima and Nagasaki. The public had been given no hint of the existence of these weapons, and we were all expecting the war to go on for another year or two. I was as astounded as everyone else. But I had done enough physics and higher mathematics to understand the popular-science explanations that some of the newspapers and magazines were giving, and it was now a question of me explaining things to my father rather than the other way round. It was obvious to everyone that a new historical era had opened. If ever the term 'cataclysmic change' had a literal meaning, it was now. No other public event in my lifetime has imposed with such iron certitude the instant feeling that the world would never be the same again. These astonishing weapons had suddenly, out of the blue, ended the war, and we were all glad of that – we had been expecting tens of thousands more deaths on our own side, which did not now occur. But there had already been two world wars in quick succession, and if there should ever be another, these weapons would be what the combatants would start with. To us, who had just lived through six years of world war, and found the outbreak of another easy to envisage, the prospect was ungraspable. But our very inability to imagine it froze our blood. It was instantly clear that the need to avoid atomic war would exercise an altogether new kind of dominance over world politics.

Meanwhile there was uncontrollable joy that the Second World War had ended, and without the terrible further casualties on our side that we had been steeled for. On VJ Day my family felt an overwhelming need to celebrate with other people, just to go out and do something – shout, sing, laugh, dance about, punch the air, we did not know what or where. Guided by our atavistic Londoners' intuition we made our way to Trafalgar Square, where we found tens of thousands of other people who felt the same way. What we did with the time we spent there was bizarre – stroll around arm in arm with total strangers, exchange garments with them, hug people, do silly little dances with them, fall about in a lot of physical joking, shriek with laughter, sing songs, yell with bliss, work off our energy, make ourselves tired. The grown-ups around us went in for endless kissing, and anyone of either sex in a uniform was smothered with embraces. According to later analysis this scene was a prelude to massively profligate copulation between total strangers. Hundreds of new human beings must have been conceived that night.

CHAPTER TWENTY-THREE

Until I went to Oxford I had little idea of rational thought as anything different from the sort of activity you engaged in when you read a novel, or saw a play, or argued about politics. These things engaged the whole of you, part of which was your mind. But analytic thinking as itself the mode of engagement – or the primary one, the cutting edge, and a disciplined activity – was something I did not properly understand until I found myself being trained in it. Then I discovered that, used as an additional tool, it increased my understanding of everything, and usually by an enormous amount. I have valued it exceedingly – and done a great deal of it – ever since. However, the academics who trained me in it seemed to imagine that in itself it constituted the whole and sole correct approach, and this was a view that impoverished their understanding. So a crucial distinction needs to be made between the defectiveness of the academic approach when allowed to be the only one, and the immensely valuable enrichment it can bring to a fuller understanding when that is rooted at deeper levels.

For me the earliest stirrings of this sort of thinking occurred at Christ's Hospital, not in a classroom but in the school library. If I visit that library now, my spirit soars as I walk in, because this was where my mind awoke. In classrooms I was reacting, responding to instruction, doing what teachers required me to do; but browsing at liberty in the library I was pursuing my own interests, going spontaneously where curiosity led, and this was so much more enlightening. A lot of the time I followed my nose and grazed, ruminated, then wandered off to the next grazing point. Frequently I came across things by accident, as when a book just happened to stand next to another on the shelf, and my eye was caught by the colour of its binding. It gave me deep inner happiness to spend a Sunday afternoon browsing like this, with the library to myself, and I would often drop in there for shorter periods on other days.

The first book I read there that made a lasting impact on me was called *The Bible of the World*. It consisted, it said, of the essential passages in the scriptures of each of the world's main religions. What impinged on me most was the first section, consisting of Hindu scriptures. Some of the things it said were things I had thought but did not know anyone else had. Chief of these was that what actually existed was, in itself, something it was impossible to make any direct contact with, and therefore impossible to imagine. The Hindu scriptures said that all you ever had were images. These, being images, were insubstantial and ephemeral. Only what was behind them was real and lasting. But this, being not image, could never be in a mind. I was astonished that this thought had been thought thousands of years ago, and written down in what were now, it would seem, classic writings. It gave me reassurance. It was my first realisation that mine was not an oddball view, slightly mad, but a solidly based approach that was shared by large numbers of people. This took me out of the isolation I had felt myself to be in and made me feel part of something wider. But these Hindu writings went on to give an explanation that had not occurred to me. The lasting reality behind the images, they said, did not consist of what were somehow the same things only in a different, perhaps invisible, form: the *real* mountain, the *real* tree, the *real* house. There was just one big, unimaginable something. All real reality was one, and this was veiled from us by the itemised world of experience. It was only in the world of experience that separate items existed. We ourselves, individually, had emerged from the single oneness of everything at our conception, and would return to it when we died. In between, our lives were a sort of aberration, like amputations, some kind of mistake, or a sort of delusion.

I did not know what to make of this. Even on its own showing we could not know if it were true, I thought. Nor could we know if it was untrue. I could see no reason for rejecting it, but felt no inclination to believe it either. I was passionately attached to the life that it told me was illusory, in fact I held it more dear than anything else; but I knew only too well that it was ephemeral; so I had to concede that it could not, in itself, be lasting reality. I was left agnostic on the question of how, if at all, this life and what was not this life were related. Even so, what had spoken powerfully to me was the fact of the distinction: the fact that an uncrossable gulf exists between this world of ours and whatever else there is, such that from within this world we cannot get much conception of the rest. There is a sense in which I have been trying ever since to fight my way out of this impasse, but although such efforts have enriched my understanding of the problem, they have not carried me as far as a solution. Wittgenstein maintained that anyone who penetrated the problem to the bottom would find that it evaporated, and that there was, properly understood, not really a problem at all; but I am as sure as I can be of anything that this is wrong. The more one truly understands the problem the more substantial it becomes, and the more baffling and frustrating. It is the fundamental problem of experience, and of all human existence.

I suppose this must have been the first time I found myself reading about what could be called philosophical problems. I also came across two books by Nikolai Berdyaev, an actual philosopher, an exiled Russian who at that time was alive and publishing new work. These books appealed to me even though I did not understand them. They were very Russian, I thought, and although they were socialist they were anti-communist, mystical, even a bit religiose. It is possible that if I read them today I would find them mushy, but at that time I found them elusively moving – moving in a way I would not have expected writing about ideas to be.

The experience of finding that something was interesting even though I did not understand it was one I had with a lot of my reading, and was at its most intense with contemporary poetry. I discovered modern poetry because of the thinness of the volumes. When my eye first fell on them on the shelves I was startled to see volumes that were so big in format, with stiff covers, yet had so few pages. I would not have expected them to be published as books at all, but as pamphlets. I took some of these thinnies down and found that they contained poems, although it was not poetry as I had encountered it, nor had I heard of any of the poets. Poem after poem was unintelligible, yet tantalising. I re-read those that tantalised me most, then read them again – and again. Parts lodged in my mind, and I would find myself saying them over to myself at other times, especially in bed at night – still not understanding them. Why were they so interesting? It was as if these poems were enjoying a joke at my expense by playing with my curiosity, and there was something playful in my response to them, as someone might feel who was labouring at difficult but witty crossword puzzles. I became addicted. And the more I understood the poems, the more seriously I found myself taking them, until I grew into a fully fledged devotee of what was then contemporary poetry. One of the unknown writers stood out above the others, T.S. Eliot; but W.H. Auden was jolly good, and there were people called C. Day-Lewis, Stephen Spender and Louis MacNeice. All of them were not only alive but in the prime of their lives – Eliot was in his fifties, Auden not yet forty – and producing new work. This fact itself excited me – it was all happening *now*. For years after that I marinaded in the writings of these poets, trying out new ones and occasionally adding another to the central canon, the chief of these being Dylan Thomas. That kind of poetry played a more important part in my inner life than any other sort of writing for a considerable period. The nature of the poems I wrote myself was changed by it, and from having been an old-fashioned romantic I became a modern.

Because this poetry meant so much to me I started digging around in its references – because Yeats was so dear to Auden I read Yeats; and because Hardy meant so much to Dylan Thomas I read Hardy. I read Dante in translation because Eliot treated him with such deference. I also started reading criticism of the writers I most enjoyed. My discoveries spread outwards all the time. I became an excited tracker-down and looker-up of things from one book to another, and a user of the *Encyclopaedia Britannica* and dictionaries of quotations. When I found the names of the same contemporary novelists cropping up again and again I dug their books out of the library and found myself reading E.M. Forster, Aldous Huxley and Somerset Maugham – also D.H. Lawrence, who was the recently dead writer most often referred to. I read all Forster's novels while still at school.

In all this I felt an involvement and enthusiasm quite different in kind from anything I felt in classrooms, where we pursued no such matters. I talked about it excitedly to my friends, but most of these were not especially interested. Many thought it all a bit arty-farty. So in this respect, at least, I found myself again in a world of my own.

The feeling that I myself was a writer in the making began to grow in strength and confidence. I started to publish poetry in school magazines, indeed to think of myself as a future poet, and perhaps a novelist too. At no time did it enter my head to think of such things as connected with classwork, or having anything to do with school. I saw writers as being different sorts of people from academics. Real writing, it seemed to me, was creative writing – poetry, plays, novels, short stories – and people who wrote other things did so because they could not manage the real thing. Biographers, historians and the rest were in this sense failed writers, usually novelists manqué.

At the same time as all these things were happening – though unaware of it, mostly, since my interests were only intermittently engaged – I was getting a good education of an old-fashioned sort in the classes I attended, one that provided me with a solid academic foundation for the rest of my life. In the central tradition of public-school teaching, it was heavily weighted towards languages; in fact all I was learning now apart from languages was higher mathematics, history and geography. Two of the more memorable teachers – memorable chiefly because they were the only ones I was frightened of – taught me Latin in two successive years: Derrick Macnutt and the headmaster. I have since been an object of awe to devotees of the crossword puzzle for having been taught by Macnutt, for he is regarded by many, still, as the greatest setter of puzzles there has ever been. He was Ximenes of the *Observer*, author of the still-classic book *On the Art of the Crossword*, and was at the height of his powers during the period when he taught me. In the classroom he was a terrorist. He shouted nonstop (his nickname was Boom), and after asking a boy a question he would stride across to his desk and stand over him, shouting down at him, then beating him about the head if he gave the wrong answer, or if, understandably in these circumstances, he became tongue-tied. The only way not to be beaten by Boom was to come up instantly with the right answer. All the boys were terrified of him and dreaded being asked a question, because if you even so much as paused to think it was *Whack! Whack!* 'Come on, boy.' *Whack! Whack!* 'Don't leave me just standing here.' *Whack! Whack!* 'We haven't got all day.' *Whack! Whack!* The blows were delivered hard, with the butt of the hand against the side or back of the head. If in desperation you came out quickly with what you hoped would be the right answer but wasn't, he would shout, '*Think*, boy, *think*. Why don't you *think*?' and give you an even harder whack on each repetition of the word *think*. If you made many mistakes in your written prep he would beat you on the bottom with a cricket bat. In the house of which he was housemaster he caned boys on their bare buttocks until they bled, and was notorious for doing this arbitrarily and unjustly, especially to boys who happened to be good-looking. He would position them for the caning with great meticulousness, making them crouch face down in an armchair with their naked bottoms sticking up into the air. There is no doubt that he was a sadist in the literal sense of that term, a person who got sexual pleasure (including, if some of the stories were true, orgasm) from the infliction of pain. Yet the fact is that I learnt more Latin from him than from anyone else: he just made me do it.

Under the headmaster we read Book Two of Virgil's *Aeneid*, a lifelong possession in some ways, though the Latin itself has gone. He was another shouter, also frightening. But, unlike with Boom, there were strands of civilisation in his method. It was from him that I acquired a genuine understanding of why satisfactory translation is impossible – basically, because words have their meanings in terms of observation, experience and activity, the living circumstances in which they are learnt and used, not in terms of other words. As he liked to put it: 'Words don't mean words.' My studies in Latin literature, such as they were – mostly Caesar, Livy, Virgil and Ovid – had a lifelong effect on my view of the relationship between moral behaviour and personal integrity. If you knew what was right, you ought to do it regardless of the cost to yourself, even if that was greater than your life. If you commanded an army in which your son was serving, and he committed a crime for which any other soldier would be put to death, the right thing to do would be to execute your son, even though everyone expected you to invent some excuse for not doing so. Needless to say, I have never come anywhere near to living with such alarming rectitude; and if I were in the Roman general's situation I would spare my son. But I would do it shamefacedly. There is something about the Roman notion of impersonal justice that commands my assent, whether I like it or not; and it has had an influence on me, even though I am incapable of living up to it.

The teacher whose classes I enjoyed most taught us English: a very young woman called Helen Tyrrell. She was preparing us for School Certificate, the rough equivalent of the more recent GCSE. There was always a Shakespeare play, in our case *Richard II*, and a set book, which was usually in prose but in our case was Book Four of Palgrave's anthology *The Golden Treasury*, the section devoted to the Romantic poets.

I had an odd relationship to the Shakespeare play. I already loved his work with a passion, but had never been a reader of it, indeed never thought of it as something intended to be read. I had always taken it for granted that theatre was a performing art, and that plays existed only in performance: their texts were recipes for performances, no more intended to be read for their own sakes than food recipes. Shakespeare himself never published any of his plays, though he published, and was very keen to publish, his poems. The plays existed to be acted, to be seen, not read. On the stage they came alive: on the page they were not there. So this whole business of treating them as if they were reading matter seemed to me to go against their nature. During school holidays I was seeing Shakespeare played by the greatest actors of the day, and finding the experience thrilling beyond words; but here at school I was being confronted with slabs of cold print and told that this was Shakespeare. If only I could have seen *Richard II*, which unfortunately I never had, I could have re-enacted bits of it in my head each time I read some of the text. As things were,

I felt like a gourmet who sits down with relish to eat his dinner and finds himself handed the recipes to read instead. I got to know *Richard II* as a text without knowing it as a play, and felt my relationship to it unnatural and alienating. This spoiled the play for me for decades. For half my life it remained the odd one out among Shakespeare's plays, the only one I could not spontaneously relate to. It was only after I had seen it many times that I was able to respond to it in the same way as I did to the others.

The pleasure for me of Miss Tyrrell's classes lay in the Romantic poets. I was, or had been, a bit of a Romantic poet myself, and they came as meat and drink to me. I swilled their stuff down, licking my chops between gulps. Some of the poems, or chunks of them, have been part of me ever since – a quotation from one was the title of my last book. Miss Tyrrell's approach helped this process by being fresh and engaging, unlike many of the fuddy-duddies we were used to being taught by. She had come to Christ's Hospital straight out of Oxford, at the age of twenty-two, in the full flush of enthusiasm for her subject, and this was her first teaching experience. She was only a few years older than I was, but I did not think of her in that way. For all her youth and sympathetic manner she was an authority figure merely by virtue of being one of the teachers. But one day, when I was talking to her after a class, it came out that I was a reader of modern poetry, and at once she started referring to Eliot and Auden. It was the first time I had heard these names on anyone else's lips, and it gave them an independent reality they had not had before. I became excited and voluble. She asked me to come and talk to her in her study: to have anything like a serious conversation we needed to be somewhere other than a classroom. And there she gave me, in brief outline, an overview of contemporary poetry. What she said caused me to realise that, by what seemed to me sheer chance, I was already reading the most interesting of the writers she talked about – but of course they had been pre-selected by the school library. She even knew about Dylan Thomas, who was younger than the others – little more than thirty at that time – and when I left her she lent me one of his books. So now I knew someone who not only knew about these poets but actually bought their books. Scarcely had this happened when Dylan Thomas published a new volume called *Deaths and Entrances*, and I bought it myself, and thought it contained his best poems of all.

I took the School Certificate in eight subjects, half of them languages. The subjects were Latin, French, German, English language, English literature, history, elementary mathematics and advanced mathematics. When I went to the headmaster's class-room at the beginning of the following term to find out what my results were, there was nothing but a row of misprints beside my name. I sought out a master and told him that the copying-out of my results had been garbled. He peered at the results book, disappeared to the school's office, came back, and said no, this was not an error, these were my results. The possibility of these being my actual results had not occurred to me, even when I saw them on paper. I had got a distinction in every subject except the two mathematics papers, in which I had credits. I looked at the other boys' results to see if any were like mine. None were, except for those of a boy called Pickens: he had seven distinctions to my six. I was dumbfounded. For days I was unable to talk about it even to my friends, being in a state of shock. Something basic to my conception of myself had been shaken to the foundations. I failed to take the new realisation properly on board, and made what was in essence the same mistake at Oxford six or seven years later. Then, when I found myself being given a long viva for my degree in philosophy, politics and economics, I took it utterly for granted that this meant I was a borderline case between a second and a third, and it was only later that I learnt to my incredulity

that I had been vivaed for a first. At no time in my life have I
thought of myself as an academic person. At school especially I
found most academic work boring. The small part of it that interested me I would work at joyfully, but for the rest I did as little
as would keep me out of trouble with my teachers – and did not
always manage to do that. I had no desire to shine in class, or
come top, or win prizes: that whole mode of being seemed to me
a dim one. When prizes started coming my way, towards the end
of my school career, they seemed to me unrelated to my interests, in fact unrelated to *me*.

After School Certificate there were two or three subjects in
which my teachers thought I was bound to get a place at Oxbridge,
and each wanted me to specialise in his, but by that time I knew
which one I was going to pursue. This was history, though I chose
it not because of the subject but because of its teacher, David
Roberts. He had the reputation of being, and certainly was, the
best teacher in the school. He did not teach his specialists in a
classroom but gave them individual tuition, as if they were already
at Oxbridge and he was their tutor. Each met with him alone at
frequent intervals and would be given individual tasks, individual
essay subjects, individual reading lists. The boy would then spend
history periods working by himself in the school library, and would
write his essay. During these periods Roberts would always be
around in the library, seeing how each one was getting on, available to all. When an essay was finished the boy would have another
session with Roberts, and they would go through the work
together, the boy being also questioned about his reading. In all
these respects the life of a history specialist was quite unlike that
of other boys in the school. For that reason Roberts would take
on only those who he thought could handle the independence,
these being by no means always the cleverest. Some of the other
masters resented him for being so presumptuous and highfalutin
as to carry on so differently from themselves, but the fact that he

got nearly all his boys into Oxbridge, including some unpromising and even recalcitrant material, when none of the others had anything like so good a track record, made it difficult for them to do more than snipe.

Roberts's methods attracted me immensely, and for the rest of my time at Christ's Hospital I was a history specialist. Two-thirds of my school periods were devoted to history, the rest to languages, and only the latter pursued in a classroom. The history I was launched on was unusual. Roberts required all his boys to study chiefly, though not exclusively, medieval European history, and I found this a revelation. Being taught by him was a milestone experience in my life. His particular aim was to unlock the capacity for self-development of each individual; and he could find a boy's hidden potential like a water-diviner. Other teachers would nearly always encourage a boy to do what he was best at, or, failing that, what he was most interested in, and thus to develop along the lines that came easiest to him. David explored until he found what a boy was capable of being interested in but had never turned his mind to, and then put him on to it, thus enlarging him, his mind and his outlook, yet always on a basis that was rooted in the boy himself, and was not factitious. In the course of questioning me about my passions for music, theatre and poetry, he realised that I had never woken up to the visual arts. So he came one day and sat beside me in a corner of the library with an art book full of high-quality reproductions of Old Masters, and spread it open before the two of us. Our conversation went something like this.

'What would you say about that painting?'

Me silent, gawping at the picture. Nothing to say.

'You're looking straight at it, so you must be able to say *something*. Say anything that comes into your head, it doesn't matter how obvious. Don't be afraid of being silly.'

Me: 'Well, this half of the painting is light and that half's dark.'

'Good. Now why do you think the artist has done that?'

Me speechless again. Mind blank.

'Well, what effect does it have?'

Me: 'Well, contrast, I suppose.'

'Good. Now why might the artist have wanted to get an effect of contrast? What, for instance, could he be contrasting here?'

And from such laboured beginnings, with painful, bumpy slowness, we were off. He drew me in. For the first time I started looking at a picture and thinking.

He judged that, for me, it was best to start by getting me to *read* a picture.

'These hands over here are beautifully painted, in very fine detail. But those over there are hardly more than sketched in. And, after all, it's the same picture. Why do you suppose that is?'

And then, in response to yet another blank-minded silence: 'Well, how does it affect your eye now that you notice it?'

He soon had me fascinated, then excited; and by an ingenious selection of pictures he managed to give the whole process a relationship to the history I was supposed to be studying. Next time I was in London during the school holidays I was off to the National Gallery and the Tate, and other galleries, to look at originals. I had never been in the habit of going to art galleries, preferring museums: nor was it something my family ever did. So it was almost a new world: at any rate, the eyes with which I was seeing it were new. From that day to this I make for the main art gallery in any town I visit. Paintings do not have for me the compulsion that music and theatre do, but they have enriched my life nonetheless: the interest I take in them is real, and so is the pleasure I get from them.

Another quite different thing that David Roberts did for me was to challenge some of the basics of my thinking, not so much my assumptions as my concepts. When I spouted my schoolboy socialism at him he would say something like: 'What do you mean when you say equality? Equality in what respect? Equality of opportunity? Equality of possessions? Equality of income? Equality of status? Any two of the above? All?' And needless to say I did not really know what I meant by equality, except in the most vague and emotional way. He did the same to me with the concept of freedom, which had always been my idée fixe, and I found this an impossible nut to crack. At first the sort of thing I would say was: 'Everybody knows what freedom is. It's silly to *ask* me what it is. Freedom is just freedom, that's all.' He had no difficulty in showing me that not only were there various sorts of freedom but that some were incompatible with others, so that when different people talked about freedom they were sometimes in conflict with one another. Which sort, he wanted to know, did I stand for?

In the early stages of this my reaction was one of frustration. I had never been challenged to analyse my own thinking in such a way, and had no real idea how to do it. I did not see how one *could* do it, or be expected to do it. Your basic concepts, it seemed to me, were what you started from, so they were, as I might now say, irreducible. From that starting point it was your emotions, nourished by your moral sense, that drove your ideas forward. Of course you had to respect logic on the way; but so long as you did that, it was feeling that was all-important; and this seemed to me how things should be. My commitment to the ideals of freedom and equality was so passionate that the mere questioning of them presented itself to me as an act of hostility, to which I reacted with resentment, a resentment that easily became anger. David was quite unruffled by this, in fact he understood perfectly what I was going through, and he was putting me through it deliberately. For me it was a process of real emotional difficulty, painful, slow. It was years before I got through it, and there is an important sense in which such a process can never be completed; but in me it was started by David. It was the beginning of my higher education. This is a process that most people do not embark on until they go to a university – and not always then. The awakening left me with a lifelong feeling of indebtedness to him, as the person who made me start thinking, very much against my will. Being a schoolmaster, he always linked his teaching to reading of some kind, but he never allowed anyone just to start from books: he always made sure first of all that they were infected with a serious problem that arose from the breakdown of their own immune system, and only then pointed them towards a book or books in which they, eager by now to get some help with the problem, might find it. In my case it was John Stuart Mill's *On Liberty*, which I guzzled greedily.

Almost everyone who studied under David has stories like this to tell, yet the stories themselves are uniquely different according to the personality of the teller. He helped each of us to discover ourselves – sometimes against our resistance – and then go on to develop, critically, whatever it was we had discovered. I cannot imagine a better teacher. He became a lifelong friend, as he did to several of his pupils. I went to his home many times, and got to know his wife and children. A dozen years later, on a visit to him when I was a parliamentary candidate, I found myself engaged for an unforgettable afternoon in a conversation with his father, Lord Clwyd, now in his nineties, who had been in the House of Commons as a Liberal MP under the leadership of Gladstone – and before that had spent a year and a half on a single round-the-world journey, made in great comfort at a total cost of £350. David, the younger of twin brothers, missed inheriting his father's peerage by twenty minutes. He also had a younger brother, Melvyn Roberts, who was a composer good enough to merit an entry to himself in the *New Grove Dictionary of Music*.

In physique, David was portly, and reminded everyone of a well-known comedy actor of the day called Robert Morley, still to be seen in some old films. Without being himself at all actory he had a certain sparkle and dash, and always a twinkle in the eye. His speech and mannerisms were much imitated, especially his way of putting a finger to one side of his nose, or his reiterated injunction to history specialists, 'You've got to get a general picture', waggling a hand at arm's length with the fingers splayed as he spoke. The fact that his relationship to his pupils combined clear-eyed detachment with personal concern brought a high level of irony into it, and much humour, which he was anxious should not be hurtfully misunderstood. Given that he was, in his way, a sort of genius, it is not surprising that he had not himself had much academic success before finding his vocation as a school-master. I have been told (I have not checked this) that he got a third-class degree at Cambridge and became a prep-school teacher. He told me himself that he had been a plodder at university who never gave serious thought to what he was doing. It is obvious that what he needed was a teacher like himself, and did not have the good fortune to find one.

The only other teacher who impinged on me significantly at that age was an American, Al Blackmer. As soon as the war ended, Christ's Hospital resumed a regular relationship with the oldest private school in the USA, Phillips Academy in Andover, Massachusetts. Each year a boy would go from one to the other, and also a master accompanied by his family – the two families swapped homes. The Christ's Hospital master who changed places with Al was the only one I felt a regret at not being taught by. He was Edward Malins, a young cavalry officer recently returned from the Far East. Casual yet elegant, refreshingly tolerant in outlook and attitudes, a lover of the arts, especially music, good-looking, and married to an equally attractive wife, he seemed too sophisticated to be a schoolmaster. (Colin Davis seems to have had a special relationship with him rather like the one I had with David Roberts.) Even so, I think I came off just as well with Al Blackmer.

Al introduced us to American literature, which we knew nothing about. I still carry in my head the inflections of his voice as he read two classic short stories aloud to us: 'I'm a Fool' by Sherwood Anderson, and 'The Killers' by Ernest Hemingway. It was my first lesson in the relationship between American writing and American speech. When I heard him read Shakespeare – it was the final scene of *Othello* – I had culture shock. I found it ridiculous, not acceptable, to hear Shakespeare in an American accent: I felt embarrassed, and wanted to laugh. But the truth is that American pronunciation is probably closer than modern English to the way the language was spoken in Elizabethan England. In any case Al read the scene so well that I forgot about my embarrassment and became absorbed in the content. This, again, was an important first lesson, this time in the silliness of provincial cultural attitudes to America. Later, in my mid-twenties, when I spent a year at Yale, he wrote inviting me to visit him and his family, and we became friends. I think of him with much admiration and affection.

Altogether, I believe, I got as good an education at Christ's Hospital as was to be had at any school in Britain at that time. Most of the classroom work was not of much interest to me, but that would have been the same anywhere else; and here it was well taught, on the whole, though I did have my share of bad teachers. It is obvious now that I should have specialised in physics and maths, the two subjects I was best at, but that was not obvious then: the school, like all the best schools at that time, took it for granted that bright boys specialised in humanities, and I shared that foolish view. I did not feel at one with most of what I was doing for teachers until I became a history specialist – and then the individual care and attention I received were extraordinary by any standards, and my real education began. Against my own emotional resistance I started to think, to analyse, to look critically at my own ideas and my own concepts. The essays I wrote for David Roberts were my first attempts at intellectually serious writing, and each one received from him an instructively critical response. With one I was carried away and produced sixty pages

– it was on Louis XI – yet David read every word of it and gave me vigorous and detailed criticisms. He made us not only study history but reflect on its nature; and when A.L. Rowse's book *The Use of History* came out he ordered us all to read it. To my surprise I found myself revelling in academic work.

But, as must be the case with any school education worthy of the name, the most valuable aspects of it were going on outside classroom periods. I was developing across a broad front as a human being, learning to stand on my own feet in a stressful society, and to get along with every kind of person. Within myself I was trying to develop as a writer – a poet first and foremost, but also trying my hand at general essays, and a diary, all now mercifully defunct. And I was increasingly enthusiastic as a debater.

One experience I had in connection with a school debate had an important effect on my life. Bob Pitman, an Old Blue currently prominent at Oxford as a debater, was invited back to the school to speak, and I was detailed to debate on the same side as him. I remembered him vividly for his star performances in Gilbert and Sullivan. He knew nothing about me, but he wrote and suggested that we meet on the afternoon of his arrival to make sure that our prepared speeches were not going either to repeat or contradict one another. We went for a long, meandering walk across Big Side. During most of this he was bubbling with enthusiasm about the Oxford Union. I had heard of it without actually knowing what it was, and he gave me a wonderfully sharp, though also beglamoured, description of that club-cum-debating-society – its atmosphere, its debates, the coruscating wit, the outsize personalities. Incomparably the highest achievement open to any undergraduate while at Oxford, he said, was to become president of the Union. From that day onwards I thought that if I went to Oxford the Union would be one of the centres of my life there, and I would become its president. What actually happened was that on my first day as an undergraduate I took the cheque for my student grant to a bank in the centre of Oxford, opened my first bank account, then walked the two hundred yards to the Oxford Union and wrote my first cheque, for life membership. In a crowded, many-sided life at Oxford the Union meant more to me than any other institution, and I did indeed become its president.

There were visiting speakers at Christ's Hospital of other kinds who made a lasting impression on me. The then provost of King's College, Cambridge, a fellow called Sheppard, told us that what more than anything else distinguished human beings from animals was language, and that the first people to understand this had been the ancient Greeks. He quoted, from a play by Sophocles, a passage that makes the point, a chorus beginning:

> Wonderful are the world's wonders, but none
> More wonderful than man . . .

I was mesmerised by it. It was the first time I had heard any such significance attributed to language. For me it was counterintuitive, and the more I thought about it the more I disagreed with it – today I would say that if one thing more than another distinguishes man from the animals it is morality – but it is a fascinating idea nevertheless, and it opened up all sorts of possibilities in front of my eyes. Also, I thought that the Sophocles, my first tiny glimpse of Greek drama, was marvellous – it gave me goose pimples. Even Sheppard's manner swept me away. Instead of standing behind the speaker's table as usual, he sat on the front of it dangling his legs. I had never seen a speaker do this, and was hugely impressed – it seemed a triumph of informality and direct contact with us. It became my own practice in subsequent years, in the role of teacher and political speaker. But it was many years before I saw anyone else do it.

There was a Captain Harry Rée who talked to us about his

adventures with the French Resistance during the war. Years later he became a friend. Colin Davis returned to give more of his profoundly musical performances on the clarinet, and I later got to know him too. Altogether it was as if our surroundings were opening up after the hunkered-down, closed-in years of the war. No doubt part of this feeling was due to the age I was at, and the fact that I was growing up, so perhaps I would have had some of it at that stage of my life anyway; but the school really was turning outwards. The sandbags and blackout shutters had gone; younger masters with fresh, alert faces were reappearing after years in other countries. Quite other things were coming back too, like ice cream and bananas, which had not been seen for years. We acquired an American boy at the school, then half a dozen French boys. Foreign visitors became common. As it had done every year before the war, the school started visiting London every St Matthew's Day and marching behind its band through the City to the Mansion House, to be greeted by the Lord Mayor for tea and a celebration, each of us being handed a coin by him (I forget how much). A month after that we marched into Horsham, again behind the band, for a special showing of the film of Shakespeare's *Henry V.* It was the only occasion during my time when the people of Horsham saw the whole school – which was, so to speak, reasserting its existence in the eyes of the outside world after the deliberate obscurity of the war years.

The school was more famous then than now. For hundreds of years it had been one of the biggest sites (and sights) in the City of London, and the only school in the country that offered a five-star boarding education to the children of hard-up parents. Added to that was its remarkable uniform, familiar to everyone in the capital. Inevitably, people became less aware of it after it moved to the countryside. But the biggest change in its position came after the Second World War, when the academic opportunities it offered were opened to the population as a whole. Christ's

Hospital ceased to serve a unique purpose, though it continued to meet special needs. Its distinctiveness now was as a charity. The post-war revolution in secondary education was launched by the Education Act of 1944, in the middle of my time at the school, so I knew Christ's Hospital in the last years of its special greatness.

Well known though it was, those of us who were there had an exaggerated idea of its outside reputation. We were more aware than others of our old boys who were making a name for themselves in the world, and we supposed them to be more famous than they were. I think this is true of all schools. And we thought of our old boys as being somehow continuous with ourselves – they represented the future towards which we were heading. There were quite a few on the current scene. The actor establishing himself as the leading young man in British films, Michael Wilding, was a recent Old Blue (and, enviably, was to marry both Margaret Leighton and Elizabeth Taylor). Keith Douglas, who had been killed in the war, was being talked about as the outstanding poet to have come out of it. Keith Vaughan had had his first one-man exhibition, and was launched on his fame as a painter. Constant Lambert had more reputation than any of them, at least as a personality – social figure, wit, author, composer, regular conductor at the Proms, director of Sadler's Wells Ballet (and, had we but known it, secret lover of Margot Fonteyn). Almost undisguised, he was to turn up later as one of the leading characters in Anthony Powell's twelve-novel epic of mid-twentieth-century Britain, *A Dance to the Music of Time*. There were older established celebrities such as Barnes Wallis, the prototype of 'Q' in the James Bond films, inventor of the bouncing bomb and other devilishly ingenious wartime inspirations; the poet Edmund Blunden, an already classic writer from the First World War, though still not old; and John Middleton Murry, man of letters and husband of Katherine Mansfield. Those of us who cared about

sport – which was a majority – were proud of the fact that the
Old Blues rugger team was generally regarded as the best of the
public-school old boys' teams during the 1940s. Those more
academically inclined were aware that the school sent something
like thirty boys a year to Oxford and Cambridge, where quite a
number became professors and heads of colleges. Whatever our
separate inclinations, we saw ourselves as going into a world in
which Old Blues flourished. (The City, we knew, was teeming with
them.) During the time I was there I do not think it occurred to
me to doubt that Christ's Hospital was the best school in the
country. It was an ignorant opinion, of course. But there can have
been no other that offered so good a boarding-school education,
leading to such excellent life chances, with no consideration whatsoever of money or social class.

CHAPTER TWENTY-FOUR

At the end of one school year five of the six house monitors in Barnes A left, so I and my contemporaries became the government. By now Hudson, Courtier and Mercer had left too, but all the rest of my year became monitors simultaneously. Griffiths was house captain, with Erskine-Tulloch and me in charge of the seniors, and Cavendish and Batts in charge of the juniors. For the first time I had to organise other people, and punish lawbreakers. Learning to do these things fairly and responsibly had always been an essential part of a public-school education, and so it still was in the Britain of those days, and would have been a turning point in the personal development of anyone. We came into the perks of office, chief of which, as far as I was concerned, was the freedom to stay up late, since we had to supervise the other boys going to bed and then to sleep. And we acquired fags, smaller boys to make our beds, clean our shoes, post our letters, and run our errands.

All this was, as it had been developed to be, a training in growing up, because it was learning to accept responsibility and exercise authority. My friends and I had our own views about this, and we ran the house in what was really rather a grown-up way, allowing the boys more individual freedom than in other houses (and in return being regarded by them as 'slack'). We became a house known for personal rather than shared attainments: we were the individualist's house. It was during this period that Richard

Cavendish and I became particular friends. Almost inevitably, given his interests, he became a history specialist like me and entered David Roberts's kingdom in the school library. Because David did not teach his specialists in the classroom that had been allotted to him for that purpose, he turned it into something approximating a junior common room for his older pupils, and now Richard and I were the only two members of it from Barnes A. Back at the house we came to be thought of as the two 'intellectuals', though people were still well disposed towards us. Unlike me, Richard was quite good at sport, and this helped, I think.

The newness of our regime was underscored by the fact that our old housemaster, Snugs Burleigh, had retired at the same time and been replaced by an air force officer newly back from the war, Eric Littlefield. His nickname, which he brought with him, was 'Pongo', the genus name for orang-utans, and an armed services word for an ordinary chap, a bloke. I fell foul of him in the first few days, in a way from which I never recovered in his estimation. On his first tour of the dormitories he had been sitting on the end of a boy's bed chatting, and idly fingering the number card at the foot of the bed, when he noticed some handwriting on the back of the card. He looked closer, and found himself reading an obscene limerick about the boy he was talking to, about him being the object of another (named) boy's lustful desires. Without showing it to the boy, Pongo asked him if he knew what this writing was, and the boy said no, he had not realised it was there. Pongo – who believed him, on the grounds that if he had known it was there he would have erased it – said nothing more, but slipped the card into his pocket. During the next couple of days he hunted around to find whose handwriting it matched. It matched mine.

I was summoned to his study. The conversation went something like this.

'Have you been writing anything, er, shall we say indiscreet recently?'

'No, sir.'

'Are you sure?'

'Yes, sir.'

'Search your mind. Can you think of anything, er – well, I'll be blunt, *indecent*, that you've been unwise enough to commit to paper?'

I was baffled. 'No, sir.'

Pongo produced the card and handed it across to me. 'Is this your handwriting?'

I was discombobulated. I went lobster red. I had written that limerick a full two years before, in a different life. At that age, and in a school, two years is an aeon, and I had long ago forgotten all about it. Obviously I had written the limerick on the boy's bed card for him to stumble across at some future time, but he never had, and then I had forgotten about it myself.

Almost lockjawed with embarrassment, I explained this to Pongo, who told me in return how he had found the card. At the end of it all he said: 'I believe you. I accept that you wrote this a very long time ago. In fact I think I can see the difference in your handwriting. But the question is, is it true?'

'What do you mean, sir?'

'Is what you've written on the card true? Did these things actually happen?'

This was a shock. I was trapped. And I was tongue-tied. What I had written contained much truth, if exaggerated, but our schoolboy code made it impossible for any boy to say such things about another boy to any master.

Pongo tried to help me out.

'The boy has no idea what you've written here, still less who has written it. If you tell me, I give you my word I'll never say anything to him about it. But I want to know if it's true.'

'No, sir, it isn't.'

'Not any of it?'

'No, sir.'

'Not a word of truth in any of it?'

'No, sir.'

I could see he was angered and frustrated by the fact that he had no way of knowing whether what I was saying now was true or not. He decided to put the boot in.

'What you're telling me is that all this is nothing but the product of your dirty mind?'

'Yes, sir.'

The lobster blush, which had started to fade, came back more intensely than before. But Pongo was not going to let it go at that. To me standing pillar-box red in front of him he said: 'You made it all up? It's all lies – entirely the creation of *your* filthy imagination?'

'Yes, sir.'

As ordeals go it was quite a prize-winner, with me a brand-new monitor and him a brand-new housemaster. For starting off on the wrong foot with a new boss in his and your first few days it would be hard to beat. Pongo always disliked me after that, disapproved of me and distrusted me; and if it comes to that I was never a fan of his. But he never said anything to the boy. For obvious reasons I did not do so either. So no harm came of it, to anyone except me. But I felt myself to have been disastrously unlucky.

To complete the total clear-out at the top of the house, we acquired a new junior housemaster called Ronald Styles. He was a young teacher of music with an ambition to become a concert pianist. His playing was so good that this would have been a worthwhile hope but for his personality, which was too neurotic and unstable to thrive in the stressed, competitive world of international music-making. He had the worst stammer I have ever come across: when talking to him, one had to wait for what seemed like an endless time while he repeated the same ghastly, gasping sound

innumerable times in his attempt to get a word out, his lower jaw
flapping right down to his chest. It was painful. But he took his
ambitions seriously, and worked hard at them. At the time of his
arrival he was teaching himself to memorise the solo part of
Brahms's Second Piano Concerto, a massive work, unusually difficult as well as unusually long. He would often seek me out in the
dayroom and invite me to his study to listen to him play it: he
said it helped him to have someone listening, because he played
differently if projecting to an audience, even an audience of one.
I would turn the pages for him, but since he was trying to avoid
looking at the music he never prompted me, and I had to concen-
trate. I learnt the work almost by heart myself. Being a music
teacher he could hardly stop himself from instructing me, so in
addition to the score-reading and his performances I was given a
lot of analysis. It all added up to quite an intensive study of the
concerto on my part, and I found this hugely satisfying. It was
already a work I greatly loved. Just as my favourite violin concerto
was Brahms's, so this became my favourite piano concerto.

I still carry in my mind another performance of it, by Claudio
Arrau, that I heard at about the same time, on the radio in the
dayroom. Under Snugs Burleigh we had not had a radio, because
he would not allow it, and this had been a source of some bitter-
ness on our part; but then, to our astonishment (and, I must say,
exasperation), he made us a present of one when he left. It made
a huge difference to my life. My new-found freedom to stay up
late meant that I could listen to concerts when almost no one
else was around – and a lot of the classical music on radio was
broadcast late in the evening. The starvation of orchestral music
during term-time that had plagued me throughout my time at
Christ's Hospital came to an end.

Another of my important new freedoms was the freedom to go
out of bounds by myself. With money I got from my father I
bought a clapped-out old bicycle from a boy who was leaving, and

spent hours cycling around the villages in the surrounding countryside. (This, incidentally, was the only time in my life when I have
had a bicycle.) My studies in medieval history were giving me an
interest in village churches, and I was learning to read the history
of a village from its church. The sheer number of medieval
churches in England is unique, simply because no large-scale war
has ravaged its countryside for nearly a thousand years. And it
was always villages or towns that I was most interested in, not the
scenery that I cycled through in between. Other people were
always going on about how beautiful the countryside was, and I
liked it well enough, but countryside has never been an object of
much interest to me in itself. I am, I know, an excessively urban
person, and I wish this were not so, but the only natural surroundings that set fire to my imagination are large-scale things – water-
falls, lakes, deserts, mountains, and heavenly bodies outside our
orbit altogether. Otherwise, the only things in my environment
that switch me on are human activities.

I suppose it was during this period of my life that I began to
find my feet as a person – to become myself. Obviously my age
was the central factor in this, but there were other things too –
a combination of freedom and responsibility which, though they
came because of the age I was, might not have come in other
surroundings. I was well educated, which again could easily not
have happened. I knew I was lucky. I remember one day standing
in the school library and thinking: I can choose any path in life
that I want, do anything I'm capable of. If I want to be a doctor,
I can be a doctor. If I want to be an architect, I can be an architect. If I like, I can be a lawyer – or a teacher – anything. It's up
to me. I've got the choice. All doors are open. I won't be in this
position always, and it may not last for long, but I'm in it now. I
was past the age at which my father had had to leave school and
start work, in a job that bored him; and here was I, no more
deserving than he, enjoying a life full of all the opportunities that

he had been denied. This was one of the things that helped give me a sense of my own differentness, a sense of self, a feeling that I was on a path of my own. I was even beginning to look like a young man now, nearly six foot tall, still growing. People were beginning to talk to me as if I were a grown-up.

Because of my greater freedom, the difference between life at school and life at home narrowed. Instead of being two different environments to which I belonged equally, and adapted alternately, it was now more a case of me being the same me in both places regardless. I did not yet know Nietzsche's injunction: 'Dare to be who you are,' but it was what I was beginning to do, with increasing confidence.

It was unlucky for me that, just as I was finding my feet in this way, the ground beneath them was shifted permanently by two earthquakes in quick succession. Within six months of one another the two people I loved most in the world died; first my grandfather and then my father. It was like two shocks of the same earthquake, and it created a chasm in time, such that for years afterwards I was inclined to think of life before and life after my father's death as two different lives, both of them lived by me, the first in a welcoming world in which I was growing up and which contained this person that I loved so much, the second in a colder world that did not contain him and in which I was a grown-up myself. In a way it was as if I replaced him. But I was not an improvement, and the loss was irreparable.

Something about my father changed during the last full year of his life, which was 1946. Looking back, it seems fairly clear that he fell into a depression. It might have been the earliest symptom of the cancer that was going to bring his life to an end in May 1947, but I do not think so. It was more like what is now called a mid-life crisis, the male menopause. The challenges and tensions of wartime were over, but for him a return to normality meant a return to boredom. Everyone was talking about the brave new world we were going to create, but to him the future offered nothing either brave or new, merely a reversion to the rut he had been in between leaving school and the war. His youth was over, he had been too old to serve in the armed forces, yet at forty-four he was still an employee of his father, on a weekly wage. And when, in due course, he should inherit the shop, the work itself would go on being the same. His marriage had been a long-running disaster, and was now falling to pieces. His children were becoming grown-ups, increasingly independent. It could even be that he felt I was overtaking him: I was now as tall as he, with the youth he had lost, and better educated, and was apparently moving into a future rich with opportunities – a future that at the same time offered him nothing. It would be little wonder if he was depressed. Before his own father, whom he dearly loved, was diagnosed with cancer, my father had already become quiet and withdrawn. My grandfather's death sentence added one more grisly fact to his life.

To me, living away from home, my grandfather's illness was something that happened at a distance. I would receive occasional bulletins but be unaware of day-to-day realities. Some of the information reaching me was misleading. It is difficult nowadays to get people to understand this, but at that time serious illness was a taboo subject – especially mental illness and cancer – even within families: people simply did not talk about it, if they could avoid it. When they did talk about it they used euphemisms and evasions: they would hint and imply, and expect you to understand what they meant, without them having actually to say it. It was considered especially necessary to shield the old and the young from bad news. It was not the exception but the rule for a person dying of cancer not to be told – perhaps even not to want to be told – although his next of kin would be informed. All this has now gone, or most of it, but it was then the atmosphere that we all lived in. To me it seemed as if my grandfather had died before I really knew what was going on. It came as a great shock.

It happened in November 1946, and he was seventy. I was sixteen. He was buried in St Pancras Cemetery. I went to the funeral in my Christ's Hospital uniform because those were the only clothes I had that were suitable for such an occasion. I remember the stony misery that filled my heart on the way to the cemetery as I sat in the undertaker's car with Bill and Peggy Pett. When I turned away from the graveside my eyes filled with tears. Bill, moving alongside me, gripped my hand and squeezed it painfully hard. Only that prevented the tears from flowing. This was unprecedented in my experience within my family, a physical gesture of emotional understanding. I was astonished by it, especially coming from Bill, whom I had never liked. I looked on him differently after that.

I had always taken it for granted that when my grandfather died, the family shop would come to my father. And so had my father. But it did not. After the usual brief delay, during which everyone waited and wondered, the contents of my grandfather's will were disclosed, and it turned out that his whole estate had been left to my grandmother. I was not present when my father was told this, but the description I heard was so lurid that it has remained with me all my life, as if I had been there. He went green. And then, for just a moment before recovering control, he looked as if despair overwhelmed him. At the age of forty-five he found himself embarking on a new life as an employee of his mother.

I do not know exactly what went on within the family after that, partly because I was away at school, though most of it would have been hidden from me anyway. Certainly there was a lot of electricity in the air, and I knew that high-tension diplomacy was going on. My father made it clear that he was not prepared to carry on in this situation, except for a transitional period. My grandmother was now an old lady who had had nothing to do with the management of the shop for many years, and could not conceivably run it herself. If my father was not prepared to run it for her, her (exceedingly powerful) instinct was to sell it for as much money as she could get for it. Her other children would benefit more from this – eventually, at her death – than from any of the alternatives. On the other hand, they themselves felt that it would be unjust to my father, who had given his life to the shop in a way that none of them had, and had been in effect its manager for a long time – he would now be left with nothing, not even a job. It was one of those family situations where everyone's honest and genuine interests are at odds. What natural justice would have decreed was fairly clear. My grandfather should have left some money to each of his daughters and the shop to my father, with the proviso that a proportion of the income from it should go to my grandmother for the rest of her lifetime – a share smaller than the one he had been drawing for the two of them, but enough for her needs. He had in any case left her the house they lived in, and the value of that could eventually have been divided between the two daughters. I believe that what my father tried to do was to broker a deal along these lines – but of course he was in the invidious, mortifying position of asking for sacrifices from everyone else while seeking advantages for himself. It was painful all round. These were, I know, bruising times for everybody: I heard some damaging exchanges and some bristling silences. We were back to family drama at its worst, as in the old days.

At what stage my father was diagnosed as having cancer is something my memory has blotted out, but while all these things were going on he was becoming more and more seriously ill. All his adult life he had been practically a chain-smoker, and now he was found to have lung cancer. In those days the two things were not known to be connected. As in the case of my grandfather, the full reality of the situation was kept from me. It so happened that the three months before my father took to what turned out to be his deathbed coincided almost exactly with one of my school terms, so I was away from home for that period and did not know what was going on. When nightmare forebodings invaded my mind, I tried to shake them off, and told myself that I was being irrational – that if things were as bad as that I would have been told something by now. When only four days of the term were left, Pongo called me into his study in the late afternoon. Our conversation went roughly as follows.

'I've got some bad news for you, I'm afraid. Your father is seriously ill.'

'I know, sir.'

'Your mother telephoned. They want you at home. I think you'd better go tomorrow.'

I thought: why? There isn't anything I can do about it. I said: 'But I shall be going home on Tuesday anyway. He's been ill all term.'

'Your family think it would be best for you to go straight away. The doctors have just seen him, and they think he's very unwell.'

I tried to avoid engaging with the implication of this, but it got to me just the same, and my vision swam.

Tears seemed to fill my whole head. In a voice that I heard cracking about all over the place I said: 'Can you tell me any more, sir – what the situation actually is?'

He started fiddling with a packet of cigarettes, taking a long time to get one out. He always did this when he was embarrassed. But he was always shy when talking to a boy.

'There's nothing more I can tell you,' he said. 'The doctors are concerned, and your family want you at home. I think you ought to go tomorrow morning by the . . .' and he told me what train to catch.

Whether it was that evening or after breakfast next morning I do not know, but I went to an ordinary daily chapel service before catching the train home. Being surrounded by people singing hymns and psalms was too much for me, and I stood there with tears pouring down my face. Still, no one had actually said anything – no one had said my father was dying, or even that his life was in danger. So I still struggled to tell myself that my fears were exaggerated, that they were reactions based on ignorance, that if things were really as bad as all that someone would have said something to me by this time. Yet part of me – a still-only-just-submerged part – knew what I was steeling myself against. I have been told that people who face death often go through such feelings. I was like a condemned man half aware that he was in denial.

When I got off the train at Victoria my sister Joan was on the platform. Walking up to her I made a for-God's-sake-tell-me-what's-happening gesture, eyebrows raised and eyes wide open, hands moving outwards and upwards.

'Don't worry, Bryan,' she said feelingly. 'He's going to die quite quietly.'

Victoria station spun round me, then my vision blacked out (or rather greyed out) and I thought I was fainting. I groped blindly at Joan for support, and she led me to a bench in the station concourse, where we sat for some time while I cranked myself up into coming to terms with the shock. My father was not just dying, he was dying *now*, and I was immediately about to see him dying, and he would be dead in a couple of days.

Joan was deeply upset. 'Didn't you know?' she asked, distraught. 'I thought you knew.'

Haltingly, and with long silences, she told me what had been going on in my absence. The story ended with our father taking to his bed the day before, and the doctor saying to my mother that he would live for only another two or three days, whereupon my mother telephoned my housemaster.

'I was the one saying all along that you mustn't be given a shock, that you must be told,' Joan said. 'And now this.'

During all that time my mother had put off telling me because there was nothing I could do, and she saw no point in upsetting me to no purpose. Joan had protested to her: 'Yes, but Dad's going to die quite soon, and when it does happen it mustn't come to Bryan as a total shock, a bolt from the blue.'

When, the previous day, they had decided to telephone the school, they had agreed that they would ask my housemaster to break the news to me that my father was on the point of death, and to send me straight home. After making the telephone call my mother had told Joan that she had done this. I do not know whether the failure of nerve was on her part with Pongo or on Pongo's part with me. Both would have been in character, but I think, given the circumstances, the latter is more likely. Anyway, Joan had assumed that Pongo had told me. When she met me on the platform her first concern had been to assure me that our father was not in pain, and that I was not on the point of witnessing nightmarish death throes – she had interpreted my facial expression and hand gestures as a way of signalling shock-horror at what I was about to face. Her first words had been intended to put my mind at rest.

'There's nothing to be frightened of,' she said. 'He's quite calm, and he looks normal. He's being given a lot of morphine. The doctor says he'll just drift away. If he's not asleep, he'll talk to you quite naturally.'

But I was terrified. To see my father and know that he was about to die was more than I believed I could bear. But there was no alternative, at this point, to going home and facing it. Dragging myself away from that bench in Victoria station was one of the hardest things I have ever done.

As it turned out, my father lived not for two or three days but for six weeks. He was dying throughout the whole of that school holiday and well into the following term, and at no point did he or the rest of us know how much longer it – he – was going to go on. It was always true that he might die next day. I was at home throughout it all, eventually coming to an arrangement with Pongo that I would return to school the day after the funeral, whenever that might be.

My life contains two episodes which were literally traumatic in the effect they had on me, and this was one of them. The other was to come in my twenties, and had to do with my marriage. After each of them, I was not the same person again. With the death of my father, the human being I supremely loved, loved unconditionally, was dying in front of my eyes. At one point he said: 'It feels to me as if I've been in this bed half my life,' and that was how it felt to me too. I was in a state of intolerable and yet – of course, it had to be – tolerated anguish, unbearable yet borne, and so always at the end of my tether. I stayed at home most of the time, helping out, sitting for long periods with him, unable to think of anything else, not much wanting to go anywhere else. There were, however, a few times when I was overwhelmed by a need to get away from it, and then I would just go out, it scarcely mattered where. On one of those occasions something happened that I have always remembered with gratitude.

It was a Sunday afternoon. I took a tube train to Green Park, blind with misery, and wandered around the park for a while. Then I crossed Piccadilly and began to drift through the empty streets of Mayfair. In those days London's West End was notorious for its street prostitution, thick on the ground at every time of day, and since I had grown to adult height I was used to being accosted. For any full-grown male walking alone it was, literally, an everyday occurrence. I was ravenously tempted, but I had never been with a prostitute, not out of anything to do with rectitude but from fear of venereal disease. One of the salient themes of wartime propaganda had been the dangers and horrors of this, and it was also the subject of many schoolboy jokes, so I thought I knew about it. On me, at least, the propaganda had its effect.

Occasionally I might be lured into conversation by one of the girls, especially one close to my age – sometimes they stopped you by blocking your path, and then it was difficult not to speak – but in any case they were usually (not always) asking for more money than I had. It was only by the narrowest margins that my resistance stayed unbroken. My custom, when accosted, was to veer past the girl saying nothing at all, possibly shaking my head, usually avoiding her eyes, and no doubt looking as scared as a rabbit. But on this occasion, lost in grief, I hardly noticed.

One, however, caught my eye. She was standing looking at me as I approached her: older than the others – old enough to be my mother – and very expensively, yet well, dressed. When I drew level with her, instead of the usual opening she said: 'You're unhappy. What is it?'

I stopped beside her.

'My father's dying,' I said. I made no effort to remove the devastated look from my face, but I did, as it were, engage with her.

'Do you love him very much?'

'Yes.'

She began to talk to me about this with ordinary sympathy. She had a French accent and was a person of warmth and charm. There was a fellow feeling here that I was not used to. After a few minutes of this we turned and walked along the pavement, very slowly, side by side; and for something like half an hour we wandered the streets, she comforting me. Because I was in the state I was in, I do not remember anything she said; but she provided me with such solace as no one else did in all that terrible six weeks. When I got home I found it bordering on the impossible not to talk about her, and yet I had to stop myself. I knew that my family would be unspeakably shocked at the very idea of my spending time with a prostitute, and would probably not believe that all we did was talk.

Most of the time my father spent dying he was sitting up in

bed, and always had someone sitting in the chair beside him. He assured us he was not afraid of death, and I think it was true. When he said it he did not seem to me to be protesting too much; and he was concerned for us, reassuring us. I was struck by the fact that each time he said it he added that he had never been afraid of death. I envied that, and could not understand how it was possible. After my grandfather's funeral he had said to Joan: 'I've never been sure whether there's anything after death or not, but now I'm sure there is something.'

He was frightened, though, of being left alone. It was essential for him to have someone always there beside him. And he wanted to hold the hand of whoever it was, even my mother. It was always he who held their hand, not they his. Each of us in turn would sit with him for hours with our hand clasped in his, sometimes talking, sometimes not. One's hand would become cramped, or tired, or begin to feel awkward; but if we tried to change its position he would grasp desperately at it as if it were being taken away. My mother hated this, and spent as little time with him as she could, so it was usually either Joan or me, or one of his many visitors. We always warned them before they went in to see him that he would want to hold their hand.

When it was me sitting beside him he liked to talk about either my interests or my future. Why did I like Sibelius so much – what was so special about his music? How sure were my teachers that I was going to get in to Oxford? What did I want to do after that? My seventeenth birthday fell in the middle of all this, and he gave me the biggest single present I had ever received. It was a complete recording of the third act of *The Valkyrie*, on eight discs, secretly procured by my sister. I unwrapped it at his bedside, and will never forget the expression on his face, and in his voice, as he said simply: 'What you wanted.' It was something he himself would have loved to have, and had never felt able to afford.

While he was on his deathbed my grandmother sold him the

shop. This was the outcome of months of family negotiation, and was the cause of resentments that never afterwards faded. My grandmother, having agreed to the deal before she realised how ill he was, thought she had to keep her word to him before he died. The documents were signed and witnessed on his bed, with only the participants in the room, while my mother was in the kitchen. Since he was obviously never going to get out of that bed, my grandmother was in effect selling the shop to my mother, and yet not allowing her any say in the matter. I think my grandmother's point of view was that it had taken her and my father months to reach an agreement, and however favourable to him its terms were – and they were – my mother, not having been party to it, would be under no obligation to accept it, and would almost certainly not accept it, because she could be relied on to think, of any proposal, that it was doing her down. So if my father died before the deal was done, my grandmother would face the impossible task of reaching a reasonable agreement with my mother, as the only alternative to disinheriting her son's family by selling the business elsewhere. My father, I expect, took the same view. So I believe they both saw themselves as forcing a bargain on my mother. Their intentions were good, on both sides, and the financial consequences of their action were fair, even though it meant that death duties had to be paid twice in six months on the same small family business. My mother and sister bitterly resented the whole proceeding. They saw my grandmother and Aunt Hilda as acting in an underhand way, taking advantage of a man drugged with morphine, and on his deathbed. It is certainly true that my mother was shut out of a deal to which she was, in all but a technicality, one of the main parties. But she could not contest the legitimacy of the deal without, if successful, losing her own inheritance. It ensured the utmost acrimony within the family after my father's death, when my mother found herself landed with a shop that she was even more incapable of running than my grandmother had been.

The period during which my father was unable to run the shop was quite short, only the last couple of months of his life. During that time my grandmother was there nearly every day, and had the full-time assistance of Mr Davis, who had worked part-time for us ever since I could remember. My aunts Peggy and Hilda had long ago been used to helping out at Christmas, and now contributed to the best of their ability. So the shop remained open full-time. But the whole arrangement had a desperate air about it, an air of emergency. Mr Davis, though well meaning and honest, was unintelligent, and passive to a degree, with not the slightest initiative – and it is not possible for women to run a men's clothes shop. They cannot take a customer's measurements, least of all his inside leg. Fittings and alterations offer endless opportunities for embarrassment, and did this a great deal more in the social atmosphere of the 1940s than they would today. The situation was fraught with difficulty. And this was the state the shop was in when it passed to my mother, who knew next to nothing about the business. Not surprisingly, she was to sell it after a couple of years. And that is why I, born and brought up as an only son in the third generation of a family business, never inherited it.

During that desperate period before his death, my father continued to supply management consultancy from his bed. But his energies were fading fast, and his judgement must have been affected by the morphine. After several weeks of sitting up in bed he developed a bedsore, and this became a torture to him, the plague of his life. That tiny sore caused him a degree of physical pain and mental distress that was almost unmanageable, more so than the cancer that was killing him.

My problems were nothing compared to his. But I too, in my way, was living at a level of stress that I could almost not bear. My capacity to love unconditionally was being impaired, since the suffering it now involved me in was more than I could take. It was, after all, not the first time. My infant relationship with my mother had been a disaster for me – and now there was this. Drawing back from emotional involvement was not a conscious decision; in fact it was some years before I realised it had happened. I had – altogether unconsciously – become unable to give myself totally, because I had not once but twice, and before I was fully grown up, been devastated by the consequences of doing so.

There came a morning when I was woken by the sound of my mother thundering past my bedroom door to my sister's room, shouting: 'He's gone! He's gone!' Then both voices were raised, and they went back past my door to my parents' room. I got out of bed and went into the passage, and was about to go in to them when I found myself rooted to the spot outside the door. I could not bring myself to do it. I was paralysed with terror at the prospect of seeing my father's dead body. It was the same immobilising terror as had engulfed me in Victoria station.

From inside the room the women called out: 'Come in!' But I could not.

And I never did see him dead. The fact that he actually was dead, there in the next room, was itself nightmare enough. I did go into the room once before the funeral, but by then he was laid down flat on the bed and covered by a sheet. Even so, I was horrified by the knobbly bumps in the sheet where his knees and shoulders were. This experience was followed by some days when he was lying uncovered in a coffin, and most of our visitors went in to see him. One of these declined the invitation with the words: 'I prefer to keep a happy memory as the last one I have of him,' and I seized on that gratefully, docketing it in my mind for my own use.

English's, the undertakers in Hoxton Street, arranged the burial of my father next to my grandfather in St Pancras Cemetery. Again I wore my Christ's Hospital clothes. The whole occasion was so like my grandfather's funeral, which had happened six months before, that it felt dream-like. We went through exactly the same motions: the same cars, the same drivers, the same route, the same rituals; only the corpse was different. But whereas I have never forgotten the concrete-like inner misery that filled me at my grandfather's funeral, I remember nothing at all of what I felt at my father's. Or perhaps, rather, I felt nothing. It was as if my whole world were dead, and my feelings dead too.

Nor do I remember anything of the journey back home: I think we must have travelled in silence. The first memory I have is of my mother and me entering the flat and flopping down in the living room. She looked at me for a long time, as if reflecting on a new, serious thought, then said: 'If you think I'm going to keep you at your age, you're mistaken.'

That these were the very first words she spoke to me was a shock greater than I can express. I looked at her, stunned. This was an aspect of my father's death that I had not considered, the implication that henceforth I would be financially dependent on my mother. It was as if an ice-cold waterfall poured over me. In an instant, the feeling that everything was finished was superseded by the realisation that a whole new, unlooked-for world was about to begin.

I just sat there taking it in.

She went on: 'You're old enough now to look after yourself.'

I still sat there, trying to come to terms with the fact that my life was being transformed even more than I had bargained for. From now on everything was going to be different, in startling and unpleasant ways that I had not begun to consider.

'As far as I'm concerned,' she said, 'you're on your own from now on.'

In existing circumstances, the only place I could go to from home was school, and I had anyway arranged to go there next day. Years later I discovered that it was already an established policy with Christ's Hospital to waive all further fees for any boy if either of his parents died while he was at the school; so the reality of my situation was that I could live at school free henceforth, until the normal time came for me to leave. But I had no idea of this. No one told me. Communication on this point between the school and my mother was not mentioned to me by either party. Transactions at such a level had always gone on above my head, without anyone talking to me about them. The consequences of this piece of ignorance on my part were to distort my life for several years. All I knew was that my fees had been raised by the school to £24 a year, and I took it for granted, without even thinking about it, that if the payments stopped I would have to leave. In any case, apart from money, my mother was now my legal guardian, the one with the power to make decisions for my life. And if she refused to keep me on at school it would put paid to my hopes of going to university. My heart was now firmly set on going to Oxbridge; and David Roberts thought I was pretty well bound to get in. He was going, he said, to enter me for a scholarship to Balliol when I was ready, which would be in about eighteen months' time, when I was eighteen and a half. He said he was pretty sure that even if Balliol did not give me a scholarship they would offer me a place; and in these new days of government grants that came to almost the same thing. In the event, my complete failure to understand my situation resulted in my not going to Balliol. But that is a story that will have to wait until we come to it. I went back to school the next day, assuming that my fees had been paid only until the end of term.

CHAPTER TWENTY-FIVE

On the train back to Christ's Hospital I found myself disturbed not only about my father's death and my endangered future but about what I was going to say regarding my mother's attitude. It seemed to me so base, so ignominious. I felt not so much ashamed of her as ashamed *for* her – and I did not want others to see her in this light. I came to the conclusion that although I could see no farther ahead than the end of term, I nevertheless did have until then before being compelled to make the decisions that I was going to have to make; and therefore it would be foolish not to give myself the full time to consider them. I ought to do this before rushing to talk about the situation to other people. It was characteristic of my young self, then and for some time after, to make my most important decisions inside myself, without discussing them with anyone else, or asking for advice. I took it for granted that only I could know what I wanted to do, and I did not see what anyone else could contribute. In my experience, people always tried to get you to do things you knew you were not going to do, and then themselves became part of the problem.

As a matter of routine, the first thing I had to do when I got back to school was report to my housemaster. He had unexpected news for me. I was to go to France for several weeks, and as soon as could be arranged. Christ's Hospital had set up an exchange with the Lycée Hôche in Versailles, and a number of seventeen-year-olds were going from one to the other for the remainder of the school year. Four boys from Christ's Hospital had gone already; and in my absence a decision had been made that it would be good for me to go too. Indeed it was. I was plunged immediately into the distractions and practicalities – and excitements – of preparing for it.

Never had I been out of England. I needed to get my first passport; but in this and other respects the school had already made preparations: since I was under age, and legally the school was *in loco parentis* when I was there, it had acted for me. David Roberts was especially supportive. He gave me excellent advice, and not too much of it, about what to see and do in Paris. He also commanded that I send him regular reports in the form of a long letter once a week; and if, he said, I did this to his satisfaction he would give me my buttons when I returned. This was Christ's Hospital parlance for making me a Grecian, one of the school's elite. It meant I would hand in the standard blue coat I wore in exchange for a longer one of finer material, with velvet collar and cuffs, and an outpouring of big silver buttons down the front. Grecians were Olympian figures. They trod a different earth from the rest of us.

I could not bring myself to talk even to David about my mother's refusal to keep me, so although I expected to have to leave the school I accepted his offer with what I hoped would appear a good grace. It also seemed to me that going away would help me to think. In any event I was caught up in the excitement of the coming trip. Between 1939 and 1945 none of the inhabitants of Britain had been allowed out of the country except on war service, unless they had some extra-special reason. The fact that the whole of Europe was under the heel of fascist dictators doubled the feeling we all had of being cut off, as well as different, living in a fortress with the drawbridge up. During those formative years of mine, between the ages of nine and fifteen, I lived in a society in which private foreign travel did not exist, and could be thought about only in daydreams. I had had many such daydreams. But we were still scarcely two years from the end of the war, and still living on a semi-war footing: hundreds of thousands of people were still in the armed forces (the post-war Labour government staggered demobilisation over a period of years to prevent civilian unemployment); the whole population still had food rationing; there were almost prohibitive currency restrictions on foreign travel. It had not as yet occurred to me to think of such travel as available to me. In any case, aside from all this, and leaving the war aside too, people had travelled independently a great deal less until then than they do now. Before the war a majority of people in all social classes took their holidays in the British Isles – those who went abroad had a high profile but were a minority even among the well-to-do. The other members of my family, and almost everyone else we knew, had been abroad either once or not at all; and I believe this was typical of the population as a whole – I am talking, of course, of private travel. So I was now on the point of a tremendous experience, a Big Thing, to a degree not easy to convey.

Nearly all international travel was then by train and boat, so I travelled to Paris via Newhaven and Dieppe. It was typical of the wartime nature of conditions still obtaining that to get from Christ's Hospital, in Sussex, to Newhaven, also in Sussex, I had to travel on five different trains (with a great deal of luggage). The school had decreed, as it always did, that I should wear Christ's Hospital uniform on the journey, and not change into other clothes until I arrived. This made me an object of interest on the boat. The French passengers assumed I was some kind of cadet priest – I was now six feet tall. I was to find that I was taken for something of that sort whenever I wore those clothes in France, and it caused me to be treated with a tiny but noticeable touch of respect, especially by women. It helped to alleviate what would otherwise have been a gruesomely self-conscious ordeal.

At the Gare Saint-Lazare I was met by the headmaster of the lycée. This impressed me: it was unthinkable that the corresponding thing would have happened at Christ's Hospital, despite the fact that the school had its own railway station. His title was Monsieur le Proviseur, his name Casati, and he looked like Humphrey Bogart, complete with fedora – which made him un-headmaster-like, conferring higher status. He had taught French for many years (I think twenty) at one of the Scottish universities, so he felt at home in Britain and spoke the language effortlessly. He led me straight to another train in Saint-Lazare, a suburban commuter train between Paris and Versailles, which was to become my lifeline.

The Lycée Hôche is regarded as one of the best lycées in France. It has quite a grand set of buildings on one of the three great avenues that converge on the front gates of the Palace of Versailles, and is only a few hundred yards from the palace. It was built as a convent in the seventeenth century, but the French Revolution liquidated the monasteries, and some time after that the buildings were turned into a school (whose origins are therefore quite like those of Christ's Hospital). It has, or had when I was there, no playing fields or gardens, and only one open courtyard, so the boys – of whom there were at least as many as at Christ's Hospital – were indoors nearly all the time. Many were day boys with homes in Versailles; but many came from other parts of France, and some from Africa: all these were boarders. There were no such things as separate houses, dayrooms or studies. If you wanted to be by yourself you found an empty classroom. The amount of time we spent working was exactly twice what it had been at Christ's Hospital: there, on our heaviest days, we had done five and a quarter hours' work, whereas here we did ten and a half. We got up at 6.00, did an hour of supervised prep from 6.30 to 7.30, and only then had breakfast. From 8.00 to midday we had four one-hour classroom periods, with breaks of three minutes between each. At noon we had lunch. From 12.30 to 1.30 we were free. From 1.30 to 2.00 we had prep, and then two one-hour periods. From 4.00 to 5.00 we were free again. Then we had three hours of prep, followed by dinner at 8.00. At 8.30 we were free for half an hour, and then went to bed.

There was no sport, no organised games of any kind. Nor was there a monitorial system, so none of the boys had any responsibility. This resulted, inevitably, in their behaving irresponsibly, especially since the boarders were not allowed out of the school between Sunday evening and Saturday lunchtime, and had nowhere to let off steam except in the classroom. Most of the masters found it an unending struggle to keep order, though a few had natural authority. Outside the classroom they had no contact with the boys: all other organisation and discipline were in the hands of a separate profession, the *surveillants* (supervisors), who did not teach, but ruled over the boys and kept them in order, shepherding them from one place to another, and doling out punishments.

There was no bath in the lycée, but we were allowed one shower a week. The only sit-down lavatories were in the dormitories, but there was no toilet paper in them (nor in any of the others, which were Turkish-style – you crouched over a hole). The dormitories were kept locked during the day, so one could never change a garment.

The first thing we did when we got out of bed in the morning was shake hands with one another, all of us, standing around in our pyjamas. Hand-shaking between boys went on perpetually: two friends would shake hands each time they met, so it was normal to shake hands with the same person several times a day. The boy in the next bed to me came from Algeria, and while we were shaving in the morning he taught me to write obscene Arabic words on the mirror in shaving soap. The food, of course, was better than I was used to, but we had the same plate throughout a meal and ate successive courses off it; even with meat and vegetables we were given first the one and then, when we had finished it, the other. At dinner red wine was set out on the tables in giant carafes, and this seemed wonderful to me. It was the cheapest institutional *vin ordinaire*, so sour that until you were used to it a single mouthful clenched your face into a fist. The smaller boys would drink it heavily watered, and then slowly reduce the proportion of water as they got older, until in their mid-teens they were drinking it neat. I went through a telescoped version of the same process: it was three weeks before I was able to drink the wine neat. By then I was enjoying it, as you might enjoy a rough and powerful cider.

The classroom work was so challenging that at first I found it tiring, an unprecedented experience for me. In Latin periods we naturally translated Latin into French, and French into Latin; mathematics was, again naturally, mathematics in French; and so on. Even English lessons were not the walkover I had anticipated, because the French boys had been taught English grammar, which I never had, and they and the master were perpetually astonished that I did not know things about the English language that they regarded as elementary. It amazes me now that I was able to keep up in all these subjects, but I just about did, though by the end of each day I was exhausted. And of course I was all the time living my ordinary daily life in French. The English boys had deliberately been put in different classes, so we saw little of one another, and I was speaking French all day. By the end of that term I was talking French with a fluency I have never recaptured.

Two of the boys in my class were from one of France's central African colonies, and were the first blacks I ever talked to. At first it gave me culture shock to hear them bubbling over in voluble and perfect French. One, Coulibali, was very black indeed, and gravely serious; the other was lighter both in colour and personality. They gave the impression of being integrated into the surrounding community with few hints of the racism that would certainly have existed in the Britain of that day. I soon discovered that, because of this difference, Paris was in the process of becoming once more a haven for black Americans, as it had been before the war.

The best of the teachers taught the older boys and were given the title Professor. They were indeed professorial, with thick three-piece suits even in summer, bow ties, and in many cases little pointed beards. The one I liked most was the Latin teacher, a handsome, austere, acidly intelligent man who commanded perfect attention without raising his voice. He was compelling to listen to, and I suppose must have been the first charismatic French intellectual I encountered. And he was the genuine article: unlike most of those I was to come up against later in the world of philosophy, he was a person of real intellectual seriousness and integrity.

I only just missed studying philosophy at the lycée. The boys a year older than me, the eighteen-year-olds, were doing it for their *baccalauréat. Philo*, they called it, and what it meant (quite rightly) was reading Descartes. At that time philosophy was not taught to schoolchildren in England, and I was impressed.

The young are uncannily adaptable. Ever since I was nine years old I had been plunged into one new world after another, and had always adapted quite happily. The Lycée Hôche was no exception. But once I got used to it I began to feel that in one important respect the whole arrangement was point-missing as far as I was concerned. The heart of Paris was twelve miles away, twenty minutes on the train: surely getting to know it would do immeasurably more for my education than would mastering the French vocabulary in mathematics? Little opportunity of doing so had come my way. I decided to take action.

I went to see the headmaster, whom I had always found sympathetic, and put it to him. He took the point at once, but was doubtful whether anything could be done without causing trouble with other people in the school. We had more than one meeting, and he made enquiries, and then shifted his ground. What moved him, I think, was not so much anything to do with me as the fact that any concessions to me would have to be made to the other Christ's Hospital boys, some of whom were proving unable to cope with the ten-and-a-half-hours-a-day, all-of-it-in-French work. Typically, at the Christ's Hospital end, they had not been chosen with that in mind. (Nor had I.) They were floundering, and in need of rescue. Perhaps what I was pressing on him would provide a solution to their problem.

Once Casati decided to change our schedule he decided boldly. He summoned all the English boys to his study and told us that, since much of our supervised prep was for examinations that we were not going to sit, we would be excused two hours of it every day, out of the four and a half of prep. These would be the hours from 5.00 to 7.00, thus giving us three consecutive hours of freedom every afternoon, from 4.00 to 7.00. We could also ask for the whole of each Thursday off, provided it was for a purpose of approved educational value, such as visiting museums or art galleries in Paris. And we could go into Paris on Saturday evenings to a performance by any of the national companies, which would mean classical drama, opera or ballet. We would have to account for where we had been, and be ready to describe what we had seen. We would do this to Mr Rogers, a congenial and very young Scottish student-teacher at the lycée who had been in France for more than a year and spoke excellent French. We would spend two classroom periods a week with him, in which we would raise whatever questions we had about the lycée, and French life generally – manners, customs, food, clothes, transport, politics, anything, and especially the language.

It was an astute arrangement. We would still be doing eight and a half hours of schoolwork on four days of the week, plus

Saturday mornings, but we now had a real chance to get to know Paris. And get to know it I did. At first I rushed in there every afternoon, to spend a couple of hours just wandering the streets and avenues. Paris is significantly smaller than London, much easier to walk across and around, and to get to know. On my wanderings I would go up or inside anything I walked past that was free – monuments, churches, museums, art galleries, department stores – or at any rate free to me as an *étudiant anglais*. Often I would devote the whole afternoon to going back to a place that had caught my fancy the previous day. The entire experience was a feast, and I lived in a state of satisfied greed. It was the only city I had been in that could begin to compare with London, and yet it was fascinatingly different. The cost of these daily excursions was no more than that of a tube journey from Arnos Grove to Piccadilly Circus, which I was used to doing on a daily basis. Once in Paris I rarely took a bus or metro, but walked everywhere.

However, I was taking in so much during these three-hour afternoons that the time limit became more and more irksome. Getting back to the lycée became a scramble. Sometimes I was late, and began to receive warnings from the *Surveillant-Général*, Monsieur de l'Eau, that my permission to go out would be curtailed. Holding his wristwatch under my nose, and beating time in the air between the two with his fingertips, he would say, with dramatic emphasis and pauses worthy of the Comédie Française: '*Vous êtes – en retard. Il ne faut pas être – en retard. Il faut prendre un train – qui arrive – à l'heure.*' And stalk off. That was it. He meant it. So I changed my habits. There was also another consideration. I had so little money that I was beginning to feel the need to reduce even my small daily expenditure – I needed to have quite a few days when I spent nothing at all. So I stopped going in to Paris on most of those short afternoons, and left my visits for Thursdays and weekends when I had more time. Instead, I went to the Palace of Versailles, or rather to its park, which was huge. The summer of

1947 was one of the hottest on record, and I found it wonderful
to be able to get out of the lycée and go somewhere nearby where
I could wander around, or lie about, in a vast and beautiful park,
and do that every day. I would usually take a book, or something
to write with. I remember the deeply satisfied disgust with which
I hurled a hardbound diary that I had been keeping for months
into one of the ornamental canals.

The whole experience of being in France turned from being
a partially frustrating one to being something wonderful. I loved
Paris. And friends among the day boys were now inviting me to
their homes in Versailles. Lunch parties were given for me, which
was a new experience. One was given by the headmaster, at which
I was entertainingly taught the basics about wines and brandies –
and given food of a quality I had never experienced. At one such
party, which was in a Paris restaurant, I saw a steak for the first
time. I thought it a clever idea – I must remember, I thought, to
alert people to this when I get home. There were several operas
I saw for the first time: *Rigoletto* and *Il Trovatore*, *Thaïs* (for the
only time) and my first Wagner opera, *Lohengrin*. This last was an
extraordinary experience for me. Since I had been an impas-
sioned lover of Wagner's music for half my life, and never seen
any of his operas on the stage, simply seeing one was an epoch-
making event. In addition to that, *Lohengrin* had been my first
love with Wagner's music, and for that reason had always had
special significance for me. And here it was – being sung in French.
I had never heard Wagner in French before, and rarely have I
heard it since. It does not sound at all well. Since I knew only the
extracts I had heard on records, or as bleeding chunks in concert
programmes, to begin with I knew every note of the prelude, but
then came a very long stretch of music I had never heard before
– followed suddenly by Elsa's Dream, which I knew well. This
disconcerting pattern was repeated all evening, and was at its most
extreme in the last act. A long outpouring of wonderful music

that I had never heard in my life would suddenly become four minutes of music that I knew by heart, which would then issue in more music that I did not know, followed by another four minutes that I knew by heart – and so on, over and over. It was almost disorienting, an experience I was to live through with each of Wagner's operas in turn over the next few years. It caused me to hear music I knew already in a new way, because hearing it in context for the first time. The supreme revelation was the moment-by-moment integration of orchestra with stage action. Sometimes the orchestral music seemed to be radiating out of the characters. Up to now I had taken in Wagner as music alone, but from this time onwards I was to experience the music as part of a larger whole. The conductor on this first occasion was Inghelbrecht, the leading interpreter (and a personal friend) of Debussy: he gave the music an eloquent combination of forward drive and delicacy. Delicacy was something I was not used to in Wagner.

Straight theatre in Paris made less impression on me, chiefly because I disliked the style of acting, which was inflated and rhetorical – operatic, in fact. It was melodrama, the actors shouting and posturing. The only thing I now recall is Racine's *Britannicus* performed by the Comédie Française. What made more impression was the cheapness of the cheapest seats, costing less than sixpence in English money. This was also true of the Opéra, though you would not necessarily be able to see the stage. It made me realise the potential of national theatre.

The paintings of Paris opened up a new world. For me the visual arts were being newly discovered, and I was in the first flush of my enthusiasm for them. The Impressionists came as a gift from heaven. Their paintings had recently been separated out from the others in the Louvre and given their own museum in a smaller building in the Jardin des Tuileries. I went back to it again and again. The celebration of life, of colour and light, above all of seeing, shouted from the canvases. Some of them, with their direct emotionalism, moved me almost as if they were music. I loved them in a way I had not realised I could love a visual object.

A work of an entirely different sort that had a strange and lasting effect on me was the sculpture in the Louvre known as the *Winged Victory of Samothrace*. I saw the popular classics there, from the *Venus de Milo* to the *Mona Lisa*, and enjoyed them all, but apart from the *Winged Victory* they had nothing like the effect on me that the Impressionists did. But of course the Impressionists are themselves now popular classics. At that time they were still thought of as 'modern', or almost so.

All the walking and standing I was doing was tiring, the more so in what was abnormally hot weather. The temperature touched 100 degrees in Paris on one day that summer – something it had never yet done in Britain. When my legs ached I would find a place to sit and read. I have a special memory of sitting in a metal chair at the end of the Tuileries, looking over the Place de la Concorde and reading *Great Expectations*. I had recently seen the David Lean film, but the novel was even better. At that moment there was nowhere in the world I would rather have been, and nothing else in the world that I would rather have been doing.

Paris was still run-down from the war and Nazi occupation. Buildings were dirty, mostly grey or black, and public places neglected. Most people looked poor, and were drably dressed. All this was true even by comparison with London, which itself was drab. But the most striking thing of all was the level of aggression in public behaviour: people snapped and snarled at one another, aggressive and defensive at the same time. If you bumped into a stranger only slightly in a crowded place, he or she would quite likely round on you with startling viciousness and spit the equivalent of 'Can't you look where you're going?' straight into your face. It was always unpleasant, and, in the end, hateful. People whose job it was to serve the public were deliberately unhelpful, and took pleasure in denying their customers what they wanted.

Repressed aggression, bristling hostility were everywhere, always ready to explode – and on a public scale as well as a private one: daily life was constantly strike-bound, and there were always public protests and demonstrations. Aggression, aggression, aggression was the air we shared and breathed; and it was the nastiest kind of aggression, not big-boned and hearty, but spiteful and mean. Ten years later I came across a quotation from Camus saying that spitefulness was a national institution with the French, and this fitted my experience exactly. By the end of my time in Versailles and Paris I loved the places but not the people, at least not in their public aspect. When I discussed these things with French friends, or at the homes of families in Versailles, the usual response was to agree that it was indeed so, and to explain it in terms of the humiliations of national defeat and Nazi occupation. Most people, I was told, had done things to survive of which they were ashamed, and this was so recent that nobody trusted anyone else.

Throughout my visit to France, all I ever saw was Paris and its environs, except for one day which I spent in and around the cathedral at Chartres. Even so, the range of things I managed to fit in was wider than I have been able to indicate. For instance I went to the Grand Prix at Longchamp, and the Folies-Bergère, and a large public meeting at the Sorbonne addressed by famous politicians. The whole experience was so multifarious, and meant so much to me in so many different ways, that I have remembered it ever since as one of the formative periods of my life, and can easily lapse into thinking of it as if it went on for months and months instead of its actual seven weeks. It was the best possible therapy for the death of my father. During it I thought of him every day, often painfully – unbearably so at *Lohengrin*, and unbearably at Longchamp. But every day I was also taken out of myself for long periods, forgetting everything else, either sunk in the struggle of having to do classwork in French or rollicking in the pleasures of Paris. However, although I was able to lose myself in what I was doing, or in my surroundings, for some reason I was not able to do so in other people's company. I dealt with people in whatever way I had to, but without really taking them in. There must have been a huge disparity between the liveliness of my responses to what I was seeing and my lack of response to other people. For instance, I now know from independent sources which I have used to check my memories that several of the things I have already recounted I did with this or that companion, but even after being reminded of it I cannot recover any trace of the companion in the memory I have of the event. I recall the occasion itself vividly – the place, the atmosphere, above all the paintings, the operas, or whatever I was there for – but it is as if I were there alone.

The kind of detailed recall on which this book and my last one have been largely based begins to peter out at this stage of my life. I have always assumed that this had to do with the trauma of my father's death; but perhaps it would have happened in any case. I now learn from other people's responses to my work that it is quite common for individuals to retain full, detailed memories of their childhoods but not of their ongoing lives after that; and perhaps I am simply one of those people. Whatever the reason, from the time I emerged into adult life the completeness of my recall fades, and my memory becomes more like what I suppose other people's to be. It is still quite good, still detailed and secure in many ways, but now there are gaps, some of them long, and also muddled periods, and periods when everything seems to swim into a single, homogeneous, not-very-distinct flow. In this and my last book I have treated memory as a first draft, a starting point to be subjected to detailed checking – and it is surprising how many different ways there are of checking memory when one confronts it as a serious task – but after the age of about eighteen there is no such first draft available.

The school term ended earlier in France than in England, so

when the time came for me to leave the Lycée Hôche I went back to Christ's Hospital. There, for the first time, I met the boys who had gone there from the lycée, nine of them, and we fell on one another and compared impressions. They looked on their time at Christ's Hospital as a junket – getting up in the morning a whole hour later, with no prep to do before breakfast; and in the entire day only half the amount of work. There were games and sports every day, a thousand acres of open air to wander around in, pupil power in the form of a monitorial system. Life was a spree for the English boys, they thought, and terrific fun, and they themselves enjoyed it immensely – but surely no one could think that this was education? Not seriously. Surely *I*, having been to the Lycée Hôche and seen the proper thing for myself, must realise that this was not real education at all. It was just a highly organised way of having fun. What use was any of it going to be in later life? The English were notoriously not *sérieux*, and here was the explanation . . . At bottom, the attitude of the French boys came down to a disbelief and derision that we could take education so unseriously as to think it was *this*. That provided them with an explanation for the lack of civilisation that they found among the British generally. Like nearly all French people at that time, they tended to equate civilisation with French culture, so the general ignorance of things French that met them on every side (especially in a school where most boys did not even learn the French language) flabbergasted them, and seemed to them a form of barbarism.

When my second end of term came, and I returned home, I found that, for the first time in my life, I had a bit of money. My father had left everything to my mother except for two small but significant bequests to Joan and me. To Joan he left fifty pounds and all his books; to me fifty pounds and all his gramophone records. Joan said he had done this because he had been so upset at his father not leaving him anything, but our bequests were so apt that there seemed to me more to it than that. Because of mine, I have had a sizeable collection of records ever since, no matter how hard-up I have been. What came to me in addition were all the masculine accessories that were of no use to my mother or sister. It never occurred to any of us that I might wear my father's clothes – the nature of our family business made second-hand clothing taboo for us, even if it had belonged to family or friends. We wore only new clothes. But his silver cigarette cases and leather cigar cases (he had two of each), his cufflinks, black bow ties, and other such odds and ends became mine as a matter of course at just the age when I was in sight of wanting such things. The biggest treasure trove of all was his ties. He always had an eye for these as being the only dash of colour in a man's dress, and whenever an especially good one came into the shop he collared it for himself. He had always let me wear some of them, those he cared least about. Now they were all mine – and by the time of his death there were something like two hundred of them. Ever since, I have had a ridiculous abundance of ties, an absurdly large number. As fast as they wear out or get lost (or stolen), or become dowdy or out of fashion, they are replaced by new purchases or presents. But I still have one, nondescript (it must have survived because it was scarcely ever worn), that has the family shop's label on it.

CHAPTER TWENTY-SIX

My mother had no connection now with my staying on at Christ's Hospital, but because I failed to understand this I misunderstood the conversations I had with her about my situation.

I told her at the beginning of the holidays that I regarded it as essential that I get a university education. It was much rarer then than now. No more than five per cent of the population went to university – even from the best public schools the great majority of boys did not go – but I was determined to get there. I wanted to go back to school for the next term in order to set about securing a university place – which, I said to my mother, I would do as quickly as I possibly could. In my mind, what I was doing was pressing her to go on paying for me to be at school a tiny bit longer, trying to bring home to her how much was at stake for me, and assuring her that I would make such demands on her for as short a time as I could manage.

To my amazement she replied that whether or not I went back to school was a matter of indifference to her, and entirely for me to decide. If I did, she said, she was not going to keep me during the school holidays. If I wanted to, I could go on staying in a room in her flat (as she put it), and she would not charge me for that; but she would not provide me with any money, so I would have to earn what money I needed. What I thought she was saying was that although she did not care whether I went to university or not she would not go so far as to take away from me

357

the possibility of doing so. However, this was the furthest she was prepared to go: she was determined to make the minimum sacrifice that such relenting required of her.

By misunderstanding her in this way I was not thinking ill of her. In fact she was offering a great deal less than I was attributing to her. All she was offering was to let me go on using my own room (in what would normally have been regarded as my own home) rent-free for a quarter of the year.

My relief was intense, but still apprehensive. She had said nothing about keeping me on at school for as long as I might need, which could be for another year or more. She had not addressed herself to that point at all. She had referred only to one more term, the following term – I could go 'back' – and even that with an ostentatious lack of benevolence. Further than that she had not committed herself. Perhaps she happened to be in a good mood at the time. In any case, I knew from experience that she was effortlessly capable of making promises about such things and then breaking them. But that meant also that there was nothing to be gained by pressing her – in fact, to do so was more than likely to be counterproductive. So I deliberately, anxiously refrained from raising the matter further. I was holding my breath. I could go back to school for the next term, at least, that was clear. Then I would have to hope for the best. Some time, any time, she would inform me that she had stopped paying my fees and that I had left school (my grandmother had done exactly this to my aunt Peggy). I felt vulnerable, on a tightrope still, but at least upright, and in with a chance.

I kept myself that summer, as before, by working in the income tax office in Tottenham, and living in my rent-free room. Ken Connor was also working at the office, and he and I went to the Proms together. It was at the Proms that year that I heard a complete Mahler symphony for the first time, the Fourth, in which, for the only time, I saw Elisabeth Schumann. I do not remember whether Kathleen Ferrier sang in that season, but she was at her peak at about that time, and I went to everything of hers that I could get to. I had never heard such a beautiful voice in live performance. It had a rare mix of attributes: although exceptionally full and rich, it was not sensuous but poignant, a combination that pierced the heart. I would sit (or stand) enraptured during her performances. I have heard few better voices since.

When I got back to school for the following term I told David Roberts that I wanted to sit for the very next Oxbridge entrance exam, whenever it was. He was dismayed. The normal age for candidates was eighteen and a half, and I was a bare seventeen and a half, a whole year short of peak form. He regarded me, he said, as a near certainty – but in a year's time, not now. It would be stupid to sit the exam when I was not ready for it. As far as preparing for it was concerned, I had just missed the whole of the previous term by being in France. Why do it?

His reference to my time in France gave me an idea for an excuse. I still found it impossible to tell him the truth about my mother, I found it so humiliating. If only I had told him, I would have discovered the reality of my situation. But what I said was that my time in France had brought me to the point where I had outgrown being a schoolboy. I was now just longing to leave school. He already knew about my intensive life of theatre and concerts in London, and how much I missed those when I was at school: I now implied that the parallel experience I had had in Paris had compounded this, to the point where I could no longer bear the constraints of school life. I had to get away, go out into the adult world. Being only seventeen, I spoke in the terms typical of late adolescence, with violently uttered sentences like 'I can't bear this dreadful place a minute longer' and 'I've simply got to get out of here.'

David was hurt. I was rejecting him and everything he was trying to do for me. The stupidity of my attitude seemed to him unworthy of me, and he said everything he could to dissuade me. I was adamant. In my mind, getting a university education depended on my not giving in to him, so nothing he could have said would have made me change my mind – unless he had told me that my mother was not paying for me to be at school. Alas, he never did. I knew how silly my behaviour appeared and was deeply embarrassed. My real feelings were the opposite of what I was saying. I loved the school, and had always been happy there – more than ever now that my father had died: in fact, this was the only place where I felt wanted. I was profoundly upset at making David feel that I was sweeping him out of my life – this again was the opposite of my real feelings: I was devoted to him, and appreciated everything he was doing for me, including what he was trying to do now, with so much concern, to prevent me from damaging myself. But at the moment I could think of no other way of asserting my will. In any case, having grabbed at the straw of this excuse, I was stuck with it, and had to go through with it.

With the new academic year a new master arrived to assist David with his history specialists, and David handed me over to him to see if he, as a much younger man, could do anything to dissuade me. He was twenty-six, I think, and had just got a first in history at Balliol, having gone up to Oxford late because of ambulance service during the war. He was Ralph Davis, son of H.W.C. Davis, the Regius Professor of Modern History at Oxford. Ralph was to spend one year only as a schoolmaster, and the rest of his career as a university teacher, first as a fellow of an Oxford college, then as a professor elsewhere. He was, in fact, unfitted to be a schoolmaster, and it turned out to be a piece of ill luck that I fell into his hands. He made much worse the damage that I was doing to myself. When I was handed over to him I was making myself appear headstrong and difficult, brash, rejecting, full of false values, and he did not have the maturity or temperament to take this in his stride and brush it to one side. Instead of weighing me up dispassionately and thinking how he could get me to behave in my own best interests, as David had been trying to do, he took against me, and became antagonistic. From him I learnt that the next entrance examination for Balliol would be held in six months' time, in March, and so I set my sights on that.

During the interim, something entirely unconnected with any of this happened, something that transformed my life – and incidentally constituted a new threat to my staying on at school. I became involved with one of the school's female staff. Our relationship had to be kept a deadly secret. If we had been discovered we would both have been sacked on the spot, with no question or discussion, and we both knew this.

It happened as a result of a game of rugger. I was still, as I had always been, a bad player, though not as bad as before, and my height gained me an undistinguished place in the house XV. Because I was thin, and could run quite fast in short bursts, I played as a three-quarter. The ground on the day of the match was frozen hard as concrete. I and the winger outside me were tossing remarks to and fro about the dangerousness of this as we lined out for the first throw-in, and I, referring to my well-known hatred of being compelled to play, said: 'Perhaps I'll break my leg and be excused the rest of the game.' These were to become famous last words. Within a matter of seconds I had received the ball and, twisting the upper part of my body so as to pass it while accelerating away from the pass, was crash-tackled by a six-footer from the other side and went down with an almighty smash. I had, indeed, broken my leg – a joke which had the winger chortling throughout the rest of the time I knew him.

I was carried off to the infirmary, where the doctor said they would X-ray me not immediately but the following day. Meanwhile, to keep my weight off my feet, I was put to bed in one of the wards. I quickly found that if I moved my leg in the bed, the two broken ends of bone ground together and gave a stab of excruciating pain. So I just lay there, moving my leg either not at all or slowly and carefully.

This was all very well until night fell and I wanted to sleep. I then found that when I nodded off I would unconsciously change position and be jerked awake by the stab of pain. After two or three repetitions of this I decided that real sleep was impossible, so I would force myself to stay awake. I sat up in the bed and made myself as comfortable as I could against the pillows. The ward was now in total darkness, and the boys in the other half-dozen beds were asleep. But there I sat, bolt upright, with my hands folded across my lap, busying myself with my thoughts and waiting for the night to pass.

After a long time, in the depths of the night – it must, I suppose, have been about three o'clock – a soft illumination appeared on the other side of the glass panels at the end of the ward. The sound of footsteps came from farther down the corridor, from somewhere out of sight. A torch was approaching. When it came into view its light plunged everything behind it into blackness, so I could not see who was holding it. It floated along, three or four feet above the ground, with footsteps coming from the darkness beneath it. It approached the door, which silently opened. It hung in mid-air in the open doorway, and from that position beamed itself on each bed in turn, revealing one boy after another curled up asleep – until it came to me, and there I was, sitting bolt upright, fully awake and gazing directly back into its beam. The torch evinced soundless surprise, and lingered on me for a moment. Then it approached me, with the footsteps below it again, until it got to my bed, and then I was able to see a nurse standing over me.

'Why are you sitting up?' she whispered. 'Is everything all right?'
I explained.
'You mean they haven't put you in a splint?' she said. 'That's

the first thing they should have done. I'll do it now.' And off she went.

She came back with the splint, and keeping her words and movements quiet so as not to disturb any of the other boys she wrapped up my leg. It was all done by torchlight.

'There,' she said. 'You'll be able to sleep now.'

Then, as an afterthought, she said: 'I was just doing a round before making myself a cup of hot chocolate. Would you like some? It might help you sleep.'

'I'd love some,' I said.

Off she went again, and came back this time with two mugs of chocolate. She sat on the settle beside me, and – there was no need now for the torch – we carried on a conversation in whispers and sips in the dark.

Her responses had been sympathetic, and at the same time practical, and I liked that. While she was putting the splint on I had seen her in enough light to find her pleasant-looking. She asked me about myself, and then told me about herself. She was thirty-one, still unmarried, and lived in the infirmary with other unmarried nurses. One snag about the job, she said, was that the infirmary had been deliberately set apart from the rest of the school, and the life of those who worked in it was so different from that of the teaching staff that the two rarely met. With patients they were seldom able to have even the kind of conversation she and I were having now. It was all rather a cut-off existence as far as personal contacts were concerned. In fact, she said as she was leaving, this conversation had itself been a tonic, and she might look in again the following night, after the others had gone to sleep. If I was still awake I might like to have another chat, though of course, if I was asleep she would not disturb me . . .

At school I was always conscious of being starved of female company, so this prospect was an attractive one. Next night I deliberately stayed awake. It was especially easy to do this, since I had

363

been in bed all day. She came, and again we held a whispered conversation in the dark, this time for a couple of hours. And this time she brought the hot chocolate with her. I cannot now remember how long I stayed in the infirmary altogether, or why it was longer than expected – there must have been some complications with either the fracture or the treatment. I feel, uncertainly, that it was a couple of weeks. Whatever it was, she came every night, and we talked at great length . . . One night she gave me a blanket bath, and this involved some fairly intimate bodily contact between us. After that we necked and canoodled night after night with increasing intimacy. On my last night, when we knew I would be leaving the next day, she got into my bed.

It was a crazy thing for us to do. We were surrounded in the darkness by other boys, and although they had slept soundly through all our previous neckings we had no guarantee that they would sleep through this. We were making a great deal more noise. Nobody stirred, though – adolescent boys, and very young men, sleep like the dead, in a way few other people ever do – and by the end we felt sure none of them had heard us. I went on believing this until, more than half a century later, at a school reunion, a forgotten acquaintance – old now like me – came up with a twinkle in his eye and a quiet, warm chuckle and told me how he had woken up in that ward and heard these unmistakable sounds coming from my bed. He had been startled out of his wits, not daring to move – hardly daring to breathe – and just lay there in the darkness listening. I asked if he had told anyone, and he said he had not, though on reflection it seemed to him very strange that he had not. Thinking about it now, he said, he realised that he had actually been shocked.

Another bizarre aspect of the whole thing was that my right leg was encased in plaster of Paris from foot to mid-thigh. So that was how I had my first sexual experience. My leg remained in plaster throughout the early weeks of our relationship – for we arranged, of course, to go on meeting, and did so for the rest of my time at the school.

Apart from anything else, I found the affair monumentally exciting. After dark, and after the other boys had gone to bed, she (let's call her Jill) and I would meet in one of our secret places. I was now the deputy house captain, which meant I had a study, but this was approachable only through the dayroom, so it was impossible for us to meet there. In any case, we felt we needed to keep our meetings away from the house. At first we met in the open, in woods and copses on the edge of the school's extensive grounds. She would bring blankets, and we would wrap ourselves together in them. After one such tryst I returned to the house to find two of my fellow monitors, Richard Cavendish and Dick Gerrard-Wright, still up. They were bending over Richard's desk in the dayroom, discussing something that lay on it, and as I walked in Richard looked up and called out: 'Here, look at this.' I bent over the table, my head between theirs. Wright sniffed, unselfconsciously surprised at first, then ostentatiously, and said in astounded tones: 'You smell of scent!' In that moment I smelt it too.

'Do I?' I said with as much unconcern as I could muster. 'It must be this soap someone's given me,' and turned away and disappeared into my study. I thought it was obvious that I had fled, and I expected Wright and Cavendish to pursue me about it later, so I prepared things to say, but neither of them mentioned it again.

That winter, 1947–48, was one of the coldest there had ever been, with the deepest snow I have known in England. (The previous one had been exceptionally bad too, so the two last winters of my time at school were almost the wintriest of my life.) It was no longer possible for Jill and me to make love in the open. But in any institution such as Christ's Hospital there are always disused rooms, in fact whole disused buildings, and we found it fun to explore for them, and discover safer and safer ones. She went on bringing blankets, and our meetings were very happy. We remained, so far as we knew, undiscovered and unsuspected.

The whole relationship was a key experience in my life. We were both actively involved, and equally responsible for what we did; but if there was one rather than the other who tended to take the lead it was her, because of the difference in age. Perhaps for that reason I never felt that I was taking advantage of her, nor did I feel any guilt towards her, not then nor when we parted. The whole thing always had something of the character of a wartime relationship. We acknowledged from the start that it could not have any long-term future, and on that basis we gave ourselves up to it uninhibitedly while it lasted. After I left school I saw her only once, when I was on leave from the army before being sent abroad. Then, in Austria, I became involved with someone else – indeed, while I was away, so did she. But between us, through everything, there was always good feeling. Four or five years later, when I was in my last year at Oxford, she sent me a telegram to tell me she had got married, but gave me no address. It was obvious from this that she did not want me to get in touch with her, and I never attempted to do so.

I have occasionally told the story of this relationship to close friends – usually women friends who have quizzed me about my first relationship – and they have nearly always asked if I think Jill had similar relationships with other boys, before or after me. For reasons too detailed to go into here, I am certain that her relationship with me was a one-off. To begin with, it was not only about sex. From our first meetings we devoted hours and hours to talking about other things too, and with intense interest. We discussed not only ourselves and our past lives, and the individuals closest to us, and the school itself, and the people we knew in common: we talked also about books, films, whatever was in the newspapers, life in general, politics, whether or not we believed in God. And this meant that we got to know each other exceedingly well. If I may so put it, we became close in spirit. It was not the sort of relationship that was interchangeable. For me it was a piece of incredible luck, and I look back on it with nothing but pleasure.

In spite of this life-changing love affair I still thought it essential to secure a university place before my mother delivered on her promise not to keep me any longer – and indeed before my affair with Jill was discovered, which we feared it might be, at any moment. I had no choice but to take the examination in history, because that was the only subject I was well enough advanced in; but I was beginning to feel that I wanted to change subjects once I got to university. I was devoting two-thirds of my working time to history, and already this felt excessive. I was interested in it, but no more so than in a number of other subjects. I had chosen to specialise in it not for the subject, but to be taught by David Roberts, and now that I was not being taught by him anyway, but by Ralph Davis, I had had enough of it. I began to wonder what else I might do instead.

I assumed it would have to be one of the subjects in which I had got a distinction in School Certificate, because I would not be able to reach university standard quickly enough in any of the others, and therefore would not be accepted. But although I had got a distinction in Latin, classics was out – I had repudiated Greek anyway, and had seldom enjoyed Latin. Modern languages was a possibility, with my good French plus decent German. But this felt like a waste of opportunity. I had become used to speaking and reading French, and expected to go on doing so for the rest of my life (with increasing mastery, I assumed, though in fact the reverse has happened). Because of my passion for Wagner I intended to get into a similar position with German, and did in fact do so the following year, in Austria. It would be a waste of university, I thought, to do there what I intended to do in any case. My aim should be to gain something extra from university, to expand, get broadened out, learn things I would not have learnt otherwise. That scuttled the only remaining alternative, English. I was already a gluttonous devourer of poetry, novels, and performances of plays; and I knew I would go on doing that for the rest of my life. Also, I had by now developed a low opinion, something approaching a contempt, for the academic approach to such things, which I saw as point-missing in a way that was fundamental to their nature.

So what was I to do?

I took my dilemma to Ralph Davis, who invited me to discuss it with him in his study. The evening on which I did so was to have deleterious consequences for me for years to come. He referred early on to the PPE course at Oxford. I had never heard of it, so I asked what it was. He explained: 'Philosophy, politics and economics.' As someone interested in politics I was instantly alert, and quizzed him about it. My eagerness leapt higher when he told me that virtually none of the undergraduates who did PPE would have studied any of the three subjects at school – and higher still when he told me that the course was a recently intro-duced one aimed at people who were thinking of going into poli-tics. Here was my solution, I thought, and said so, bubbling with enthusiasm. Thereupon Ralph Davis poured a barrel of cold water over me. No, *no*, NO, he said: I should on no account do PPE.

He expanded on this at length, with dismissive scorn. The most important thing a higher education could do for anyone, he said, was to lead them to the frontier of human knowledge, the fron-tier with the unknown, and then engage them with their subject at that point. On the way, you would do a lot of work to cover the already existing territory, and absorb a general education in the subject at a high level. In whatever specialism you selected, you would follow that path as far as it would go, until you were shoulder to shoulder with the people who were doing original research. It was at that point, said Ralph, that you would start thinking at the deepest level of all, grappling not just with what you did not know but with what nobody knew. From that point on you had to do everything for yourself: identify and formulate your own problems, decide on your methods, find your materials, make fruitful yet critical use of them, produce your own ideas. This was the true goal of higher education, and it was to this point that everything had been leading. It developed your capacity for independent thinking at the deepest level, the level of original thought, and in a disciplined way; and trained you in how to work hard at it. History was ideal for these purposes. It constituted an almost perfect education, even for someone who had no intention of becoming a historian. There were other subjects that could achieve it too – for instance classical scholarship, or physics (which would always include higher mathematics). Whatever the subject, the process was one that needed a long time: it could not be gone through in less than three or four years. The trouble, he said, with a course like PPE, which tried to cover three different subjects in three years, was that it doomed itself to failure from the outset. In the time available, a student could not go far enough, or dig deep enough, in any one of the subjects. He was given no possibility other than to remain at a first- or second-year level in each, being led through the sort of general introduction to it that ought to have been, but in this case was not, a transition to something deeper. So the entire course consisted of introductions. And this betrayed the students.

Ralph was passionately eloquent about all this, and heated, as if a burning resentment against PPE had built up inside him. And I accepted the whole argument. It made luminous sense to me. I had reached an age when I wanted to develop my mind, but did not know even what that meant, let alone how to do it. The school, except for David Roberts, had not done it, I knew that. But now that Ralph explained it to me I understood what I needed

to do. I wrote off PPE as an option. It was years before I was able
to reconsider that: I was for a long time convinced, because of
what Ralph had said, that whatever I chose to do it would need
to be a single subject. I still did not want that subject to be history,
and could not decide on an alternative; but because I had to go
into the army before going to university I would have a long time
to think about it – and I was now, I believed, in a position to do
that with understanding. I went away from that evening in Ralph
Davis's study with a light step, and not the slightest realisation
that he had just sent my life off the rails for the next few years.

CHAPTER TWENTY-SEVEN

The Christmas break of 1947 was my last holiday from school, though I did not know it. Christmas itself raised difficulties about what to do, not only for me. For decades our extended family had spent Christmases together: the four of us from Arnos Grove plus what we referred to as 'the Southgate contingent'. This consisted of two households, one of my grandparents and maiden aunt Hilda, the other my father's favourite sister Peggy and her husband, Bill Pett. The nine of us had always gathered, with a guest or two, at one of our three homes, and had a good time. But now, within six months, both the Southgate and the Arnos Grove contingents had lost their patriarch. The family was doubly bereft, and, with that, depressed. We agreed that any attempt to hold our usual family Christmas would be painful. Nobody wanted that. So it was suggested that we put up together at a hotel where we could make our own little world but be surrounded by people enjoying themselves, and have all the work done for us by other people. I was included in this for no other reason than that it would have been embarrassing for everyone if I had been left out. We all discussed where to go. It would have to be a modest hotel, one suited to our means, yet we wanted a place with character.

It was Joan who suggested Stratford-upon-Avon. She had been there two or three times with friends to see plays, and had taken a liking to the town. It had all sorts of hotels, she said, and they were half-empty in winter – in fact some of them closed down –

so we should be able to get a bargain rate at quite a good one. In those days there was nothing like the general demand for hotels at Christmas that there is today: quite the contrary. So it was agreed: we would spend Christmas in Stratford-upon-Avon.

Joan found the hotel. It had once been a grand private house on the bank of the Avon, with a long garden that ran beside the river to the churchyard wall of Holy Trinity (where Shakespeare lies buried). There could scarcely have been a more attractive setting, or a more convenient one.

Almost at once, dissension broke out in the family. The Southgate contingent found my mother impossible to make the arrangements with, and concluded that a Christmas spent with her without my father would be disastrous. They pulled out and made other arrangements. So only three of us – my mother, sister and me – went to Stratford. I fell in love with it, and have remained so ever since.

Scarcely any of the Shakespeare sites were open to the public in those days, but we went around looking at them all. I found it inexpressibly moving to see Shakespeare's birthplace, and his school, and the site of the house he bought when he returned to Stratford towards the end of his life; and also the homes of people related to him; and above all his gravestone – and to think of him actually *there*. On Christmas Day, pagans though we were, we went to a service in Holy Trinity and sang carols, throughout which I thought of him lying there a little way in front of me . . . We did a lot of non-Shakespeare things too. On the clear, frosty morning of Boxing Day we watched a fox-hunt gather to drink a stirrup cup before setting off – a magnificent sight. Stratford in those days was quite different from the tourist centre it has since become. At Christmas the streets were empty. When I went out of doors I felt almost as if I had the town to myself.

By sheer coincidence our hotel was where I spent a whole summer five years later when, as a penniless undergraduate, I worked as a waiter during the Long Vacation of 1952. It exists no longer. It and its beautiful garden have been replaced by a housing estate.

That Christmas remains the only one I have spent in a hotel. The three of us got on well enough, and did a lot of things together, though I also went out alone. A fellow guest, a businessman who got into conversation with me, took me to what he said was the best pub in Stratford. It was my first experience of hearing businessmen talk about the Labour government. The sheer venom of it, even when surrounded by good Christmas cheer, took me aback. A typical joke was: 'Why is the Labour government like a bunch of bananas? Because they came in green, they've turned yellow, and there isn't a straight one in the whole bloody bunch.'

The winter of 1947–48 was a difficult time for me in many ways, and the viciousness of the weather made everything worse. My life was a mass of adolescent tangles. The death of my father hung weightily over it all like a cloud of poison gas, but in addition to that there was my uncommunicating relationship with my mother, and the secret relationship I was involved in at school – where I was also, on the basis of yet another false pretence, perceived as rejecting the teacher to whom I was most devoted. In every area things were not only emotionally dramatic but, except for Jill, intensely unpleasant. It may indeed have been that I was too grown-up now for the life I was living. Other events bore this out. Covent Garden announced that it was going to stage Wagner for the first time since before the war, but all the performances were scheduled to fall within termtime. There was to be *Tristan and Isolde* and *The Valkyrie*, neither of which I had seen, and both of which were to be staged with international star singers, Hans Hotter and Kirsten Flagstad. Her voice was the best I had heard on records, but of course I had never seen her in the flesh. It was simply unacceptable to me that this should be happening and I not go. So I bought a single ticket for each of the last two performances – a couple of days apart, just before the end of term – and insisted within myself that somehow I would get there. To ask to be let off school to travel up to London alone for such things (when they had not even been arranged by a senior member of staff) was not only unknown but unimaginable. I said nothing about it until the time drew close, and then asked Pongo. He was not so much disapproving as nonplussed. He said he needed time to think, and would let me know. When he did let me know he said that two such outings would be excessive. However, just this once, as a very special favour to me personally, and not to be counted as a precedent, even by anyone else, let alone me, and only because it would be near to the end of term, and because I would then be not all that far off my eighteenth birthday, I could go to one of the operas, but to one only. He left it to me to decide which.

I was thrilled and devastated. After a lot of self-torturing I plumped for *Tristan*, if only because it was a self-contained work. With limitless reluctance I posted the ticket for *The Valkyrie* to Ken Connor. It turned out to be a lucky decision, because I was able to see the same production of *The Valkyrie* at Covent Garden the following year, as part of a complete *Ring*, when I was on home leave from Austria. And the *Tristan* was unforgettable, not least because of the voice of Kirsten Flagstad. After nearly sixty years it remains, I think, the best voice I have ever heard, as sumptuous as Ferrier's but with more bloom, more sheer beauty of sound, and also a greater variety of tone colour. She was particularly good at darkening her voice and expressing feelings and thoughts that were specific yet concealed by the words. For the rest of her career I took every opportunity of hearing her (and was therefore present at the world premiere of Richard Strauss's *Four Last Songs* in May 1950). Her voice was so beautiful in itself, regardless of what she was singing, that I would sit there unable quite to believe what I was hearing. I remember thinking once: I'm nineteen now, but when I'm ninety I'll still want to be able to relive this sound. I must impress it on my memory now for the rest of my life – and trying to do so. I must have had some success, because it gives me gooseflesh just to remember it.

Back at school for what was to be my last term, I found life mostly taken up by two things: my relationship with Jill and my preparations for the scholarship to Balliol in March. Ralph Davis, backed up by David Roberts, carried on trying to persuade me to put off the exam, and I persisted in refusing. When the time for it drew near, and I asked Ralph some idle question about what being at Balliol was like, he replied nastily that it would make little difference to me since I would not be going there. The conversation continued something like this:

Me: 'I know you don't think I'm going to get in, but just supposing I do.'

Ralph: 'If you get in, it won't be to Balliol, because you won't be putting down for Balliol.'

Me: 'What do you mean?'

Ralph: 'Look here, the fact is you're going to do badly in this exam. You're not ready for it. If your papers are read by the people at Balliol they'll get a low opinion of you. And if you try there again next year they'll already have decided they don't want you. You'll never get in. If we can't stop you taking the exam now, you've got to put down for another college if ever you're to get in to Balliol.'

I was dumbfounded. For well over a year I had been told I was destined for Balliol, and I had taken this for granted. It was now part of my conception of myself. I protested strenuously. Ralph Davis protested back. It emerged that the credit at Balliol that he was most concerned about was not mine but his. He had come to us straight from there, and his tutors, who were now personal friends, would be my examiners. If the very first candidate he sent them was below standard, what would they think of him? Furthermore, these were the people he would be asking to be his referees in any job application he might make. (He was, unknown to me, already applying for university posts.) He became angrier and angrier, and finally shouted at me in tones that closed the conversation: 'I *FORBID* you to put in for Balliol!!'

Actually, he had no power to do that, but I did not understand this at the time. In places like my school no one frontally disobeyed so direct an order from a person in recognised authority, and it did not enter my head to do so.

What college should I put in for, then? The Oxford colleges organised their entrance examinations in groups: candidates wrote down an order of preference on their application forms, and their papers were read first by the college of their first choice. When it decided not to take someone it passed his papers on to the college of his second choice; and so on. The group I had been targeted at consisted of Balliol, Magdalen, St John's, Wadham and Keble. I had heard of only two of the others apart from Balliol – Magdalen and St John's – and knew nothing even about them.

In his anger during our argument Ralph had so bitingly, and at such length, rubbished my chances of passing the exam that it damaged my self-confidence. I had always known that by taking it earlier than I ought to I was increasing my chances of failure, but I still thought it was my only chance of ensuring a university education. Now that I found myself staring into the cold eyes of the probability (the certainty, according to Ralph) of failure, I knew that the most important thing was simply to get a place, any place, at Oxford. Which college it was at was a trivial matter by comparison. I asked Ralph which of them was the easiest to get into. He said the one with the lowest standards in the university was Keble – so, he said decisively, I should put in for that.

I went to Oxford to take the examination. The candidates stayed in the college of their first choice, so I stayed in Keble. We all sat the same papers together, but that was in Keble too, in the dining hall. I did not have any preconceived idea of the college as a place, but I found it actively depressing. Built on the largest of scales, it was Victorian gothic throughout, and clamantly ugly. The endless corridors were loweringly institutional, with rooms opening off them that you found yourself reluctant to go into, as in a hospital or a prison. The windows, much too small, were designed as if to keep out the light, which they did; and the arti ficial lighting everywhere was a dull, dirty orange. The whole place was murky, like a Victorian prison. My soul descended into my shoes as I wandered round it.

I had never felt such dismay as this in a new place. It was compounded when the candidates started discussing the colleges they were staying in. Some were positively excited about them. And when they started comparing them with Keble, or talked about the differing reputations of the colleges, it began to sound as if Keble were some sort of joke college, notorious not only for its ugliness but also for low standards of every other kind. People said it consisted largely of students who could not get in anywhere else. Everyone I spoke to had either put it down last or left it out altogether, because they would rather risk another try for a better college than accept a place at Keble. Their talk piled horror upon horror. Keble was, they said, churchy: something like a quarter of the undergraduates there were going to become vicars. The whole reputation of the place had something of Aldwych farce about it. If I went there, they said, I would find that all I had to do was say I was at Keble for people to laugh. (Every one of these things turned out to be true.)

By the end of my visit my hostility to Keble was implacable. I had made a ghastly mistake. Going there was unacceptable. I found myself grabbing in a new, wholly unexpected way at what Ralph Davis had been saying all along, that there was no chance of my passing the exam. Thank God, I thought. I told myself that, with his knowledge of my work, and his knowledge of Oxford, he was bound to be right. But what a close shave! I began to form plans of finding ways to keep myself if I had to leave school, and then trying to arrange through the school, through David Roberts, to take the exam to Balliol. Now that I knew how the system worked I felt I had a chance of doing something along those lines. Having met the other candidates, I felt that my hopes of getting into a good college were not less well grounded than most of theirs. I might not get a scholarship, but I was likely to be offered a place, which was all I needed.

Although by the time I left Oxford to return to Christ's Hospital I wanted desperately to fail the exam, I had come only slowly and reluctantly to that conclusion. While writing my papers I had done so as if my life depended on it. And, prickly adolescent though I was, my predicament vis-à-vis my mother had aroused in me enough good sense not to try to show off, but to write as well as I could. I surpassed myself. The examiners later told David Roberts that I had written the best papers they had seen in more than ten years, since well before the war.

Two days after I got back to school I went in to breakfast and there on my place at the table was a telegram from Keble. They had given me their top scholarship. I was distraught. With a rush of blood to the head I plunged straight out of the dining hall to look for David and tell him that I was going to refuse the scholarship, and explain to him what I planned to do instead. By an extraordinary coincidence he was directly outside the door, crossing the lawn on his way to the masters' common room, and I nearly knocked him over as I came rushing out of the door. I stood there pouring it all out, and he stood there listening to it. Then, for a long time, we walked very slowly up and down on the grass outside the dining hall, to and fro, to and fro, against the muffled backcloth noise of a thousand people having breakfast, while he talked me out of what I had decided to do.

I knew enough now, he said, to understand that there was always an element of chance in examinations. However probable a candidate's success, it could never be guaranteed. One or two of the ablest pupils he had ever taught had been undone by exams. He was, indeed, virtually certain that I could get a place at Balliol, if not a scholarship; but he emphasised the word 'virtually'. He could not be sure. Nor could I. That being so, just suppose I turned down the Keble scholarship, then sat for Balliol the following year, and was not offered a place? What would I do then? The truth, he said, was that *then* I would give my eye teeth for a scholarship to Keble. But then it would be too late. In any case, what mattered about a college was not what people said about it, and not even the quality of its architecture, but the quality of its teaching. I had written my papers in medieval history, and this meant that if I went to Keble I would have as my tutor one of the most distinguished medieval historians in Britain – certainly one of the two or three best in Oxford – the great J.E.A. Jolliffe. To be taught by him would be a privilege – and a privilege I could get only at Keble. Meanwhile, in the university at large, I would be just as free to do whatever else I wanted as I would be at any other college. Only plodders lived within their colleges. What I was being offered was something truly valuable, and it would be wrong to gamble it against the possibility of getting nothing at all. I would be allowing myself to be governed by false values. On this point he was withering. Imagine, he said, someone risking the very possibility of an Oxford education because he disliked the architecture of a college, or because other people made unpleasant jokes about it. What would I myself think of any other person who did that?

This conversation was a turning point in my young life. At one moment David said: 'Don't you go looking any horses . . .' then stumbled and stopped, having taken the wrong turning with the words, so I said, '. . . gift horses in the mouth.' Ever since then I recall this whole conversation whenever I hear that phrase.

My respect for David was beyond words, as was my affection for him, and I knew that his only concern was for what was in my best interests. Eventually my arguments against him dried up, and I felt myself, though somehow still against my will, being talked round. My Achilles heel was my lack of self-confidence. I caved in, and accepted the scholarship. In due course, after service in the army, I went up to Keble. What this whole story and its antecedents signify is that if Ralph Davis had simply left me alone, to follow my own choices along the path I was already on, I would have gone to Balliol and plunged straight into the study of philosophy, politics and economics – which, in retrospect, is obviously what would have been best for me – whereas, because of his double intervention, I went to Keble and spent my first three years at Oxford taking a degree in history (having been blocked at the last minute in my attempts to switch to music). I did then take a degree in philosophy, politics and economics, but it was only after these years-long diversions that I found the path that my own inclinations had pointed me to in the first place – and which was, for me, the right path. These were seriously wrong decisions; and in each case I fought against them hard at first, but in the end went along with them, so I carry a full share of responsibility. What started the whole mess was my mistaken assumption that staying on at school was dependent on my mother's being willing to carry on paying for me after she had told me directly that she would not. It was a catalogue of errors on all sides; and their combined consequences were to cause me prolonged setbacks during my early years. I think I eventually got over their ill effects, but they did me a lot of harm in the short run.

Having written so harshly of the Keble of that time, I must in fairness add that the college has long ceased to be as it was then. Its rise to excellence was one of the supreme success stories of Oxford in the second half of the twentieth century.

Acceptance of the scholarship there changed everything else

for me at once. In those post-war years the universities were straining to take in, direct from the armed services, people of widely differing ages who in normal times would have gone up in different years, but whose higher education had been interrupted or postponed by the war. Colleges were stretched to their limits, and to help themselves cope they were refusing to take most school-leavers straight from school. These were still subject to military service at eighteen, unless they received exemption on health or other grounds, so the universities required most of them to do their service before coming up as undergraduates. The standard life-path for my generation of students was to be at school till eighteen, then go into the army for two years, then go to university at the age of twenty.

This was the path that now opened before me. However, I had not yet got to my eighteenth birthday, and this prompted the hope that with luck I might be able to take advantage of a quirk in the system. If a conscript's two years of service took him so far into a new academic year as to leave him unable to start university until the following year, but still with an awkward gap to fill (without occupation or source of income), he could apply for an early release, to catch the beginning of the earlier year. This was known as a Class B Release. I hoped that if I could persuade the authorities to call me up on the earliest legal date, which was my eighteenth birthday, that would maximise my chances of getting a Class B Release, and enable me to start at Oxford in October 1949 (it being now March 1948). It would be cutting it fine, because I would be missing half a year's military service, and I was by no means sure that the authorities would allow so much. But it was worth having a go. I wrote and asked to be called up on my eighteenth birthday.

We were now under two weeks from the end of term, and my birthday was about to fall in the vacation, so now I knew I would be leaving school for good in less than a fortnight. All this was disconcertingly sudden. My relationship with Jill made it agonising too, even though we had always known that such a day must come. We had been very happy together, and our relationship was the one wholeheartedly good thing in my life at that time. But there seemed to be nothing else for it. I went around saying my goodbyes.

On the last night of every term there was a leaving service in chapel for those boys who would not be coming back. It was attended by the entire school and staff. I had always found it chokingly moving. I was liable to be got at emotionally by any leave-taking so, to me, even being only a bystander at the end of so long and deep an attachment had been distressing. Most boys left at the end of a summer term, this being the end of the school year, so the group of leavers then was always a big one; but now, at the end of the winter term, there were only two or three of us. The service consisted, as always, of the same valedictory prayers, readings and hymns; and while the last hymn of farewell was being sung, those of us who were leaving put down our hymn books and threaded our way past our fellows, out of our pews, and down the centre aisle to the altar, under the eyes of the whole school as they sang goodbye to us. There to receive us, with his back to the altar, stood the headmaster. Although we were so few, he used a voice that could be heard by everyone in the chapel to summon each of us by name to step forward and receive from his hands a large bible with the school's crest on it in gold, and our name inside – obviously meant to be our bible for life. As a Grecian, I was given also a matching copy of the Book of Common Prayer. Then came what for me had always been the most devastating moment of all, the Charge. The school remained standing while the headmaster said to us, looking into the eyes of each in turn as he spoke: 'I charge you never to forget the great benefits that you have received in this place, and in time to come according to your means to do all that you can to enable others to enjoy the same advantages; and remember that you carry with you, wherever you go, the good name of Christ's Hospital. May God Almighty bless you in your ways and keep you in the knowledge of his love.' My eyes were now full of tears, but luckily for me none of them spilled on to my cheeks. That scene remains with me as one of the most piercing of my life.

Later in the evening, I found myself unable to get my mind round the fact that I would never put the same clothes on again. I had lived in them for nearly seven years, and taken them for granted. Now, as I removed each garment in turn, I did so in the knowledge that I would never wear it again: first the deep-blue ankle-length coat, with all its silver buttons and velvet trimmings; then the white bands and the Hamlet-style shirt; then the mustard-yellow stockings; then the hard, tough-wearing knee breeches, grey, with those silver buttons again. I occasionally wear two of them now as a pair of cufflinks.

It seemed to me that I had no choice but to leave school and go out into the world; there was no practical alternative. But so much had been lost in so short a time. First there had been my grandfather, then my father, now my first lover, plus the world I had lived in for seven of my most formative years. I was not yet eighteen, and had lost the three people closest to me. This was not a self-pitying reflection – on the contrary, it was factual, and my attitude was stoical, accepting of the inevitable. Nor was I backward-looking: I knew I had to move on, because life moved on.

But I had been naive to suppose that because I had asked the bureaucracy to call me into the army as soon as possible they would do so. When 12 April came, the first thing I looked for in my birthday post was my call-up papers. They were not there. The rest of April passed, then the whole of May, and still no sign of them. I thought now that I had lost all chance of getting out of the army in time to go to Oxford in October 1949. My position at home was embarrassing too. I was still living in the rent-free room in my mother's flat, but it began to seem an age since I had told her that I would join the army on my eighteenth birthday and be off her hands for ever. I began to wish I could have gone back to school, where the summer term was now in full swing, and await call-up there. The fact is, of course, that I could have done, just as other boys did, only I did not know it. I became nostalgic for what I was not experiencing, and would never now experience – for what people were constantly referring to as their unforgettable last summer term, when they had secured their place at university and had nothing to do but enjoy themselves. I might have had all that and Jill too. But by forcing everything forward a year I had forfeited the whole experience of life at the top of the school. After one more term I would have been a house captain, and a school monitor, one of those god-like figures who had the world at their feet and on whom the sun shone perpetually, who were occasionally to be glimpsed on summer evenings casting long shadows across the grass of the main quad as they sauntered over to drinks in the headmaster's house while everyone else was working. They were doing it now, at this very moment, and I might have been there (as of next term) if only . . .

CHAPTER TWENTY-EIGHT

'Wakey! Wakey!'

I have never hated any other two weeks of my life so much as I hated my first two weeks in the army. It was made hateful for us deliberately, as a form of the age-old policy of 'breaking in the recruits'.

I was in a camp on Salisbury Plain, in a barrack room with a couple of dozen young men of my own age from all over Britain – except for one, Paddy, a twenty-eight-year-old from the Republic of Ireland. Having been resident in Britain for some time when the Second World War broke out, he received call-up papers from the British Army, whereupon he immediately skipped back to Ireland and spent the rest of the war there. However, the British authorities lay in wait for him throughout the war and beyond. Three years after it ended he came back, and was instantly arrested as a deserter and handed over to the army.

'The first lot of leave I get I'm going over to Ireland and I'm not coming back,' he said, openly and cheerfully. Which is what he did. There was no legal way of stopping him.

Each day began at six o'clock, when we would be fast asleep from the exhaustions of the previous day. The ear-jangling sound of a bugle blown with bursting lung power outside the window made the bones in our head judder. At the same time a six-foot-six sergeant crashed in through the door shouting, *'Wakey! Wakey!'* and ran round the room tipping everyone on to the floor with mattress, bedding and all, yelling nonstop into our faces: '*Come on, get up! Up! Hands off the joystick! Wakey, wakey!*' We came to consciousness on the floor in a heap of violence, chaos and cacophony. And from that moment we were hounded and harassed through the day. The declared object was to break any resistance we might have to obeying orders, and replace that with automatic compliance, however ridiculous the order. Hours of every day were devoted to mindless drill, old-fashioned square-bashing, during which we were roared at and abused. 'Get it together, you lot – you sound like a splatter of shit from a duck's arse! . . . No, you silly cunt, your other left! . . . You, Smiler at the back there, get with the rest of us – you're standing around like a spare prick at a wedding!' and so on and so forth. Other hours were devoted to soul-destroying tasks of deliberate pointlessness. One day we spent half the morning lugging heavy crates from a warehouse at one end of the camp to a warehouse at the other, and as soon as the job was finished, and we were exhausted, we were ordered to carry them back again. Another day we were instructed to blanco our webbing the purest white: we were berated, each one separately, for not getting it white enough, until finally, when we all had it perfect, a sergeant major marched us to a coal tip, stirred our webbing around in it with his swagger stick – to a running commentary of sadistic derision – and then ordered us to start again. Another day we were all issued with nail scissors, marched to a lawn, and ordered to cut the grass; and there was nothing for it but to get down on our hands and knees and cut the grass with nail scissors.

These ploys, I was later to discover, were all well-known and old-established spirit-breakers of long tradition, but to me they were new, and they had the opposite effect: they induced hatred and revolutionary violence. I have never felt such hatred: I would have blown the whole place up if I could. My rage was so colossal that it is difficult now to believe that the entire experience lasted

only a fortnight. But that was only for me: for the others it lasted
six weeks. We had embarked on a six-week course of so-called
basic training, during which our future in the army would be
decided; and I had no idea that I was about to be taken out of it
so soon. In my mind the hell of it stretched for all those weeks
ahead, so I dug myself in for a long campaign of endurance. We
were not even permitted the solace of creature comforts at the
end of a long day. We slept between the roughest of blankets,
without sheets, and washed and shaved in cold water. The latrines
were an offence to high heaven. I cannot pretend that the food
was worse than at Christ's Hospital, because that would not be
possible, but it was not much better. Many of the men bolted their
lunch in ten minutes so as to have the rest of the hour to themselves, as being their only haven of sanity in the day.

It was a degraded and degrading existence, hideous beyond
anything I had been capable of imagining at that age. Once,
behind the scenes in the cookhouse, I saw one of the hags who
worked there put on a public performance of squeezing a giant
parsnip slowly up her vagina to the encouragement and applause
of her colleagues, and sign off the act by tossing the vegetable
into the cookpot for the men to eat. All around were corruption
and petty thieving on a monumental scale, and people who said
'fuck' several times a sentence (sometimes in the middle of a
word, as in abso-fucking-lutely), and furtive, desperate sex in
corners with women who worked in the camp. I began to realise
that this was probably what armies had been like since the beginning of time. But for the authorities to allow it to go on to the
extent that it did showed unbelievable contempt for the soldiery,
the assumption that they were little better than animals.

And they were, I have to admit, a rough lot. Inevitably, they
were chiefly from families of the industrial poor, because that was
what most people in Britain were in the 1940s. Several were not
able to write a letter home, and one or two could not read. I was

the only individual in my barrack room to have pyjamas: the rest slept in their underwear. The young man in the next bed to me had never seen pyjamas, and asked what they were. Another remarked that it was ancy-fancy of the army to break our meals up into courses. He had never seen that before, he said: at home there was one good plate of something and that was it. He could not see the point of this courses business. Most of the men were away from their families for the first time in their lives, and had known only one background up to now. They were also, because they were out of their element, unsure of themselves behind their tough, yobbish exteriors, and this made them easy to lead and to influence.

The sergeants who trained us were a hardbitten bunch in their late twenties who had fought through the war. They had achieved a degree of promotion and authority which they now preferred to keep by staying in the army rather than go back to civilian life. Some had had horrific experiences, and had killed people. My platoon sergeant, Sergeant Smith (or, as he gave his name, Sarnt Smiff, had shrapnel holes in his face, and what with this and being six-and-a-half feet tall looked like a monster in a horror film. The sergeants in general looked on us eighteen-year-olds with benign contempt: we were milksops who had seen nothing and knew nothing. They liked to needle the well-educated ones, because the assumption in those days was that these were going to be officers, certainly most of them. Once, when I had committed some transgression in the ranks, and was standing to attention to be reprimanded, the sergeant marched up to me, stood right up against me, his toecaps touching mine, and said directly into my face, in a voice that started under quiet control and rose to something like a scream: 'Private Magee: if I meet you in six months from now I shall probably have to stand to attention when I talk to you, and call you sir, but by fucking Christ...' and then a stream of abuse, most of it obscene, that seemed to go on for several minutes. In his own mind he was, I think, unburdening himself of his feelings about the officer class to one of them while he had the chance.

To determine our future we were given aptitude tests, and interviewed individually about what we wanted to do. I said I wanted to go into the Education Corps. I said this because I detested the whole military side of the army, and had heard that if you went into the Education Corps you found yourself either teaching illiterates to read and write or giving classes in subjects like civics. I thought these were things worth doing, and I could get some genuine pleasure out of them. I awaited the call.

Instead, a notice went up on the board informing everyone (including, incidentally, me) that I had been transferred to the Intelligence Corps. I would, it said, be reporting in a couple of days' time to the School of Military Intelligence in Sussex. I had never heard of the Intelligence Corps, or its school, and went to the Colonel's office to ask what all this was about. I would, they informed me further, be given a three-month course of training at SMI (as they called it) and would then be put to work in some intelligence job. Did this mean, I asked, that I would miss the rest of basic training? In reality, yes, they said, though in theory the rest of my basic training would be incorporated in the SMI course. (The rest of what? I wondered.) My overriding reactions were relief, surprise, and an awareness of my ignorance of the whole situation. I still did not really know what any of this meant. Throughout my years at Christ's Hospital, leavers had been going straight from school into the army – and during most of those years I had myself been training in the Officers' Training Corps – so I thought I knew about the alternatives that would face me. Now, suddenly, there was this, something completely unknown. No one else from my intake was going with me.

I made the journey to the School of Military Intelligence by train, accompanied by a corporal whose job it was to ensure that I did not desert. He handed me over and returned.

The home base of the Intelligence Corps was an army camp just outside a village called Maresfield, which in turn was just outside the little town of Uckfield. By now I thought of myself as having half grown up in Sussex, not only because of Christ's Hospital but because of Worth before that. Now here I was back again. Conditions in the camp were primitive, but I was used to that.

The atmosphere could scarcely have been more different from the camp I had just left. When I found my barrack room and sorted myself out with the other new arrivals, I found that all of us had just come from public schools or grammar schools and were heading for university. Life, after multiple fracture into two weeks of degradation, began to feel as if it might come back together again.

Next morning I was raised gently to consciousness by a quiet knocking on the door of the barrack room. I opened my eyes and found myself looking at a sergeant major standing in the open doorway, elegantly dressed. With an air of friendly diffidence he was tapping the wooden panel with his swagger stick. When a stir went round the room, and he knew he had woken us up, he said: 'It's eight o'clock, chaps. You'd better get up if you want any breakfast.' He turned round and walked away.

I thought then that I had come to the right place.